Study Guide

Robert E. Nunley
University of Kansas

George W. Ulbrick
University of Kansas

Severin M. Roberts
University of Kansas

Daniel L. Roy
University of Kansas

The Cultural Landscape
An Introduction to
Human Geography
Sixth Edition

James M. Rubenstein
Miami University, Oxford, Ohio

PRENTICE HALL, Upper Saddle River, NJ 07458

Acquisitions Editor: *Dan Kaveney*
Supplement Editor: *Wendy Rivers*
Special Projects Manager: *Barbara A. Murray*
Production Editor: *Dawn Blayer*
Manufacturing Buyer: *Ben Smith*
Supplement Cover Manager: *Paul Gourhan*
Cover Designer: *Liz Nemeth*
Photo Credit: *Guatemala, Lake Atklam, Woman weaving
                rugs in foreground.*
Photographers: *Michele and Tom Grimm/Tony Stone Images*

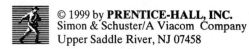

Printed in the United States of America

10 9 8 7 6 5 4

ISBN 0-13-080180-1

Prentice-Hall International (UK) Limited, *London*
Prentice-Hall of Australia Pty. Limited, *Sydney*
Prentice-Hall Canada, Inc., *Toronto*
Prentice-Hall Hispanoamericana, S.A., *Mexico*
Prentice-Hall of India Private Limited, *New Delhi*
Prentice-Hall of Japan, Inc., *Tokyo*
Simon & Schuster Asia Pte. Ltd., *Singapore*
Editora Prentice-Hall do Brasil, Ltda., *Rio de Janeiro*

Contents

Preface

The present study guide was produced by the four authors, aided by many students from the Geography Department of the University of Kansas. Ms. Roberts prepared the study guide with editing by Mr. Roy, Dr. Nunley, and Mr. Ulbrick. Dr. Nunley designed and critiqued all drafts, prepared the final draft; and assumes full responsibility for any errors or shortcomings. A web site, developed by Mr. Roy and edited by Ms. Roberts, Dr. Nunley and Mr. Ulbrick, supplements the text and study guide, and is available at: http://www.prenhall.com/rubenstein

It is suggested this study guide be used to outline the chapter for a full grasp of concepts and as a means to integrate the material with course notes. The *Key Terms and Concepts* and *Progressive Review* sections at the end of each chapter offer a tool for testing knowledge of the basic concepts of human geography.

Comments and suggestions are welcome. E-mail: (nunley@ukans.edu).

CHAPTER 1

BASIC CONCEPTS

Chapter One details the building blocks of human geography. Maps and map elements are presented--maps are the geographer's medium for study and portrayal of geographic information. Geographers study the locational relationships of the physical earth and of human cultural characteristics. The *where* of geography involves techniques for describing locations on the earth's surface. Included are the concepts of latitude and longitude which measure the location of places on the Earth's surface. The historical development of geography as a discipline is described, in part, by the scholars who contributed to the body of geographic literature and thought. The *why* of geography is investigated by using Regional Analysis and Spatial Analysis, each of which is expanded upon in this chapter. Types of regions and patterns of distribution are summarized. An introduction to physical processes and climate types is offered. Chapter One also outlines examples of human interaction with the natural environment. Globalization and local diversity are the two perspectives from which the text's concepts and characteristics will be presented.

Some people believe that geography is memorizing capitals and countries, climates and crop types, as well as other facts that may initially appear "trivial." Geography is the analysis of information that has a spatial component; it is the organization of material by place. Maps give a better understanding of the traits of places, and how those traits influence other locations around the globe. *Geography* is the scientific study of the location and distribution of people and activities across the Earth's surface. Geographers ask *where* things are, *why* they are there, and *why* their geographic arrangements are significant. As historians study the sequence of human activities through time, geographers study the arrangement of the earth's physical characteristics, human culture, and human activities across space.

Components of Geography (3-4): Geography may be divided into two primary components: Human Geography and Physical Geography. Human geography is the focus of this textbook and concentrates on cultural and economic human behavior. Physical geography is the study of climate, landforms, and vegetation. Human populations are affected by and, in turn, influence the physical environment in which they live. A balanced geographic analysis avoids concentrating all energy upon one part of geography, without considering to some degree the other parts of geography.

There are a multitude of basic concepts necessary to effective geographic thinking. Two concepts describe *where* people and activities are found. *Location* is the position something has on the Earth's surface and can be described by different methods. *Distribution* is the arrangement of people and activities across the Earth's surface. Geographers are interested in *why* each place is unique. *Culture* is the body of beliefs, traditions, political, and economic practices of a group. Distinctive cultural groups occupy particular *regions*--areas of the world distinguished by a collection of distinctive cultural and physical features.

Geographers are also interested in *why* places are similar. *Spatial interaction* is the relationships among people and objects that form across the barrier of space. The means by which the movement of people and ideas occurs is *diffusion*. *Globalization* are actions or processes that involve the entire world and result in making something worldwide in scope. *Local diversity* is the unique way people express their unique cultural traditions and economic practices. *Human-natural relationships* are the interaction of people with the natural environment.

Key Issue 1: How Do Geographers Describe Where Things Are?

Maps: Scale Models That Show Where Something Is (4): The most important tool for geographic studies is the map. Map use distinguishes geography from other disciplines. A *map* is two-dimensional or flat scale model of Earth's surface, or some portion of it, on which only selected data or locational traits are shown. Maps are a reference tool for representing where something is found. Maps also communicate geographic information using patterns, shapes, and colors to represent human activities, physical features, or dynamic processes. *Cartography* is the science of mapmaking. Mapping is essential for understanding spatial patterns-how they occur, where they occur and why they occur, at a specific location.

Scale (4-6): *Scale* determines how much area and detail a particular map represents. Scale can be displayed in one of three ways: a fraction (1/24,000) or ratio (1:24,000); a written statement such as "One inch represents one mile" or a graphic bar scale (Fig. 1.1). The scale of the map tells the distance on the earth relative to the distance on the map. *Small-scale maps* show a large surface area with less detail than a large-scale map. The *large-scale maps* represent a small land area but with much more detail than the small-scale map.

Projections (6): A *projection* is a scientific method of transferring location on Earth's surface (or any portion of it) to a flat map. There are many map projections, and each tries to minimize one type of distortion for a specific purpose. The four types of map projection distortion are *shape*, *distance*, *relative size*, and *direction*. Every map has advantages and disadvantages but each can be used appropriately. The text uses *equal area projections*. One of the most famous and most frequently misused projections is the *Mercator projection*, which was created in 1569 by a Flemish geographer named *Gerardus Mercator*. Parallels and meridians form a square grid on the flat projection. This projection is mathematically adjusted to attain conformity and was created for navigation, so it minimizes distortion in direction while wildly distorting the size and shape of high latitude regions.

Contemporary High-Tech Mapping (6): In order to communicate a geographic meaning and avoid misunderstandings, maps need to be made well, and made in such a way as to convey information competently to the map's reader. Since 1950, computers and technology contributed to two mapping innovations–*Remote Sensing* and *Geographic Information Systems (GIS)*.

Remote Sensing (7): The acquisition of data about the Earth's surface from a satellite orbiting the planet or from another long-distance method is known as *remote sensing*. Imagery produced from remote sensing may be used to evaluate water pollution, weather systems, deforestation, and many other problems.

GIS (7): A *geographic information system (GIS)* uses computers to extrapolate knowledge from different areal data, each type or attribute is created as a separate layer (Fig. 1-2). Each layer contains a certain characteristic (such as soil type, water table depth, slope, or land cover). When operated correctly a GIS can give non-intuitive and accurate answers to questions concerning such things as pollution sources, best locations for wetlands, optimum agricultural plots, potential for erosion, or which ZIP codes contain people who would like to receive a certain type of direct mail.

GPS (7): A *global positioning system (GPS)* is a system of applying special satellites and a local receiver. The piece of electronic equipment receives satellite transmissions, and calculates the latitudinal and longitudinal coordinates of the location. The elevation of the location is also calculated by most GPS units. The satellites are currently operated by the government and locations are purposely inaccurate. Vertical distortion is approximately seven times horizontal distortion. Data captured using GPS can be integrated into a GIS for better analysis of a given area.

How Geography Grew as a Science by Asking "Where?":

Historical Development of Geography (7): Early in human history, *geography* was synonymous with *navigation*. For example, Mediterranean sailors charted their voyages to distant lands by noting distinctive landmarks such as rock formations and islands. Similarly, Polynesian sailors used three-dimensional *stick charts* made of strips of palm trees and sea shells to guide them over the South Pacific (Fig. 1-3).

Geography in the Ancient World (7-9): Hundreds of years before the use of the term *geography*, the ancient Greeks were concerned with geographic phenomena. *Geography* is based on two Greek words, *geo*--Earth and *graphy*--to write. *Thales of Miletus* applied basic geometric principles to measuring land area in the 6th century BC. His student *Anaximander* argued the world was shaped like a cylinder and drew a map from sailors' information. Later, *Aristotle* (384-322 BC) demonstrated that the Earth was spherical, noting that all matter falls toward the center or core of the Earth. In 325 BC *Pytheas* sailed to Iceland and developed a method for measuring latitude by observing the positions of certain stars. *Hipparchus* (190-125 BC) developed a primitive system of latitude and longitude that is conceptually equal to our current system. *Eratosthenes* (276-195 BC) accurately measured the Earth's circumference to within a hundred miles. He is also the first person known to use the word *geography*. Additionally, Eratosthenes prepared some of the world's first known maps and divided the Earth effectively into five climatic zones. The Roman, *Strabo* (63 BC-AD. 24) extensively described the known world of his time in the seventeen-volume work, <u>Geography</u>. He regarded the Earth as a sphere in the center of a spherical universe. *Ptolemy* (AD 100-170) wrote the eight volume <u>Guide to Geography</u>. In China, geography was also developed by *Phei Hsiu*, "the father of Chinese cartography."

Geography in the Middle Ages (9): After Ptolemy, geographic thought made little significant progress in Europe for nearly a thousand years. Beginning in the 7th century AD, there was great influence of Islam upon geographic thought. Muslim writers such as *Edrisi, Ibn-Batuta*, and *Ibn-Khaldun* wrote extensively about the lands controlled by the expanding Muslim Empire.

Viking adventurers from Scandinavia did much for exploration in the late part of the first millennia AD. In 860 they arrived in Iceland from their homelands in continental Europe. *Erik the Red* sailed to *Greenland* in 981, after being banished from Iceland. *Bjarni Herjolfsson* sailed erratically south and west of Greenland in 985 and reached *Newfoundland*. He was probably the first European to reach North or South America. In 995, *Leif Eriksson* established a settlement in Newfoundland, using the former vessel of Bjarni Herjolfsson.

In 1492, *Christopher Columbus* crossed the Atlantic and set anchor near Hispanola. He died in 1506 believing he had reached Asia by using a new passage. *Vasco Nunez de Balboa* viewed the Pacific from a mountain in *Panama* in 1513. He is considered to be the first European to see the world's largest ocean. In 1522 the *Victoria* became the first ship to sail around the world. It was captained by *Ferdinand Magellan* through the Atlantic and most of the Pacific (to the *Philippines*, where he was killed in a conflict with the natives). After Magellan's death, *Juan Sebastian del Cano* piloted the Victoria for the remainder of its circumnavigation of the globe to Spain. The *Straits of Magellan* near Cape Horn at the tip of South America are named after this great explorer. Geographic thought was rekindled in the seventeenth century in Europe, inspired by the recent discoveries of the Americas to the West. The German, *Bernhardus Varenius*, wrote <u>Geographia Generalis</u>. It stood for more than a century as the standard treatise on modern geography.

How Geography Grew as a Science (9): *Immanuel Kant* (1724-1804), a German philosopher, believed that geography could be classified scientifically either logically (based on a systematic framework) or physically (based on location). His belief was that "descriptions of phenomena according to place comprise geography." Two school of thought developed in geography, one that the physical environment causes human behavior and the other that humans and the environment are interrelated.

Does the Physical Environment Cause Human Action? (9-11): In the mid 1800's, virtually all accessible knowledge of the Earth was incorporated into a large, multi-volume work called <u>Cosmos</u> by the German explorer and naturalist, *Alexander von Humboldt* (1769-1859). Von Humboldt and Professor *Karl Ritter* of the University of Berlin are considered to be the cofounders of modern Western geography. They argued geography must move beyond describing the earth into analyzing why aspects were present or absent. Additionally, these two geographers believed that the physical environment determined social development, an approach known as *environmental determinism*. Other prominent geographers who supported

4

environmental determinism included *Friedrich Ratzel*, his student *Ellen Churchill Semple*, and *Ellsworth Huntington*. The study of human-environment relationships is now called *cultural ecology*. Environmental determinism was replaced as the predominant paradigm of geography by *possiblism* which advances the idea that the environment may limit some human actions, but people have the ability to adjust to their surroundings. Possiblism is considered to be less restrictive in its thinking as well as more open to other factors that describe human interaction with environment.

In a Region, Everything is Related (11): An area of the Earth with its own distinctive landscape that results from a unique combination of social relationships and physical processes is known as a *region*. *Regional studies* were begun by *Paul Vidal de la Blache* (1845-1918) and *Jean Brunhes* (1869-1930) and further developed by *Carl Sauer* (1889-1975) and *Robert Platt* (1880-1950). The *regional studies* approach to geography organizes the Earth's peoples and environments through identification of regions and their descriptions, based on similarities and differences of human and physical characteristics. In Latin America most people speak an Iberian Language (Spanish or Portuguese) and are Roman Catholic, and the climates are mostly tropical or sub-tropical. Therefore the phrase, Latin America, may be a useful regional designation for that part of the Western Hemisphere generally known as "The Americas."

Location: Where Something Is (11): *Location* is the position that something occupies (on the Earth's surface). Placename, site, situation, and mathematical location are the four ways in which geographers answer the "Where" question.

Placenames (11): Most places on Earth have been given names, and which are known as a *placenames* or *toponyms* (literally, place names). The name of any state, county, or place is its place name. Places may be named for founders, famous people, important historical events, or features of the physical environment. Toponyms tell a great deal about the history and social customs of places.

Confusion and Change (11-12): Names can be used repeatedly in the same area, causing confusion. There may also be locally used names and unofficial names. Places may change names to be less offensive, to honor someone, or to reflect political upheavals. The Board of Geographical names, operated by the U.S. Geological Survey is the official arbitrator of names on U.S. maps.

Money and Politics (12): Places have been named and renamed to promote tourism, to encourage settlement, to glorify a town (as with land prospectors and developers), to alleviate political tensions, or to promote a place because of nationalism.

Site (12-13): A *site* is the physical characteristics of a place. For example, places can be described by site characteristics such as climate, soils, vegetation, latitudes, and elevations. Site is essential to settlements, especially for defendable or convenient locations in the landscape. Site characteristics don't generally change with time though human preferences do.

Situation (13-14): *Situation* is the relative location of one place to another, more familiar one. Situation aids in finding unfamiliar places by referential direction from more familiar ones. Situation is also important for understanding the importance of a location because of accessibility and inaccessibility and proximity to human and physical features.

Mathematical Location (15): Many reference maps use a grid system to locate places using columns and rows, often called the "A-1" system.

Latitude and Longitude (15): The Earth is a sphere with a diameter of about 12,875 km (8,000 miles) and a circumference of about 40,000 km (25,000 miles). It rotates continuously on an axis that passes through the North and South poles. Halfway between the poles lies the *equator*, which divides the Earth into the northern hemisphere and the southern hemisphere. Locations on the Earth are determined by two different measurements: latitude and longitude. *Latitude* is the angular distance measured north and south of the equator. Lines of latitude are called *parallels* as each line is *parallel* to the equator and all other lines of latitude. *Longitude* is the angular distance measured east and west on the Earth's surface. Lines of longitude are called *meridians* and they extend from pole to pole. Both latitude and longitude are measured in degrees, minutes, and seconds. Latitude measures degrees north and south of the equator up to 90 degrees at the poles. In most places, longitude is measured starting at the *prime meridian* that passes through Greenwich, England. Longitude measures degrees east and west of the prime meridian up to 180 degrees, the international date line.

U.S. Land Ordinance of 1785 (15, 18): The *U.S. Land Ordinance of 1785* partitioned much of the U.S. into a system of townships and ranges to encourage settlement of the west. *Principal Meridians* and *Base Lines* were used as reference points to delineate the individual townships (Fig. 1-7). These serve the same purposes as do X and Y for a mathematical or geometric chart. A *township* contains 36 sections and measures 6 miles to a side (36 square miles). Each square mile is known as a *section* (Figure 1-8). Each section is divided into quadrants (northeast, northwest, southeast, or southwest quarter) each of which consists of 160 acres (.25 square miles). "Quarters" were the most common plot sizes homesteaded by pioneers.

Distribution: Spatial Regularities (18): Also known as *locational analysis*, it searches for worldwide patterns in the distributions of human actions and environmental processes. The arrangement of any phenomenon across the Earth's surface is called *spatial distribution*. Human activities and environmental conditions are dynamic, therefore the *movement* of people, goods, ideas, energy, and natural materials (like water) is a subject studied by geographers. Spatial distribution possesses three main components: density, concentration, and pattern.

Density (18): The frequency with which something occurs in a measured area is called *density*. There are several ways of measuring density. *Arithmetic density* is the number of objects in a given area. *Physiological density* measures the number of people to area of arable land (land suited for agriculture). *Agricultural density* measures the number of farmers per unit area of farmland. *Housing density* is the number of dwelling units per unit of land. Large population does not necessarily mean a high density, nor is high population density related to poverty.

Concentration (18-21): The dispersion of something over an area is called *concentration*. Things found grouped in a small focal area in a landscape are said to be *clustered*. If objects are located far apart from each other they are *dispersed*. For example, the population of the United States has long been clustered in the North-East but, due to economic changes and aesthetic appreciation for warmer weather, the US's population density has increased in the Sunbelt and California.

Pattern (21): *Pattern* is the geometric order of the objects across space. Some objects are placed in a *regular, geometric* pattern while others are more *randomly* or *irregularly* distributed. Some things such as cities have *linear* distributions when located along rivers or a primary road, and others have a *grid pattern,* such as the county lines and roads of the Midwestern plains.

Key Issue 2: Why Is Each Place Unique? (21): Culture and the division of the earth into regions are two things geographer's use to analyze the uniqueness of each place.

Culture: People's Beliefs and Traits (21): *Culture* is the body of customary beliefs, material traits, and social forms that together constitute the distinct tradition of a group of people. *Culture* is from the Latin word *cultus* and means "to care for."

Geographic Approaches to Studying Culture (21): Geography looks at two aspects of culture--what people care about, and what people take care of.

What People Care About (21-22): Geographers study why cultures are distinctive in particular areas of the world. Cultural values are derived from a group's language, religion and ethnicity. *Language* is a system of signs, sounds, gestures, and marks that have meanings understood within a cultural group. *Religion* is the principle system of attitudes, beliefs, and practices through which people worship in a formal, organized way that is important to the group. *Ethnicity* is the collection of a group's language, religion, physical traits, and other cultural values.

What People Take Care Of (22): There are two elements of material artifacts interesting for study--daily necessities of survival (food, clothing, and shelter) and leisure activities.

Cultural Institutions (22): Political institution are created to maintain the values of a group of people and protect the material artifacts. Cultural identity includes political affiliation. Political boundaries do not, however, always coincide with the boundaries of a cultural group which can cause political problems.

Cultural Identity (22-23): Self-identification by cultural identity is a source of pride and an inspiration for personal values. Cultural identification is important for other people because people want to identify the people with whom they share similarities. Cultural identity is also the means by which groups of people can be identified across the landscape. People sort themselves in space by choosing places in which they can comfortably live. Cultural groups move in distinct patterns as well. People choose towns, neighborhoods, and houses based on their cultural identity, which includes race, religion, economic status, and sexual preference.

Cultural Ecology: Relations Between Cultures and Environment (23-24): The study of interactions of culture with the natural environment is *cultural ecology.* Cultures impact the environment by their use of *resources*--substances with usefulness. *Pierce Lewis*, a leading landscape geographer, states "the cultural landscape is our unwitting autobiography." Humans' approach to the natural environment has a cultural basis. Culture affects the decisions people make about house location, agricultural practices, and environmental management. Wealth affects people's ability to modify the landscape. The cultural ecology, or human-environment, approach to world issues allows for more information to be included in a thoughtful consideration of a problem.

Physical Processes (24): Understanding the physical environment in which humans live helps geographers understand the ways culture affects the landscape.

Climate (24): Long-term weather conditions at a particular place are known as its *climate*. The German climatologist *Vladamir Koppen* said the world was host to five different climate types (Figure 1-12): tropical, dry, warm mid-latitude, cold mid-latitude, and polar. Humans aren't adept at living in places with extremes of rainfall or temperature. The map in People are less attracted by weather that is too wet, cold, hot, or dry. In Southwestern India, Bangladesh, and Myanmar (formerly Burma), *monsoon* rains come each year to replenish the water supplies, and usually flood many parts of the area. The Monsoons of South Asia last from June through September and provide the area with water and (due to flooding) widespread fertilizer (silt) for their crops.

Vegetation (24): Most of the Earth's land surfaces support some type of vegetation communities, called *biomes*. Earth's vegetation consist of four biomes. The *forest biome* contains trees forming a continuous canopy. Forest biomes are found in North America, Europe, Asia, and the tropical areas of South America, Africa, and Southeast Asia. The *savanna biome* is a mixture of trees and grasses that are prominent in Africa, South Asia, South America, and Australia. *Grassland biomes* cover much of North America and don't support many trees due to lack of precipitation. *Desert biomes* support plants and animals adapted to dry environments.

Soil (24-25) The natural terrestrial surface layer containing living matter and supporting–or capable of supporting–plants is known as *soil.* *Erosion* and the *depletion of nutrients* are the main agents that tend to destroy soil.

Landforms (25): The science that studies Earth's landforms is called *geomorphology.* *Relief* is the difference in elevation between two points. *Slope* is the angle at which land is inclined. Slope and relief are shown on topographic maps, which are used to study physical and cultural features of landscapes (Fig. 1-8).

Human Environmental Modification (26):

The Netherlands: Sensitive Environmental Modification (26): Few places on the planet have been modified to benefit people as much as the polders of the Netherlands. A *polder* is a piece of land that has been created by draining water from an area, and then encircling it with dikes to prevent it from becoming periodically flooded. A *dike* is an elongated dam that prevents water from lakes or the ocean from flooding areas of lower elevation. Like much of the Netherlands, New Orleans is protected by dikes because much of its topography lies below the water level of the Mississippi River. The Dutch have been transforming the North Sea into land in this way since around 1200 AD, mainly in the *Zuider Zee Works* and the *Delta Plan*, the two primary polder projects in the Netherlands. The famous windmills associated with the Netherlands were used for pumping water from polder areas. Once dried, the polder can be used for construction, agriculture, or recreation.

Florida: Not-so-sensitive Environmental Modification (26-28): Due to periodic flooding, the State of Florida asked the federal government to straighten the 98 mile-long *Kissimmee River* which meandered from Orlando to Lake Okeechobee (Fig. 1-21). During times when annual flooding was great, the river would immerse 45,000 acres of nearby land, much under agricultural production. In 1971, the channel opened and changed the environmental landscape of Florida. Water drained from cattle farms defiled the canal. The river, in turn, polluted and fouled *Lake Okeechobee*, the source of fresh water for half of the state's population. Since then the Army Corps of Engineers has spent hundreds of millions of dollars in attempts to rectify their mistake by restoring the river to its original course. Barrier islands run parallel to the coast of the southern and eastern states of the U.S.. People build homes upon them for the view and aesthetics of a nearby ocean. With human occupancy erosion is exacerbated, and many of the homes are periodically destroyed by storms.

Region: Areas of Unique Characteristics (28-29): A *region* is an area of Earth defined by one or more distinctive characteristics. Geographers use the regional studies approach to identify similarities and differences across the landscape. Regional analysis begins by identifying important characteristics then advances explanations for variations between regions.

Types of Regions (29):

Formal Region (29): A *formal region* is an area in which selected characteristics are present throughout. It is also known as a uniform region or a homogeneous region. People in a politically-delineated area such as a county, state, or nation belong to a distinct formal region. Although a substantial number of people of a certain characteristic live in such a region, there usually are others present (i.e. minorities) not described by the name and traits given to a formal region. This mixing of cultural identities is known as *diversity*.

Functional Region (29-30): A *functional region* is a nodal area which influences and serves a larger area. The concentration of influence tends to be strongest at the core of the region and declines with distance away from the core area. The center of the node is called the *core* while the outlying area of influence is called the *periphery*. Functional regionalization is used to describe newspaper and television areas, dominant economic activities, or transportation and communication systems.

Vernacular Region (30-32): A *vernacular region* (*perceptual region*) is one that is culturally identified by the people of some area. Examples of vernacular regions include the "Bible-belt," "Sun-belt," and "Frost-belt." Analysts have difficulty identifying boundaries of vernacular regions; there are a multitude of perceptions for each region, owing to the numerous perceptions of any one labeled area by different groups of people. *Mental maps*, internal representations of a portion of the

Earth's surface, portray individual knowledge and perception of a given area and often reflect how people organize their daily lives.

Regional Integration (32): In the real world, geographers understand that characteristics are integrated. For example, geographers divide the world into two economic regions: *more developed countries (MDCs)* and *less developed countries (LDCs)*. MDCs, such as European countries, U.S., Canada, and Japan are located mainly in the northern latitudes. Regions dominated by LDCs are located in mainly southern latitudes. Consequently, there is a north-south partition of the world's social or economic problems. Geographers build models to identify relationships between the distribution of one trait of development with others. A primary objective of geographers is to better understand the areal associations of different regions.

Integrating Cancer Information (32-33): Geographers recognize that local environments may cause their residents to be affected by local physical phenomena. For example, core areas of water and air pollution seem to cause more people nearer the source to suffer greater from associated symptoms than do people located further away from the origin of the pollution. Maryland has the highest cancer rates among the fifty states. When cancer rates within Maryland are mapped, decisive internal variations can be visualized. Westernmost Garret County has a lower cancer rate than does Baltimore City (Fig. 1-17). Most of the high rates of cancer are in metro areas which, it turns out, are more inclined to suffer from air pollution and water pollution.

Key Issue 3: Why Are Different Places Similar? (33): Studying spatial interaction and diffusion of people and ideas helps geographers identify why regions can display similar characteristics.

Spatial Interaction: Interdependence Among Places (33-34): *Globalization* is an action or process that involves the entire world and results in making something worldwide in scope. Areas must be connected to each other in some way.

Globalization of Economy and Culture (34): Actions or processes that provide worldwide accessibility of something are called *globalization*. With freer trade, people around the world have more access to a greater diversity of goods; innovations in communications allow people to share ideas, knowledge, and concepts more readily. Such things integrate the world's environments, economies, and peoples, thus *"shrinking"* the world.

Economic Interaction (34-35): In today's world, many large businesses place parts of their companies all around the world, depending upon where each will be most profitable. For one firm, manufacturing could be in Mexico, marketing could be in the U.S., and headquarters could remain in Amsterdam. These traits are linked to better transportation and communication, as well as to the globalization of the world's economy. Firms that manufacture their goods, conduct research, and sell products in many different domains around the world are known as *transnational corporations*. Most transnational corporations are based in North America (mainly U.S.), Western Europe, and Japan. Current trends show that transnational corporations move many operations to countries where labor is comparatively less expensive. At least one of the three financial centers of the world–*New York, Tokyo,* or *London*–is open nearly 24 hours a day, with differing schedules and time-zone differences. With more competition encouraged by freer trade in the world, firms locate their operations in more profitable locations.

Cultural Interaction (35): Globalization of the landscape is occurring because of the proliferation of material artifacts and cultural values. International corporations purposefully maintain uniformity of appearance because they can be readily recognized independent of location. Uniform consumption preferences may result when the television sets provide billions of people around the world similar information about cultural elements. For example, today there are many culturally different people on the planet who yearn for Nikes, jeans, and Sony electronic products. The globalization of religion and language are especially interesting topics. English is increasingly important as the international language. Three *universalizing* religions--Buddhism, Christianity, and Islam--are the predominant world relations.

Networks (35): *Networks* are chains of communication and transportation that connect places. Televisions, telephones, road networks, and airlines rapidly connect people across large distances. The further one group is from another, however, the less likely they are to interact. *Distance decay* is the diminishing of contact with increasing distance.

Enhanced Communications (35-36): *Enhanced communications* result where travel is much quicker than in earlier times (Fig. 1-20). *Time-space compression* is the time it takes an innovation to diffuse to a distant place. Also, telecommunications and computers make inter-global communication instantaneous and seemingly limitless. Still, many people in the world don't have access to the media and computer networks to the same degree as do people in MDCs. Consequently, intellectual and economic disparities derived from this resource have increased the socio-economic disparities between LDCs and MDCs.

Diffusion: Movement Between Places (37): The process by which a characteristic spreads from one place to another over time is *diffusion*. The original location of an idea, technology, or innovation is a *hearth*. As an innovative idea emerges in one place, if well received, it will *diffuse* to other places.

Types of Diffusion (37):

Relocation Diffusion (37-38): *Relocation diffusion* is the spread of a phenomena through the movement of people from one region to another. When people relocate, they take with them their culture, language, religion, and ethnicity. AIDS and other diseases are often spread by people who relocate.

Expansion and Related Types of Diffusion (38): The spread of a trait through a region is *expansion diffusion*.

Hierarchical diffusion (38): *Hierarchical diffusion* is the spread of phenomena from a node of origin, often from the spread of the ideas of political leaders, socially elite people, or other important people.

Contagious diffusion (38): *Contagious diffusion* is the extensive diffusion of something through a population. It is analogous to the spread of a disease.

Stimulus diffusion (38): *Stimulus diffusion* is the spread of an underlying principle, but not the specific idea. Due to quick transportation, computers, telecommunications, the internet, expansion diffusion can be achieved almost instantaneously. The reduction in the time it takes for an idea to disperse is called *space-time compression*.

Diffusion of Economy (38):

Investment Flows From Three Core Regions (38-40): Modern communication and transportation systems organize the Earth and expedite transfer of capital, goods, services, raw materials, and finished goods. The three hearth regions of the global economy are North America, Western Europe, and Japan. Nearly three-fourths of the world's population and nearly all of the world's population growth is occurring in Africa, Asia, and Latin America. The differences in infrastructure and available capital place the LDCs on the periphery of the global economy. The disparities between economies and increasing gap in economic conditions is increasing because of *uneven development*.

Specialization in the Location of Production (40): Every place in the world has distinct assets and opportunities which can be taken advantage of. Transnational corporations often take advantage of the individual strengths of locations. The global economy has heightened economic differences among places. Transnational corporations make use of varying skills possessed by laborers around the world and make locational choices to use the natural resources and laborers as best as possible.

Diffusion of Culture (41): Nearly everyone in the world is aware of the existence of televisions, telephones, and motor vehicles, though there are extreme disparities in access to them.

Unequal Access to Cultural Elements (41): People are aware of cultural elements, though relatively few people in the world have enough wealth to purchase them.

Maintaining Local Traditions (41): Globalization of technology and cultural elements changes local traditions. Some are threatened with extinction, while other localized cultures differently interpret global culture and technology. Not everyone wants the same things. Communication and transportation systems provide opportunities for local cultural traditions and languages to be reinforced by being shared across large distances. Some traditions may be modified to encompass aspects of global culture. When two groups attain a higher degree of interaction, the stronger and more influential culture will greatly affect the development of the other culture—a concept known as *acculturation*. When acculturation occurs, the weaker culture can either be completely replaced with the dominant culture, or it may be become greatly modified, with old features of the former society surviving within the framework of the newer, more influential culture.

Cargo Cult (41-42): . Some primitive tribes in remote areas of the world were so impressed with the arrival of humans in airplanes or ships that they were worshipped as gods or had spiritual meaning. Such adoration for technology from advanced societies is termed *Cargo Cult*. The classic example is Papau New Guinea and other Pacific islands because American ships and airplanes brought goods and technology during World War II. Some still believe that if they remain faithful, the planes will return with their vast wealth and build wooden "female" planes to lure the "male" airplanes to land.

Tension Between Globalization and Local Diversity (42): Tensions arise between the need to participate in the global economy and culture and the desire to preserve local traditions and cultural beliefs.

Summary: The concepts presented in Chapter One impart an understanding of how geography was developed historically, how geographers answer the "Where" and "Why" questions, and how the human-environment and regional studies methods answer the "Why" questions of geography. It is very important to learn the ideas presented in this introductory chapter; future chapters in the Rubenstein text build on a foundation of the fundamentals of geography. If any one component of this chapter incites a special curiosity, be assured that a more detailed exploration of related material is found in one of the remaining chapters!

CHAPTER 1
KEY TERMS AND CONCEPTS

Geography: The scientific study of the location of people and activities across the Earth's surface, the reasons for their distribution, the organization of material by place, and the analysis of regional similarities and differences.

Map: A two-dimensional, or flat representation of the Earth's surface, or a portion of it. It can be used to show physical traits of the landscape, or to display thematic data.

Cartography: The science of making maps. In the past most were made largely by hand but, with computers and software, they are now mostly created electronically.

Scale: The relationship between the size of an object on a map, and that object's true dimensions on the Earth. Large-scale maps show more detail for small areas; small-scale maps show less detail for larger areas.

Projection: The system used to transfer locations from the globe onto a map. Projections distort the shape, distance, relative size, or direction of the Earth. Some projections minimize one or more types of distortion.

Equal Area Projection: A projection maintaining the relative areas of the Earth.

Mercator Projection: It is computed so all meridians and parallels intersecting at right angles distorting land areas in polar regions while maintaining direction.

Remote Sensing: The process by which images (captured by electronic equipment in satellites and airplanes) can be used to observe and analyze the Earth's surface.

Geographic Information System (GIS): Computer software that facilitates the storage, retrieval, analysis, and display of geographic data, usually as an integrated series of map coverages (layers).

Global Positioning System (GPS): Satellite projection of times to hand held GPS units which triangulate a horizontal and vertical location.

Environmental Determinism: An approach to the study of geography (very popular in the nineteenth and early twentieth-century) which argued that general laws sought by human geographers could be found using approaches developed in the physical sciences. Geography was, therefore, the study of how the physical environment determined human activities.

Possibilism: The twentieth-century theory that the physical environment may set limits on human actions, but people have the ability to adjust to the physical environment and choose their courses of action from many alternatives.

The Regional Analysis Tradition of Geography: This is a way of organizing the study of the Earth's peoples and environments through identification of regions and their descriptions, based upon similarities and differences and the magnitudes thereof.

Location: The position on the Earth's surface that an object occupies. The location of something answers the "Where" question.

Toponym: Literally this term means "place name," and it is used to describe a place on the Earth's surface.

Site: The physical character of a location. Climate, soil, elevations, and others characteristics associated with a place describe its site.

Situation: The location of a place relative to other places. By using the locations of known places as reference points, the locations of unfamiliar localities may be more effectively presented.

Mathematical Location: A system that uses lines of longitude and latitude to specify the location of a place lying on the Earth's surface.

Latitude: The numbering system used to indicate the location of parallels drawn on a globe and measured in degrees north and south of the equator, the equator being zero degrees.

Parallels: Circles drawn around the globe parallel to the equator which intersect meridians at right angles. All points upon them lie equally distant from the equator (and from the poles).

Equator: The parallel with the greatest diameter; it splits the Earth into two hemispheres (half spheres)–the Northern and Southern Hemispheres.

Longitude: The numbering system used to indicate the location meridians drawn on a globe and measuring distance east and west of the Prime Meridian, which is the base meridian for the system used in most places.

Prime Meridian: The meridian which passes through the Royal Observatory in Greenwich, England; it is designated as 0 degrees.

U.S. Land Ordinance of 1785: A system based upon Principal Meridians and Baselines which divided unsettled areas of the U.S. into uniformly 36 square mile townships. Each one mile square is a section. Each square mile section was quartered into 160 acre plots, which was the size for most homesteading.

Spatial Distribution: The arrangement of a phenomenon across the Earth's surface. For example, population distribution across the Earth is clustered in many places and nearly non-existent in other, less-hospitable places.

Density: The frequency with which something occurs within a given unit of area. For example, the density of fast food restaurants would be greater in a college neighborhoods than in most non-college neighborhoods.

Arithmetic Density: This is the number of objects in a given area. For example, the arithmetic density of the UK is 240 persons per square mile.

Physiological Density: Measuring the density of people against arable land is physiological density. Japan has a large physiological density, due to its large population and small amount of arable land.

Agricultural Density: The number of farmers per unit area of cultivated farmland is agricultural density.

Concentration: The extent of spread of a phenomenon over a given area. For example, much of the U.S. population is concentrated in the Northeast, around the Great Lakes, and in southern California.

Pattern: The geometric arrangement of something. Regular, random, and linear are the three main types of patterns.

Culture: The body of customary beliefs, social forms, and material traits constituting a distinct complex of tradition of a racial, religious, or social group.

Language: A system of signs, sounds, gestures, and marks (sometimes writing) that have meanings understood within a group.

Religion: The principle system of attitudes, beliefs, and practices through which people worship in a formal, organized way that is important to the group. Most religions convey three things: how to be a good person, how to behave in a group, and what is bigger than the individual (sometimes called god).

Ethnicity: The collection of a group's language, religion, physical traits, and other cultural values.

Cultural Ecology: The study of the interaction of culture with the natural environment.

Resources: Things that yield value or are useful. People, fossil fuels, solar energy, trees, and water are all examples of resources.

Climate: The long-term weather of a particular region. Climates are greatly influenced by latitude, elevation, and relative location in relation to mountains, bodies of waters, and ocean currents.

Monsoon: The wind patterns that affect South Asia blowing landward in the summer (bringing rains) and seaward in the winter (rendering drought).

Biomes: A large community of Earth's land vegetation. Included are the 1-forest biome, 2-savanna biome, 3-grassland biome, and 4-desert biome.

Soil: The material that lies on Earth's surface between the air and rocks. It contains living matter and is capable of supporting plants.

Erosion: The removal of mineral particles and/or soil from bedrock by rain, ice, wind, or water.

Geomorphology: The study of Earth's landforms.

Relief: The difference in elevation between two points. Relief measures the extent to which an area is flat or hilly.

Slope: Relief divided by the distance between two points: slope measures the steepness of hills.

Polder: Land created by the Dutch by draining water from an areas formerly covered by shallow seas or lakes.

Dikes: An elongated dam that encircles polders and prevents flooding by restraining rivers, oceans, seas, and lakes. Currently also applied to any elongated dam along a river course.

Region: An area distinguished by one or more distinctive characteristics. Areas with similar climates, agriculture practices, or religions may be classified as a region.

Diversity: Even in a "homogeneous" region there are minorities within that region or culture that deviate from the stated rule. These additional cultures add more flavors to the final cultural product of a society. These influences represent the diversity of a region.

Formal Region: An area in which a selected characteristic is present throughout (a.k.a. uniform or homogeneous region). Cities, states, and nations are formal regions, due to many uniform traits they possess.

Functional Region: An area in which an activity has a focal point. The characteristic dominates at a central node; it diffuses toward the outer part of the region, diminishing and eventually disappearing.

Vernacular Region (Perceptual Region): An area that people believe to exist as part of their cultural identity. For example, "Dixie" is the name that many people give to most parts of the former Civil War Confederacy, though it has no government or specific delineation.

More Developed Countries: Countries that are more developed economically. These countries tend to be found in Western Europe, North America (U.S. & Canada), and East Asia (Japan).

Less Developed Countries: Countries that are less developed economically. They are also called "developing countries." High birth rates, low income, lower literacy rates, and poorer health care tend to be traits of LDCs.

Spatial Interaction: The movement of people, goods, and ideas within and among regions. With recent innovations in television, computers, and telephones spatial interaction has increased dramatically, thus rendering the planet "smaller."

Globalization: Actions or processes that provide worldwide accessibility to something. Technology and its utilization increase levels of globalization.

Transnational Corporations: Firms which locate different parts of their organization in various places in the world, due to the comparative advantages of those places.

Financial Centers of the World: New York, Tokyo, and London have tremendous influences upon the financial structure of the global economy.

Uniform Consumption Preferences: Products that are desired due to their utility and fashion, often represented by a complex structure of marketing mechanisms.

Networks: Chains of communication and transportation systems that connect places.

Distance Decay: The characteristic decrease of influence of a phenomenon with distance away from the place(s) where that phenomenon is found.

Time-Space Compression: The reduction in time required for an innovation to disperse. Increases in communication and transportation networks and their utilization decrease the time it takes for wide-spread diffusion.

Diffusion: The process of spread across the landscape.

Hearth: The region from which original ideas originate. For example: Paris, New York, Milan, and Tokyo are fashion clothing hearths, because many new types of clothing are first introduced in these cities.

Relocation Diffusion: The spread of an idea through migration of people from one region to another. For example, when French traders and settlers brought their language to Eastern Canada they were practicing relocation diffusion of the French language.

Expansion Diffusion: The spread of a characteristic among people within a region. It is divided into three components:

Hierarchical Diffusion: the spread of an idea that originates at a node of innovation within a region to other nodes in the hierarchy.

Contagious Diffusion: the widespread diffusion of a characteristic throughout a population (as with a disease).

Stimulus Diffusion: the spread of an underlying principle, even though a characteristic, itself, fails to diffuse.

Uneven Development: Uneven development describes the differences in economic activities between MDCs and LDCs. There are large disparities between economic conditions in MDCs and LDCs.

Acculturation: The modification of a culture as result of contact with another (usually a more powerful) culture. Even so, often the less dominant culture will inject some of its traits into the more dominant culture, as in the infusion of African-influenced music into the mainstream of the U.S..

Cargo Cult: A belief that the arrival of a ship or airplane in a locality has spiritual meaning.

CHAPTER 1
PROGRESSIVE REVIEW

1. The scientific study of the locations of people and activities across the Earth's _____ is known as _____.

surface, geography

2. Geography is divided into two realms: _____ Geography and _____ Geography

Physical, Human

3. A _____ is a graphic representation of an area of Earth's surface.

map

4. The science and art of creating maps is _____.

Cartography

5. _____-scale maps have large denominators and display less detail of large areas, while _____-scale maps have small denominators and display more detail of small areas.

small, large

6. In _____ projections size is greatly distorted in the polar latitudes.

Mercator

7. _____ collect data from outer space. _____ _____ is the science of processing and displaying this geographical data.

Satellites, Remote Sensing

8. _____ _____ _____ are software packages that can integrate and manipulate different sets of geographic data in map formats.

Geographic Information Systems

9. The Greek, _____, was the first person acknowledged to use the word "Geography."

Eratosthenes

10. Ptolemy wrote the eight-volume _____ to _____.

Guide, Geography

11. Juan Sebastian del Cano brought the ship _____ into port in Spain after a circumnavigation of Earth. The original captain, _____, was killed back in the islands today known as the _____.

Victoria Magellan Philippines

12. Alexander Von Humbolt and _____ _____ brought geography into the _____ era by introducing methods of _____ inquiry to geography.

Carl Ritter, modern, scientific

13. Environmental determinism is the concept that says the physical environment determines _____ _____.

social development

14. _____ is the idea that the environment may limit some human actions, but people can adjust to their surroundings.   Possibilism

15. Ellen Churchill Semple subscribed to the _____ _____ theory of human development.   environmental determinism

16. _____ describes something's position on the surface of Earth.   Location

17. A _____ is another word for place name.   toponym

18. The physical characteristics of a place are its _____.   site

19. Earth's system of parallels originates at the _____.   equator

20. Lines of longitude always intersect parallels at _____ angles.   right

21. Zero degrees longitude is known as the _____ _____.   Prime Meridian

22. The International Date Line lies mostly along _____ _____.   180° longitude

23. A survey township consists of _____ square miles.   36

24. Homesteaders generally staked out _____ acres of land, which is __/__ of a section.   160
1/4

25. The arrangement of anything across the Earth's surface is its _____ _____.   spatial distribution

26. Physiological density measures the number of people within a country against the country's _____ _____.   arable land

27. Vegetation communities of the Earth are called _____.   biomes

28. _____ is the science that studies Earth's landforms.   Geomorphology

29. In South Asia, the _____ brings heavy rains primarily during the _____ season.   monsoon
summer

30. A dike is elongated dam which keeps oceans, lakes, rivers, and seas from _____ areas of lower _____.   flooding, elevation

31. The farther you go away from the location of something, the less influence it is likely to have. This is called _____ _____.   distance decay

32. Actions or processes that provide the world with higher levels of accessibility is known as _____.   globalization

33. _____ _____ conduct different segments of business in many different nations throughout the world.   Transnational corporations

CHAPTER 2

POPULATION

Population growth and decline, reasons for population growth, differing regional population growth rates, the spatial distribution of people on Earth, and the prospect of the planet facing an overpopulation dilemma are the main ideas presented in Chapter Two. When geographers, engineers, planners, and other professionals plan cities, infrastructures, economies, and other important elements of society they plan for projected populations to prevent waste of resources (insufficient or over building) and direct and manage growth.

When the number of people in an area exceeds the carrying capacity of the land there is often hunger, poverty, and a lower standard of living. Countries with such traits are referred to as Less Developed Countries (LDCs). Countries having lower rates of population increase and higher standards of living are referred to as More Developed Countries (MDCs). Population dynamics and distributions provide a basis for understanding why economies flourish or flounder, why some people retain higher standards of living than in other areas, and why governments have difficulty aiding their populaces.

There are many terms and abbreviations in this chapter; the *Key Terms* section for Chapter Two begins on page 32. Understanding the terms is integral to understanding the concepts presented in this and further chapters.

Population: Population analysis is important for three reasons: 1-over *six billion people* inhabit the Earth, far more than at any other time in the planet's history; *2-* human population has *increased faster* in the past fifty years than at any other time in history; and 3-nearly all population growth is *concentrated* in poor, developing countries (LDCs). *Demography* is the scientific study of population characteristics. Demographers use cartography and statistics to analyze how humans and their income, gender, occupation, and health are distributed around the world. Geodemographics (analysis of demography across space) helps answer questions that may not be known otherwise.

Geographers ask where people are located, where population is increasing, and why it is increasing at a different rate in different parts of the world. Studying *overpopulation* (the number of people in an area exceeds the area's capacity to support a decent standard of living) is not a simple equation between the number of people in the world and the area. There are many variables which assist in analyzing the ability of an area's available resources to sustain people. Measures of local diversity also assist geographic analysis of areas and nations that can readily support their populations as well as those which can not.

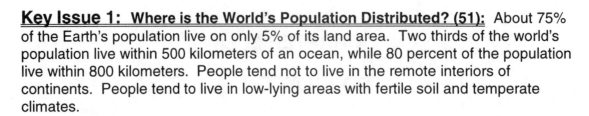

Key Issue 1: Where is the World's Population Distributed? (51): About 75% of the Earth's population live on only 5% of its land area. Two thirds of the world's population live within 500 kilometers of an ocean, while 80 percent of the population live within 800 kilometers. People tend not to live in the remote interiors of continents. People tend to live in low-lying areas with fertile soil and temperate climates.

Population Concentrations (51): Five population regions contain most of Earth's human occupants: *1-East Asia, 2-South Asia, 3-Southeast Asia, 4-Western Europe,* and *5-Eastern North America.* (See Figure 2.1 for a world map of population distribution.). The three Asian regions contain more than half of world population and comprise only 10 percent of the world's land area.

      East Asia (51-52): Approximately *one-fourth* of the world's people (1.5 billion) live in East Asia, the *largest* cluster of inhabitants in the world. Five-sixths of the people in this region reside in the *People's Republic of China*, the world's most populous country while ranking third for total area. Most of its people live near water--along Pacific coast and in several fertile river valleys draining the country's interior. There are eleven major cities though seventy-five percent of its people live in rural areas and work as farmers. In *Japan* and *South Korea*, more than one third of the people live in three urban areas accounting for three percent of their land area. More than 75 percent of the population lives in urban areas.

      South Asia (52-53): South Asia has the second largest concentration of people with over 20 percent of the world's inhabitants. *India, Pakistan, Bangladesh,* and *Sri Lanka* contain the majority of the region's land area and population. Most of the population is concentrated along the Indus and Ganges River and along the coasts. Approximately 25 percent of the population lives in urban areas.

      Southeast Asia (53): Southeast Asia is the fourth largest population cluster in the world--over one-half billion people.. The region is a string of islands between the Indian and Pacific Oceans. *Java* has the world's largest population *concentration* (more than 100 million people). Indonesia , the world's fourth most populous country, is in this cluster, as are the Philippines. Like China and South Asia, most of its inhabitants live as farmers in rural areas.

      Europe (53): Europe and European Russia contain *one-eighth* of the world's population. Unlike most of Asia, three-fourths of this region's people live in cities, while less than twenty percent are farmers. The highest concentrations of people are in the coal fields of England, Germany, and Belgium, historically the centers of energy for industry. Europeans import food and resources from other areas of the world.

      Eastern North America (53): Eastern North America includes the northeastern U.S. and southeastern Canada. The megalopolis and surrounding area accounts for about 2 percent of the world's population. They tend to be urban dwellers and fewer than 5 percent are employed in agriculture.

Sparsely Populated Regions (53): Population concentrates in areas suitable for human activities. The portion of the Earth's surface occupied by permanent human settlement is called the *ecumene*. Harsher, inhospitable environments include dry, wet, cold, and high lands. Extremely dry and wet lands tend to retard agriculture.

Dry Lands (53-54): Regions too *dry* for farming cover approximately twenty percent of Earth's land surface. The two large desert regions of the Earth extend from 10 to 50 degrees north and south of the equator and include the deserts of North Africa and Central Asia--the Sahara, Arabian, Gobi, and Takla Makan deserts. Some people survive in sparse concentrations by raising herd animals(goats and camels).

Wet Lands (54): Wet lands receive extreme amounts of precipitation--more than fifty inches per year with most receiving more than 90 inches. They are located between twenty degrees north and south latitude and cover equatorial regions. Nutrients necessary for agriculture are rapidly depleted from the soil due to moisture and heat. In seasonally wet Southeast Asia enough rice is grown in the wet season to sustain a large population.

Cold Lands (54): Much of the *cold land* near the poles of the Earth is perpetually frozen (permafrost) and covered with ice and snow, or both. The land cannot support crops; only a few hardy animals and people live there.

High lands (54-55): High lands (places with high elevations) are also sparsely settled. Exceptions are found in Latin America and Africa where elevation decreases the temperature. Mexico City, one of the world's largest cities, is located at an elevation of 2,243 meters.

Population Density (55): *Density* is the number of people occupying an area of land. Density is typically measured using three equations.

Arithmetic Density (55): *Arithmetic density* is the total number of people divided by the total land area. It is the common density assessment because it is the easiest to compute with available data.

Physiological Density (56-57): *Physiological density* is the number of people supported by a unit of arable land. *Arable* land is suitable for agriculture. Physiological density shows a region's demands on agricultural land.

Agricultural Density (57-58): *Agricultural density* is the number of farmers per unit of arable land. MDCs such as the U.S. and Canada have very low agricultural densities due to efficient farming methods. LDCs such as India and China have higher agricultural densities. The combined analysis of these three measures yield a great deal of information about agricultural demands, agricultural efficiency, potentially available food, and level of development.

Key Issue 2: Where Has the World's Population Increased? (58): Three measures are used to analyze population increase and decline. The *crude birth rate* (CBR) is the total number of live births for every 1,000 people. The *crude death rate* (CDR) is the total number of deaths in a year for every 1,000 people. The *natural increase rate* (NIR) is the percentage by which a population grows in a year (CBR minus CDR, converted to a percentage). The term *natural* means that a country's growth rate excludes migration.

Natural Increase (58-59): Earth's population is most affected by fertility and mortality rates. The *natural increase rate* (NIR) is the percentage by which the population grows in a given year. The NIR for the world during the 1990s was 1.5 percent. The *doubling time* is used to assess how quickly a given population will double. Divide 70 (a constant term) by the NIR *(Doubling Time = 70 / NIR)*. Small changes in the NIR, even a tenth of a percent, can have long term effects on population size because the base population from which the percentage is applied is so high. NIRs vary greatly from region to region (Figure 2-6). LDCs have high NIRs, often over 3.0 percent. MDCs have lower NIRs, often at or below one percent. Because of the different NIRs, virtually all of the Earth's population growth takes place in LDCs.

Fertility (60): The *total fertility rate* (TFR) is the number of births in a year, and provides a picture of society as a whole in a given year. The TFR is also the average number of children a woman will have throughout her childbearing years (roughly ages 15 through 49). The second computation of the TFR assumes women will continue to have the same number of children as did women in the past. The second computation of the TFR is used to predict population changes.

Mortality (60-63): The *infant mortality rate* (IMR)is the annual number of deaths of infants under one year of age, compared with total live births (expressed as the number of deaths per 1,000). High infant mortality rates are found in LDCs and, logically, lower IMRs exist in MDCs with better health care facilities and more nutrition available to mothers and infants. *Life expectancy* at birth measures the average number of years a newborn infant can expect to live at *current mortality levels*. Europeans and Americans can expect to live into their late seventies while most Africans can expect to live into their early fifties. The age structure of a society makes the CDR a somewhat deceptive measure of a society's care for its populace.

Key Issue 3: Why is Population Increasing at Different Rates in Different Countries?

The Demographic Transition (64): Figure 2-13 shows the *fours stages* of the *demographic transition*.

      Stage 1: Low Growth (64-65): Humans have been in *stage 1* for most of human history. Until about 8000 BC the global population increased only slightly in any given year. The population increased dramatically between 8000 BC and AD 1750 because of the *agricultural revolution*. Humans domesticated plants and animals which relieved them of reliance on unreliable hunting and gathering for food. Humans found a food source that was more bountiful and more predictable. Despite the agricultural revolution, humans remained in stage 1 because of seasonal fluctuations in food production, increasing the CDR. The NIR was low because the CBR *and* CDR were both high.

      Stage 2: High Growth (65): The *industrial revolution* occurred around 1750 AD. The world's population grew ten times faster than it had in the past (the

NIR changed from 0.005 to 0.05 percent). During this time there were innovations such as the steam engine, mass production, and powered transportation. A portion of the wealth the industrial revolution created from inventions was used to make communities healthier places to live. Machines increased agricultural production, freeing people for other types of work while steadily increasing agricultural production. The inventions decreased the CDR which increased the NIR because people were healthier and living longer.

Around 1950, the *medical revolution* began dispersing medical technology invented in Europe and North America to the poorer countries of Latin America, Asia, and Africa. Penicillin, vaccines, and insecticides decreased diseases such as smallpox, influenza, malaria, and tuberculosis which had annually claimed large portions of the population. Consequently, the populations of these continents suddenly had much lower CDRs, which, coupled with high CBRs, lead to continuing population explosions. Most countries are in stages 2 and 3 of the demographic transition with high to moderate natural increase rates.

Stage 3: Moderate Growth (65-66): When the CBR begins to drop, a country moves from stage 2 into stage 3 of the demographic transition. The CBR declines in stage 3 because of *changes in social customs*. People choose to have fewer children knowing more of them will survive. As the CBR declines, population growth begins to slow down. Many people resist having fewer children because they need people to work, especially rural families in agriculturally dependent countries. The more urbanized a country, the more people are living in urban areas in smaller living quarters with access to education and higher wages.

Stage 4: Low Growth (66): When the CBR is only slightly higher than the CDR, the natural increase rate declines. When the NIR approaches zero, it is called *zero population growth* (ZPG). The total fertility rate (TFR) needed to maintain a population without increasing or decreasing it is approximately 2.1. The number may need to be adjusted because of migration in or out of a country. Several European countries have reached Stage 4 of the demographic transition including Sweden, Germany, and the United Kingdom. The U.S. has differential NIR regionally and ethnically making it difficult to identify its stage in the demographic transition.

As in stage 3, changes in social customs changes the way people, especially women, view child rearing. Women in stage 4 enter the labor force and have increased income and leisure time. Increased education, especially about women's issues, increase demand for and access to birth-control methods. Family planning becomes a choice about life-style. Pessimism due to war or economic conditions decreases people's willingness to have children. Countries have mandated family planning and birth-control distribution programs which have been received with mixed receptivity.

The Demographic Transition in England (66-67): England is a good case study for demographic transition because its boundaries have remained static for centuries and it hasn't been greatly affected by immigration. Plagues and poor harvests kept England in Stage 1 until about 1750 AD (See Fig. 2-10). Between 1750 and 1880 England profited from the Industrial Revolution (being its hearth) and spent much money on improvements in health and better food supplies. Its population grew rapidly. England had an average growth rate of 1.4 percent during this period. England was in Stage 3 from 1880 to the early 1970's with moderate growth of 0.7 percent per year. Since the early 1970's England's growth has only been 0.1 percent annually, which means England has been in Stage 4 since that time. England experiences little growth, having now achieved low birth and death rates generally associated with MDCs.

Population Pyramids (76-68): The distribution of age and gender groups in a population are effectively displayed in a *population pyramid*. The pyramid usually depicts the population in five-year increments (*cohorts*), beginning with ages 0 to 4 at the base and placing the oldest age group at the top. Males are generally placed on the left, females on the right. The length of the bars shows the percentage of a given cohort in the population. The shape of a pyramid is determined primarily by the crude birth rate. Different stages of the demographic transition are made visual in the structural variances in the population pyramid.

    Age Distribution (68-69): The structure of the population pyramid shows a great deal about population composition, population history, and potential population changes. The *dependency ratio* is the ratio of people ages 0-14 and over age 65 (considered outside of the work force) to those 15 to 64 (productive workers). *Dependency ratio = number of dependents to number of workers.* When the dependency ratio is high, an inordinate amount of resources must be devoted to necessary services (schools, hospitals, and day-care centers). If a population is increasing too rapidly, money which could be spent on developing infrastructure and jobs must be channeled to necessary services. Without enough jobs (high unemployment) scarce resources are used to maintain the society, not increase opportunities. Stage 2 and 3 countries have high proportions of children and high dependency ratios. Countries in the latter parts of stage 3, as well as those in stage 4, experience a graying of the population with higher proportions of older people. Larger percentages of older people increase the crude death rates. In stage 2 the dependency ratio is 1:1 (one dependent for one worker) and in stage 4 it is 1:2 (one dependent for every two workers).

    Sex Ratio (69-71): The *sex ratio* is the ratio of males per 100 females. Males are placed on the left side of the population pyramid and females on the right. More males are born than females but males don't, on average, survive as long. Men outnumber women until about age thirty. In the U.S. there are 95 men for every 100 women. Places with a high rate of immigration tend to have more males than females; men are more likely to migrate further distances. There are other places with specialized activities which change the composition of population pyramids.

Countries In Different Stages of Demographic Transition (71): No country today remains in stage 1 of the demographic transition.

    Cape Verde: Stage 2 (High Growth) (71-72): Cape Verde remained in Stage 1 of the demographic transition until the late 1940s. Between 1900 and 1949 its population declined from 147,000 to 137,000. Births did exceed deaths in most years, but severe famines caused long-term population decline. Anti-malarial campaigns and more secure food supplies tripled the country's population to 400,000 since 1950 with a NIR of 3 percent, Cape Verde remains in Stage 2. Since about 1960

Chile: Stage 3 (Moderate Growth) (72-74): Chile has been in stage 3 since about 1960. Its CDR dropped sharply to about 10 by the 1970s and its CBR declined to about 20 (from 35 in the 1960s) by the late 1970s. Chileans have large families, consistent with the Catholic Church's doctrine and Spanish culture. Chile has changed from a predominantly rural society based on agriculture to an urban society. The government implemented a family planning policy in the 1950s. The NIR has remained at 1.5 percent per year since the 1960s. Further decreases in the CBR are unlikely because the majority of Chileans belong to the Roman Catholic Church which opposes birth control.

Denmark: Stage 4 (Low Growth) (74): Denmark has reached stage 4 and has a population pyramid more like a column than a pyramid. The percentage of elderly citizens is more or less equal to its younger population. Since the 1970's the CBRs and CDRs have been equal at about 12 per 1,000, indicating the country has reached zero population growth. Denmark faces interesting questions about the economy, about the effects of immigrants' differing cultural beliefs about the size of families, and about caring for elderly people.

Demographic Transition and World Population Growth (74-76): The world's demographic transition is like the different nations so far described, but on a much larger scale. The transition to stage two with a drop in the death rate has occurred nearly everywhere. In Europe and the U.S. this transformation took place long ago. In most other countries it has occurred or is occurring during the twentieth century, with many countries moving into stage 3. The second break, a drop in the birth rate, has yet to be achieved in many countries. Population is still increasing rapidly in most countries, especially in countries with a large base population. If the nations of Asia, Africa, and Latin America take 100 years to pass through Stage 2 as did Europe and the U.S., their populations won't stabilize until the year 2050 AD, at which time approximately 21 billion people will be living on Earth!

Key Issue 4: Why Might the World Face an Overpopulation Problem?

Malthus on Overpopulation (76):

Population Growth vs. Food Supply (76): Thomas Malthus (1766-1834) was an English economist concerned with the growth of human population. His essay published in 1798, *"An Essay on the Principle of Population,"* was concerned with the theorized inability of the human population to feed itself due to overpopulation. According to Malthus, *food supplies grew only arithmetically while population expanded geometrically.* He warned that starvation would reduce the human race's numbers unless moral restraint, disease, famine, war, or other natural disasters slowed the NIR.

Neo-Malthusians (76): Malthus did have grand foresight since only a couple of countries had entered stage 2 during the time of his writing. Neo-Malthusians include *Robert Kaplan* and *Thomas Fraser Homer-Dixon*. They believe that as resources become scarce due to competition, humans will vigorously compete or even go to war to obtain clean air, fuel, wood, and other resources. One target example of Neo-Malthusian thought is East Africa where population growth outpaced that of income three percent to two percent. Countries in East Africa are worse off now than they were a decade ago, in part because lacking economic growth can not accommodate the additional population.

Malthus's Critics (76-77): Many critics disagree with Malthus's essay. Marxist theorist *Friedrich Engels* dismissed Malthus's theory as being capitalistic and that it didn't consider the egalitarian distribution of resources as an alternative to starvation. Economist *Julian Simon* and *Esther Boserup* disagreed with Malthus believing an expanding population would build a better economy and develop more ideas to improve agriculture and develop innovations. Geographer *Vaclav Smil* determined that since 1950 food production growth has actually out-distanced human reproduction, in part because of advances in agriculture.

Debate Over How to Reduce Natural Increase (77): To decrease population growth, either the CDR must rise returning people to stage 1or the CBR must be lowered moving countries into stages 3and 4 of the demographic transition.

Higher Death Rates (77-78): Many people believe that sending food to starving people sustains a highly reproductive population. Eventually, a catastrophic starvation will occur slowing population. War and natural disasters also increase the CDR. Prevalent diseases could increase, mutate, or spread in LDCs where immunization, nutrition, and hygiene are not standard as they are in MDCs. AIDS is growing in number of people affected and in its areal domain; it is not medically controlled and it continues to spread.

Lower Birth Rates (78): Decreasing the CBR can be done by increasing women's standards of living in the world, increasing access to birth control, and increasing education. Family planning education and birth control reduce the CBR but are met with cultural and religious opposition.

Economic Development Alternative (78): Improved education for the entire population, especially women, means more of the population can be employed in higher paying skilled labor jobs. Increased wealth and education are the two factors most affecting beliefs and decisions about family size.

Distribution of Contraceptives (78-79): Economic growth and development is a slow process requiring capital and infrastructure building. Family planning programs is more effective more rapidly. The demand for contraceptives in LDCs is greater than the supply. Simple programs to increase availability of contraceptives, sex education, and education for women (to increase their status) are the fastest, most effective ways to slow the growth of populations. Cultural and religious beliefs make such programs difficult, though necessary.

Summary: Ultimately, population growth must slow by implementing culturally suitable programs. Overpopulation has already affected many parts of Africa, Latin America, and Asia. High population growth stresses the environment and the fragile economies. The sheer number of people living in a certain area is not necessarily an indication of overpopulation. The inability of people to work successfully with their environment and economy is a more likely indication of overpopulation.

Due to the agricultural, industrial, and medical revolutions in innovation, world population has increased dramatically. Population growth can be projected, but there are no guarantees about the accuracy of such predictions. Speculation about resource distribution and future availability further complicates the issues.

CHAPTER 2
KEY TERMS AND CONCEPTS

Census: A complete enumeration of a population. In the U.S., national population census is taken every ten years at the beginning of new decades.

Demography: The scientific study of population characteristics. Computer software allows many intricate studies to be performed by using mapping and statistical software packages.

Overpopulation: The number of people in an area exceeds the capacity of the environment to support life at a decent standard of living. Many ecologists and environmentalists believe this phenomena has drastic effects on Earth's biosphere.

Global Density: The total number of people on Earth divided by the total land area. The number yields very little information as much of the Earth is uninhabited or uninhabitable.

Arithmetic Density: The total number of people divided by the total land area; the basic form of density at which national comparisons are most often made.

Physiological Density: The number of people per unit of arable land (suitable for agriculture). Physiological density indicates the demands populations place on their agricultural land.

Agricultural Density: The ratio of the number of farmers per unit of arable land. In MDCs this figure is normally quite low; in LDCs the agricultural density is much higher.

Crude Birth Rate (CBR): The total number of live births in a year for every 1,000 people alive in society. CBRs tend to be high in LDCs and low in MDCs.

Crude Death Rate (CDR): The total number of deaths in a year for every 1,000 people alive in the society. CDRs are greatly reduced by the dispersion of medical technology.

Natural Increase Rate (NIR): The percentage growth of population in a year. The formula is: NIR = crude birth rate (CBR) minus the crude death rate (CDR), converted to a percentage. This value indicates how population increase without the effects of migration. For example, the world's population has grown at the rate of 1.5% annually during the 1990s.

Doubling Time: The number of years needed to double a population, assuming a constant natural increase rate. The formula is: Doubling Time = 70 / NIR (%).

Total Fertility Rate (TFR): 1. The number of births in a society. 2. The average number of children a woman will have throughout her childbearing years. Women in LDCs tend to have more children than women in MDCs.

Infant Mortality Rate (IMR): The total number of deaths in a year of infants under one year of age, compared with total live births, for every 1,000 live births in a society. In the U.S. high IMR rates in inner cities rival the IMRs of some LDCs.

Life Expectancy: The average number of years a newborn infant can be expected to live at current mortality levels, based on current social, economic, and medical conditions. Life expectancy at birth is a rough estimate of the average number of years an individual can expect to live. Longer life expectancy is found in countries with good medical facilities.

Demographic Transition: The process of change in a society's population from a condition of both high crude birth rates and high crude death rates bringing about low natural increase rates, to a condition of low crude birth and death rates creating a low natural increase rate. The population starts small, grows quickly, grows slowly, and ends with a high population. Sweden, Germany, and Denmark have reached the final stage of this demographic transition, while no country remains in the first stage.

Agricultural Revolution: The domestication of plants and animals enabling humans to shift their reliance for food from inconsistent hunting and gathering. The agricultural revolution first appeared about 8,000 BC and enabled the development of more complex societies.

Industrial Revolution: A series of improvements in industrial technology that transformed the process of manufacturing goods, created labor-saving machines, and converted portions of the population from rural dwelling farmers to urban dwelling workers. Europe, the U.S. and Great Britain especially, were the first regions in the world to benefit from subsequent increases in wealth.

Medical Revolution: Development of medical technology in Europe and North America to decrease illness and disease as well as to improve hygiene. Medical technology has been diffused to the poorer countries of Latin America, Asia, and Africa which suddenly decreased the crude death rate and rapidly increased the natural increase rate in many parts of the world.

Zero Population Growth (ZPG): The total fertility rate declines to the point where the natural increase rate approaches zero. At a NIR of 2.1% human reproduction maintains the population in the long run.

Population Pyramid: A bar graph representing the distribution of population by age (cohorts) and sex, placing males on the left and females on the right. Countries with large young populations are shaped like a pyramid, whereas the population pyramid actually becomes more columnar as a population reaches stage 4 of the demographic transition.

Dependency Ratio: The number of people either under age 15 or over age 64 supported by the number of people active in the labor force. High dependency ratios cause stress to the strength of a country's economy.

Sex Ratio: The number of men to 100 women in a society. Though more there are typically more male children born than female children, women tend to live longer, changing the ratio as the population ages.

Thomas Malthus: An English economist who wrote "An Essay on the Principle of Population" which theorized that food production on a world scale would be unable to serve the exploding populations of Earth, leading to mass starvation. According to Malthus, food supplies grew only arithmetically while population grew geometrically.

Infanticide: The deliberate killing of infants. In some cultures male babies are more highly prized than females. Due to the financial inability of many families to sustain numerous children, the killing of less desirable children (who are most often female) sometimes occurs.

Population Control Policies: Government's legal position on birth control. India's efforts to stem population growth have been less successful than those of China. China financially penalizes families who have more than one child.

CHAPTER 2
PROGRESSIVE REVIEW

1. Earth's population currently exceeds _____ billion.   six

2. _____ is the term for the scientific study of population   Demography
statistics.

3. The inability of an area to support its population due to
the lack of environmental and ecological factors can lead to   overpopulation
_____.

4. About _____ percent of the people on Earth lives on   seventy-five, five
about _____ percent of the Earth's surface.

5. The largest concentration of population lives in _____.   Java

6. MDC stands for _____ _____ _____.   more developed
                                                                    country

7. _____ is the world's most populated country, though it   China,
will be replaced by _____ in the middle of the coming   India
century due to a higher rate of natural increase.

8. About seventy-five percent of Europeans live in _____   urban
areas.

9. Ground that is permanently frozen is known as _____   permafrost,
and is found in large areas in the high _____.   latitudes

10. The total number of people divided by the amount of
land in their region is its _____ _____.   arithmetic density

11. Land suited for agriculture is called _____ land.   arable

12. Density that measures the number of people per unit of
arable land is called _____ density.   physiological

13. The number of farmers per unit of arable land is called   agricultural
_____ density.

14. Most LDCs have _____ agricultural densities because   high
their farming techniques are less efficient than methods
employed by farmers in MDCs.

15. It is accepted that the first revolution of innovation for humankind began around _____ BC.

8,000

16. The agricultural revolution brought about the domestication of _____ and _____ which are a more reliable supply of nutrition than the previous methods of hunting and gathering.

plants
animals

17. The dispersion of medical technology greatly reduced the crude _____ rates in many _____ developed countries.

death, less

18. The _____ revolution originated in England, bringing much wealth to the country because of new manufacturing techniques.

industrial

19. The _____ _____ _____ is the percentage a population grows each year.

natural increase
rate

20. The total number of deaths for every 1,000 people in society is known as the _____ _____ _____.

crude death rate

21. The infant mortality rate measures the number of deaths among infants less than _____ _____ old.

one year

22. The _____ _____ refers to the changing dynamics that occur to the populations of countries as the evolve form less developed countries into more developed countries.

demographic
transition

23. During stage 1 of demographic transition there are _____ growth rates, and at Stage 4 of the demographic transition there are _____ growth rates.

low
low

24. The nations of Sweden, Germany, and the United Kingdom have entered stage _____ of demographic transition.

4

25. Economic changes in stage _____ often change social beliefs so family size is smaller than in the two previous stages.

3

26. When the crude death rate and crude birth rate again approach zero it is called _____ _____ _____.

zero population
growth

27. _____ is a good model for demographic transition   England
because it has not changed its boundaries nor has it been
significantly affected by migration. It also has a good deal of
population data available for the past millennia.

28. Population pyramids measure the break down of   sex
population by _____ and _____.   age

29. A population pyramid with a very wide base and a
narrow top represents the populations in _____ developed   less
countries.

30. The number of people who don't work in a society
compared to the number of people are in their working years
is known as the _____ _____.   dependency ratio

31. Gender-wise, slightly _____ males than females are   more
born.

32. In the U.S. and Europe there are about _____ men   95
alive for every _____ women.   100

33. Since the 1950's the island nation of _____ _____ has   Cape Verde
remained in the Stage 2 of demographic transition.

34. The English economist _____ _____, wrote a   Thomas Malthus
controversial work which theorized _____ would increase   population
faster than the technological advances to supply it with food.

35. Contemporary analysts who support Malthus are known   Neo-
as _____-_____.   Malthusians

36. Improving the educational status of women will serve to   lower
_____ the rate of natural increase in LDCs.

37. A one-child policy has been employed by the
government of _____ to reduce rates of natural increase.   China

CHAPTER 3

MIGRATION

Throughout human history, people have moved from places they perceived to be less desirable to more attractive places. Sometimes migrations are within a small region, while others bring emigrants around the world to new homelands. Some people are forced to move from their homes because governments see them as a threat, or simply as an annoyance. Push and pull factors are discussed in this chapter as well as examples of migrations that have happened in the world.

Migration: *Migration* is a permanent movement to a new location. People migrate for economic, political, climatic, and other reasons when oppression or opportunity are presented. Migration is divided into *emigration* and *immigration*. *Emigrants* are people leaving a country, while *immigrants* are people who arrive at a new country. The numerical difference between the total number of immigrants and emigrants is *net migration*. A positive net migration means the region has *net in-migration,* while a negative net-migration is a *net out-migration*. The movement of people across the landscape from one place to another is called *mobility. Circulation* is the short-term, repetitive, or cyclical movements that occur on a regular basis. *Seasonal mobility* is closely tied to an the seasons; college students live at home as well as close to campus and there are a number of people who live in the south and southwest only during the winter. With modern communications and transportation, ideas and concepts spread rapidly through the world, which encourages *globalization*. People seek others who are like them which creates pockets of *local diversity*.

Key Issue 1: Why Do People Migrate?

Reasons for Migrating (87): Most people migrate for economic reasons, though cultural and environmental factors do cause some people to migrate. *Pull factors* are positive features of a foreign land that lure people to migrate.

    Economic Push and Pull Factors (87-88): If a person's native country affords little economic opportunity, migration to a country with "greener pastures" often occurs. These incentives for migration are called economic *push factors*. Places with valuable natural resources may attract workers, and the economically attractive regions may change with time. The opportunity to increase the living standards of one's family often brings people to migrate to lands of greater economic opportunity. This is the primary reason for people to migrate to the U.S. and Canada. When Mexicans and other Latin Americans migrate to the U.S. in legal or illegal channels it is most often for jobs that will pay them more than they received in their native countries.

Cultural Push and Pull Factors (88-90): *Forced international migration* is mainly attributable for two cultural reasons: slavery and political instability. Large groups of people have been forced to move across international boundaries because of political instability or shifting boundaries forcing people to migrate to countries friendly to them. People who are forced out of their country or region for political reasons are called *refugees*. Often, when people live in a repressed, totalitarian country, the existence of a democratic republic which offers many more political freedoms pulls them toward it.

Environmental Push and Pull Factors (90-91): Adverse environmental conditions often push people from their homes. When water is over-abundant (flooding) or is not present for human nourishment and irrigation, people are often pushed from their homelands. When people live on *floodplains* they are often eventually pushed out because of flooding disasters that wreck their homes and livelihoods. On the other hand, lack of rain, drought, also causes migration. In the 1930's, prolonged drought in the states of the southern Great Plains initiated the mass migration to California. Such migrants were called "Okies." The amenities offered by an area's environment often serve to pull people into those regions. For example, the beauty and recreational activities offered by the state of Colorado have lured many people to live there. Ironically, the mass migrations of recent years have produced pollution, which is what originally pushed many current residents to this destination. Many elderly people have moved to the warm climates of Arizona and Florida, where ailments associated with aged persons are less aggravating.

Distance of Migration (91): *Ravenstein* made two points about travel distance for migrants. Most migrants relocate a short distance within the same country. Long distance migrants head for major economic centers.

Internal Migration (91): *International migration* is permanent movement to another country. *Internal migration* is permanent movement within the same country. There are two types of internal migration. *Interregional migration* is movement between regions, and *intraregional migration* is movement within a region.

International Migration (91-92): *Voluntary migration* means that people have migrated due to their own free will, usually for economic improvement; *forced migration* means that a migrant has been compelled to move. *Wilbur Zelinsky* developed a *migration transition*, a series of changes in a society that is comparable to those in the demographic transition and results from social and economic changes.

Characteristics of Migrants (92): *Ravenstein* noted that most long-distance migrants are males, and most are individuals rather than families.

Gender of Migrants (92): Historically, most migrants have been male. During the 1990s, the pattern of migrants to the U.S. from Mexico reflected a larger proportion of women than of men. This is attributable to the changing roles of women in Mexican society.

Family Status of Migrants (93-94): Migrants to the U.S. are more diverse in age and family status than was previously believed. There a lesser percentage of elderly immigrants than the U.S. population. An increasing percentage of immigrants are children. Immigrants are less likely to be as educated as the average American. The countries of origin are also changing.

Key Issue 2: Why Has U.S. Immigration Changed? (93): There are two main eras in U.S. immigration. The first era, from the mid-nineteenth century to the early twentieth century, drew immigrants from Europe. The second era, which began in the 1970s, draws immigrants from Latin America and Asia.

European Immigration to the U.S. (93): In the 500 years since Columbus sailed from Spain to the New World, about *60 million* Europeans have migrated to other continents, representing the world's largest migration. After 1800, huge population growth engulfed Europe as it moved into *Stage 2* of the demographic transition. This pushed many people to come to North America, southern South America, Australia and New Zealand, where climates and soils were similar, and, therefore, more familiar. Some Europeans did settle in tropical climates, but mostly for administrational purposes. In plantation areas in Latin America and Asia, most of the workers were natives or African slaves forcefully brought to the new lands.

 Waves of European Immigration (93-95): Of the 60 million European immigrants since 1500, *37 million* settled in the United States. *Germany* was the most prominent country of origin, followed by Italy, Great Britain, Ireland, Austria-Hungary, and Russia.

 First Peak of European Immigration (94): From the first permanent colony in the U.S. in *Jamestown, Virginia* in 1607 until 1840 a steady stream of immigrants landed in what is now the United States' east coast. By the 1840's and 1850's immigration was annually over a quarter million people as the *first peak* of European migration was experienced. During these two decades, more people immigrated to the United States than in the previous 250 years. The immigrants of this time, as a whole, originated in northern and western Europe, from Ireland to Germany. Better incomes and standard of livings propelled these and future migrants.

 Second Peak of European Immigration (94-95): As the 1880's passed, the U.S. experienced a *second peak* of European immigration, again with most of the immigrants beginning their journeys in northern and western Europe. These people had ventured to America primarily because of available land that was relatively scarce in their homelands.

 Third Peak of European Immigration (95): The late 1890's and first fifteen years of the twentieth century witnessed the *third peak* of European immigration. These immigrants originated from Italy, Russia, and Austria-Hungary (which then included much of eastern Europe). This shift in the source of immigrants occurred because the industrial revolution diffused into these areas moving them into later stages in the demographic transition. The population grew very rapidly because as a result of increased technology and health care. America was irresistible.

 Impact of European Migration (95): The era of European migration to the United States ended in 1914. Ever since, the numbers of European immigrants has steadily dwindled. By the 1960s, 30 percent of immigrants to the U.S. were from Europe and, since 1980, less than 10 percent have been Europeans.

Europe's Demographic Transition (95-96): The rapid population growth of the 1800s was a result of the industrial revolution. Agricultural reforms increased farm size to increase efficiency. Displaced farmers could choose to either move to cities or to the United States. Migration to America balanced the population growth in Europe allowing Europeans to enjoy the benefits of the industrial revolution as well as helping make the transition to a lower rate of population increase.

Diffusion of European Culture (96): The emigration of 60 million Europeans has greatly altered the world's cultural landscape. Indo-European languages are spoken by half the world's population. Christianity is the dominant world religion. European-inspired economics and governments dominate in parts of Asia, Africa, and most of the New World. Conflicts in Africa and Asia are partially the result of European relocation and the construction of economic structures based on supplying raw materials to European colonial powers. Plantations in Latin America and Asia were owned by Europeans and worked by Asians, Latin Americans, or slaves from Africa.

Recent Immigration from Less Developed Regions (96): Immigration to the U.S. dropped in the 1930s and 1940s, during the Depression and World War II. Emigration exceeded immigration during the 1930s. Immigration increased through the 1970s, with rapid increases during the 1980s and 1990s.

Immigration from Asia and Latin America (96): Immigration to the U.S. is currently predominantly from Asia and Latin America, though the proportions of each vary. Five-sixths of all immigrants to the U.S. come from these two regions.

Immigration from Asia (96): Early Asian immigrants (about 1 million total) were mainly from China, Turkey, and Japan. Immigration from Asia has rapidly increased since the 1960s, accounting for approximately 7 million immigrants. Asia was the dominant source of immigrants in the late 1970s through the late 1980s when Latin America began to dominate. Most Asian immigrants came from China (and Taiwan) and India, both in stage 2 of the demographic transition. Asian immigrants of the 1980s and 1990s are mainly from the Philippines, Vietnam, and South Korea; totaling more than half of all Asian immigrants. Asians are also immigrating to Canada, accounting for more than 40 percent of Canadian immigrants. Canada, compared to the U.S., has higher rates of European immigration than Latin American immigration.

Immigration from Latin America (96-97): Latin American immigrants totaled 2 million between 1820 and 1960, and will total 10 million between 1960 and 2000. Latin American immigration peaked in the early 1990s and has rapidly declined in the late 1990s. Mexico dominates Latin American immigration, followed by the Dominican Republic, Jamaica, and Haiti. The *1986 Immigration Reform and Control Act* issued visas to people living in the U.S. who had entered illegally. In 1991 and 1990 the U.S. admitted more immigrants than at any other time in history--1.8 million and 1.5 million respectively.

Destination of Immigrants within the United States (97-98): Immigrants are clustered in California (25 percent); New York and New Jersey (25 percent);

Florida, Texas, and Illinois (25 percent); and the remaining 50 percent spread across the country. Planes and motor vehicles are currently the main modes of immigrant transportation, moving the locations of clusters of immigrants from the coasts to these six states. Immigrants cluster in locations where there are other people from the same place. *Chain migration* is the draw of migrants to a location because family members or people of the same nationality previously settled there.

Undocumented Immigration to the United States (98-99): Because demand for entry into the U.S. exceeds the quota allowed by the American government, many people enter the country as *undocumented immigrants* who possess neither the permission of the government to enter nor remain in the U.S., nor official documentation to live and work. Many cross the boarder illegally or are students or tourists who simply stay after their visas have expired. The *U.S. Immigration and Naturalization Service (INS)* enforces immigration laws and quotas. Many undocumented immigrants come from Latin America, especially Mexico. The *1986 Immigration Reform and Control Act* allows aliens who have lived continuously in the U.S. for 5 years to apply for permanent residence and citizenship. Few people have taken advantage of this law, probably fearing deportation if their applications were rejected.

Crossing the U.S.--Mexican Border (99): Crossing the border is not difficult. Most undocumented immigrants from Mexico are young males between the ages of fifteen and thirty-four who leave their families and villages in Mexico to work in the U.S. and systematically send portions of their earnings home to Mexico. Crossing the U.S.-Mexico border is not a difficult task, given its 2,000 mile length through sparsely populated desert. Once a group of Mexicans enter the U.S., they contact someone known as a *coyote* who brings them to a city within the U.S., where they hope to find employment. They accept low-paying jobs many U.S. citizens will not accept. Often the *U.S. Border Patrol* intercepts illegal immigrants and routinely deports them to border cities in Mexico, from where they attempt to cross the border again.

Intervening Obstacles (99): Migrants who are lured to a new location are often restricted from traveling due to *intervening obstacles*. Mostly, these are physical barriers which prevent the passage of human beings and their belongings to a particular area. For example, the Atlantic Ocean, Rocky Mountains, Great Plains, and many other formidable physical obstacles effectively blocked many migrants from completing their journeys to new lands. Globalization is more possible because of modern transportation, diminishing environmental features as intervening obstacles. Local diversity in government and politics requires a passport to legally emigrate from a country and a visa to legally immigrate to a new country.

Key Issue 3: Why Do Migrants Face Obstacles? (100): The long sea journey has been replaced by airplane and motor vehicle voyages. The biggest challenges faced my immigrants are gaining permission to enter and stay in a new country, and dealing with hostile attitudes toward immigrants.

Immigration Policies in Other Countries (100): Countries use one of two policies to control immigration. The U.S. quota systems limits the number of people who can permanently locate and work. Other countries permit temporary guest workers.

U.S. Quota Laws (101): By 1912, all of what is now the coterminous U.S. had been officially established as states. Many people believed there was no longer available land and jobs for more immigrants, who would strain the economy. During the third peak in immigration (when immigration sources shifted to southern and eastern Europe) established Americans often became hostile toward the new immigrants who had different origins than previous arrivals. Eventually, antagonism toward immigrants lead to the establishment of quotas in the forms of the *Quota Act of 1921* and the *National Origins Act of 1924*. *Quotas,* in this context, are the maximum number of people allowed entry into the U.S. in a given year. These quotas allowed for two percent of the existing ethnicity of the population of the U.S., according to the 1910 Census, to be allowed to immigrate each year. This procedure served to build the existing ethnic populations shaped by previous migrations. Thus, immigrants from the Eastern Hemisphere had difficulty entering the U.S.. By the 1960s, such narrowly focused laws were replaced. Statues allowed for no more than 290,000 (in 1978) immigrants each year, with a maximum 20,000 per country. In 1990, the global quota was set at 714,000 per year and in 1995 it is 675,000.

Preference System Under Quotas (101): Genuine refugees are not included in the quotas. Due to the high demand of applicants seeking to reside in the U.S., Congress has given preferential status to those immigrants who have established family members living in the U.S.. There re 55,000 lottery visas awarded each year. Asian take advantage of the family-reunification provisions and move their entire families through chain migration. Many migrants come to the U.S. because their high levels of education promise them a good living. When a large exodus of highly educated professionals leave LDCs for MDCs, it is known as *brain drain*. Ultimately, most immigrants who reach the U.S., do so to improve their economic status.

British Policy (101): Britain strictly controls immigration. Their policies are complicated by their history as a world power with colonial residents who could choose citizenship.

Temporary Migration for Work (101): Government policies sometimes allow guest workers, and Asia historically had time-contract workers.

Guest Workers (101-102): Millions of people come to the Middle East and Western Europe to work, and are known as *guest workers*. Guest workers take low-status and low-income jobs that local residents don't want. In Europe, guest workers are protected by minimum wage laws and labor union contracts. Guest workers send money home which boosts the local economy while decreasing unemployment problems.

Origin and Destination of Guest Workers (102): In Switzerland and Luxembourg, guest workers exceed ten percent of the population, in Germany 9 percent, and 6 percent in France. Two-thirds of workers in Middle Eastern petroleum industry jobs are foreign. In recent years as economic growth has slowed in Middle Eastern and Western European countries, so has the willingness of these countries to accept guest workers.

Time-Contract Workers (102-103): In the 1800s, millions of Asians migrated as *time-contract workers* with a fixed period of time contracted to work, often in mines or on plantations. They could then settle in the new country. Many Indians went to former British colonies, Japanese and Filipinos to Hawaii or Brazil, and Chinese worked in the U.S.. Today there are 29 million ethnic Chinese living abroad, mostly in Asia.

Distinguishing Between Economic Migrants and Refugees (103): Distinguishing between economic migrants and refugees is especially difficult for emigrants from Cuba, Haiti, and Vietnam.

Emigrants from Cuba (103-104): After the 1959 revolution in *Cuba,* 600,000 Cubans fled the country due to ideological differences with the new communist government. Many settled in southern Florida. In 1980 another large wave of 125,000 Cubans migrated to the U.S. in one program (*Mariel Boatlift*), when Fidel Castro permitted political prisoners, criminals, and mental patients to leave the country. The U.S. was ill-prepared to handle such large numbers of refugees, and had to accommodate them through sponsorship programs and temporary settlements.

Emigrants from Haiti (104-105): Soon after the Mariel Boatlift, thousands of Haitians came to the U.S. seeking asylum. Haitians were turned away, at which point the Haitians brought a lawsuit against the U.S. government advocating if Cubans were admitted, they should be as well. After 1991 and a change in government, many Haitians went to Guantanamo Bay to apply as refugees for migration to the U.S. After the 1994 UN peacekeeping forcer assured democratic elections, many Haitians have continued to try to migrate to the U.S., reinforcing the supposition that most Haitians are economic migrants rather than refugees.

Emigrants from Vietnam (105): When the Vietnam war ended in 1975, many Vietnamese closely associated with the American position were evacuated. Many, many other vulnerable people left by land or by boat. *Boat people* drifted into the South China Sea, hoping to be saved the U.S. Navy. Due to conflicting interpretations of immigration policy, some boat people were not rescued. In the late 1980s, there was a second surge of Vietnamese boat people with people trying to get out of Vietnam and into neighboring countries. Many countries refused them entry. Many people were accepted by the U.S., Canada, Australia, and France where many were held in detention camps. About one-half million Vietnamese have reached the U.S. since the end of the Vietnam war.

Cultural Problems Living in Other Countries (106): Citizens of a host country may be hostile and politicians often blame immigrants for economic problems.

U.S. Attitudes Toward Immigrants (106): Until the early twentieth century the U.S. welcomed immigrants with open arms, for they were a valuable factor in developing the country's economy. However, the middle and later parts of the twentieth century brought more skeptical attitudes towards immigrants who found immigration to the U.S. increasingly difficult. Attitudes changed as immigrants came from places other than European countries. The government reinforced skepticism and hostility when, in 1911, a study concluded immigrants from Southern and

Eastern Europe were racially inferior. California voted in the 1990s to deny undocumented immigrants access to public services.

Problems with Guest Workers (106-107): Many guest workers in Europe endure poor social conditions. Many are poor, single men who use their extra money to visit home. They find places to gather together with others who share their language, culture, and experiences. In the Middle East, guest workers are carefully regarded and are encouraged by some countries to marry in their native countries. Changes in the economy has increased tensions between guest workers, their host countries, and their countries of origin. Migration by Asians a century ago has created tensions in Fiji.

Key Issue 4: Why Do People Migrate Within a Country? (107): Internal
migration is easier for most people than international migration. Most interregional migration is between urban and rural areas. Most intraregional migration is from older cities or areas of cities to suburbs. *Interregional migration* is the movement from one region of a country to another, while *intraregional migration* is the movement within one area.

Migration Between Regions of a Country (107): Historically, many people in the
U.S. moved from densely settled regions to the frontier.

Migration Between Regions Within the United States (107): The settlement of the American West is the most famous example of large-scale internal migration. Through this migration, the sparse interior of the U.S. was settled.

Changing Center of Population (107): Since the first U.S. Census was taken in 1790, the *population center* of the U.S. has been steadily moving westward, and in recent years a few degrees of latitude southward. The population center stayed in roughly the same place because most settlements were along the Atlantic coast.

Early Settlement in the Interior (108): Between 1830 and 1880 people flocked to California during the gold rush. The Great Plains were called "the Great American Desert" and was considered inhospitable. People crossed through the area without settling it. The population center moved westward.

Settlement of the Great Plains (108-109): Interior settlement quickly increased and moved the population center slowly westward. Railroads and barbed wire helped pioneers to settle the Great Plains, some of the world's richest farming areas. Large-scale migration of Europeans to the East Coast offset the settlement of the West and slowed the westward movement of the population center.

Recent Growth of the South (109): Since 1950, the population center is moving more quickly to the west and somewhat southward. Many people are moving from the Midwest to the West and the South.

Interregional Migration to the South and West (109-110): Most people have moved to the South and West to take advantage of newly created job opportunities. New industries have chosen locations in the South and West, which counters the belief that industries are relocating away from the Midwest and Northeast. People also migrate to take advantage of the environment with a milder climate and outdoor recreational activities available year round.

Migration Between Regions in Other Countries (110): Long-distance interregional migration is the result of plans and incentives to develop new regions in large countries.

Russia (110): Government policy was to locate factories near raw materials, often in places with an insufficient labor pool which required a simulation of interregional migration. The Far North, which includes much of Siberia, contained 45 percent of the land area and only 2 percent of the population and was rich in natural resources. The relocation programs were not successful because of the harsh environment and difficult living conditions; many people migrated out of the area after a short time.

Brazil (110-111): Most Brazilians live in large cities along the Atlantic Coast. In an attempt to settle the interior, the government moved its capital in 1960 from Rio inland to a new city called Brasilia. Brazil has a very high rate of population increase, so people migrate to whatever area, or city, they think has available jobs.

Indonesia (111): The Indonesian government has tried to relocated people living on the most densely populated place in the world, the island of Java, to other, less populated islands. With incentives of land and materials for a house and agriculture, people took advantage of the program. Its popularity has declined in recent years and has only moved a very small percentage of Java's population.

Europe (111-112): Places attracting the most immigrants have higher per capita incomes and job opportunities. Italians move from the poorer southern region to the north, which has higher per capita incomes due to strong agriculture and industry. People in the United Kingdom move from the north to the south.

India (112): India required a permit to migrate, something left from the British colonial era. Requiring permits protects the ethnic identity of Assamese and limits international migration.

Migration Within One Region (112): People most often move to another location within their region, called _intraregional migration._

Migration Within One Region (112): In the last two hundred years most intraregional migration has been _rural to urban migration._ The urban population of the U.S. has increased from five percent in 1800 to fifty percent by 1920. Nearly three-fourths of the population in the U.S. and other MDCs live in urban areas, while approximately half of the world's population lives in urban areas. Rural to urban migration has intensified in Africa, Latin America, and Asia. Often, as with the Brazilian city Sao Paulo, cities cannot accommodate the people flocking to the cities in search of economic opportunities. They are forced, by lack of space, to live in squatter towns called _"favelas"._

Migration from Urban to Suburban Areas (112): In MDCs the intraregional trend is from the _city cores, or central cities, into the suburbs._ The suburbs area attractive because of lower crime rates, larger homes, garages, more green space, more recreational amenities, and less congestion. Suburban schools also tend to be better.

Migration from Metropolitan to Nonmetropolitan Areas (112-113): Since the 1970s, MDCs in Europe and North America have witnessed a swing in intraregional migration from _metropolitan areas to rural areas._ This phenomena is called *counterurbanization*. Like suburbanization, people move to rural areas for lifestyle reasons. With cheap modern communication and transportation, living in more isolated locations no longer isolates people economically nor socially. Retirees constitute a part of these migrants. In the U.S. counterurbanization has stopped since the early 1980s because jobs have declined in these areas. Worsening agricultural conditions have also decreased the allure of the countryside.

Summary: People migrate due to push and pull factors. Motivations to migrate stem from economic, political, and environmental reasons. When people migrate interregionally or intraregionally, it is to improve their perceived quality of life. This statement holds true for people who move from country to country or from the city core into the suburbs. Forced migration often stems from political activities. As more MDCs enter the third and fourth stages of the demographic transition, it will be interesting to note the migration that occurs--where people are coming from, why they are leaving, and where they would like to go. Migration may positively or negatively affect the stability of some populations.

CHAPTER 3
KEY TERMS AND CONCEPTS

Migration: Form of relocation diffusion involving a permanent move to a new location. The entire journey made by a person or group of persons.

Emigration: Migration from a location. When people leave a country, they emigrate.

Immigration: Migration to a new location. When people arrive in a new country, they have immigrated.

Net-Migration: The difference between the level of immigration and the level of emigration. This variable, along with rates of natural increase, determines population growth.

Mobility: The ability to move from one location to another. Mobility may be hindered by physical barriers such as deserts, mountains, and bodies of water.

Circulation: Short-term, repetitive, or cyclical movements that occur on a regular basis.

Seasonal Mobility: Movement, or migration that occurs annually and follows the seasons. College and University students often change addresses with the seasons--fall and winter at school summer at their parents' address.

Pull Factors: Factors that induce people to move to a new location. Increased political freedom and more lucrative jobs often pull people into other, more promising countries.

Push Factors: Factors that induced people to leave their former residences. Poor political, economic, and environmental conditions in one's native country often cause people to emigrate.

Refugees: People who are forced to migrate from a country for political reasons. Recently, the U.S. has harbored refugees from China, Haiti, Cuba, Vietnam and many other countries.

Floodplain: The area subject to flooding during a given number of years according to historical trends. Flood plains often have large populations that suffer greatly when flooding occurs at disastrous levels.

International Migration: Permanent movement from one country to another. During the 1800's many people from Europe migrated to the U.S. and Canada.

Internal Migration: Permanent movement within a particular country. When the people of the southern plains, "Okies", migrated to California during the Dust Bowl of the 1930's, they were internally migrating.

Interregional Migration: Permanent movement from one region of a country to another. In the U.S., elderly people commonly move from cold regions to the warmer climates of the Southwest or Southeast.

Intraregional Migration: Permanent movement within one region of a country. This can be the movement from rural hinterlands to cities, or the migration from city cores to the suburbs.

Forced Migration: Permanent movement compelled usually by political factors. People whom the government in power perceive as threatening or undesirable are frequently forced to migrate.

Voluntary Migration: Permanent movement undertaken by choice. In this case, the migrants moved for no politically-forced reason.

Migration Transition: Theory developed by geographer Wilbur Zelinsky. Change in the migration pattern in a society that results from industrialization, population growth, and other social and economic changes that also produce the demographic transition. It corresponds to stages in the demographic transition.

E.G. Ravenstein: Studied the characteristics of migrants to identify characteristics of long-distant migrants.

1986 Immigration and Control Act: U.S. policy which allowed people living in the U.S. for at least five years who had entered illegally to apply for permanent residence and citizenship.

Chain Migration: A process by which people are given preference for migrating to another country because a relative was previously admitted. Asians are known to be effective users of chain migration.

Undocumented Immigrants: People who illegally enter the U.S. to live and work. There is much debate concerning the benefits and disadvantages of illegal immigrants upon the U.S. economy.

U.S. Immigration and Naturalization Service (INS): U.S. organization which enforces immigration laws, policies and quotas.

Coyote: Person hired by Latin Americans wishing to cross the U.S. border illegally and enter the U.S..

U.S. Border Patrol: The group of agents controlling international borders, especially between the U.S. and Mexico, the U.S. and Canada, and the U.S. and the Caribbean islands.

Intervening Obstacles: An environmental or cultural feature of the landscape that hinders migration. The Berlin Wall, border patrols, border fences, and customs officers are all cultural intervening obstacles.

Quota: In reference to migration, a law that places maximum limits on the number of people who can immigrate to a country. Today, the quota for immigrants to the U.S. is 20,000 per country of origin.

Brain Drain: Large-scale emigration by talented people. LDCs complain that their more talented people often migrate to MDCs such as the U.S. due to better paying jobs.

Guest Workers: Workers who migrate to the more developed countries of Northern and Western Europe, (usually from southern or Eastern Europe, or from northern Africa), in search of higher paying jobs. Guest workers fill a niche of jobs that are often left unattended by the people in the host country.

Time-Contract Workers: A practice whereby someone would contract to work for someone else for a fixed time in exchange for passage to a new country. Though no longer practiced, time-contract workers often worked in mines, on plantations, and other hard labor positions.

Mariel Boatlift: Program whereby Cubans, when allowed to leave in 1980, were allowed into the U.S. Approximately 125,000 people immigrated through this program.

Boat People: The name given to the group of people who fled Vietnam after the Vietnam War in an attempt to be rescued by the U.S..

Counterurbanization: Net migration from urban to rural areas. People move to small towns and rural areas, due to better communications and the lure of cleaner and more peaceful surroundings.

CHAPTER 3
PROGRESSIVE REVIEW

1. The ability of humans to move from one place to another is known as _____.

mobility

2. _____ is the permanent move by people from one place to another.

Migration

3. Negative perceptions of the political, economic, and environmental conditions of their own countries that induce people to move are called _____ _____.

push factors

4. _____ _____ are conditions which draw people to move to a new location.

Pull factors

5. The three major types of push factors are _____, _____, and _____.

political, economic, environmental

6. _____ are people who are forced to migrate from their home country and cannot return for fear of persecution.

Refugees

7. It is difficult to differentiate between refugees and people wanting to immigrate because of _____ _____.

economic factors

8. Several million Irish were pushed from their homeland due to the destruction of their _____ crop by a fungus.

potato

9. The Dust Bowl of the 1930's pushed "Okies" to migrate; They moved primarily to the state of _____.

California

10. The most important pull factor for immigrants to the U.S. and Canada is _____ _____.

economic improvement

11. In the U.S., the _____ region has pulled many people to it because of the climate's reputation for low pollen counts and a mild climate

Southwest

12. The Atlantic Ocean, Rocky Mountains, and Sahara have acted as _____ _____ to people who wanted to migrate across them.

intervening obstacles

13. International migration is the permanent movement of people from one _____ to another.

country

14. _____ migration occurs when migrants have been compelled to emigrate from a country, generally due to political factors.

Forced

15. In the past 500 years, about _____ million people have left Europe for new lives on other continents.

60

16. The largest supplier of emigrants to the United States from Europe has been _____, with 7.1 million.

Germany

17. Ninety percent of the immigrants to the U.S. before 1840, came from _____ _____.

Great Britain

18. The first two peaks of European immigration to the U.S. came from _____ and _____ Europe.

Northern, Western

19. Arizona and _____ _____ were the last two of the contiguous forty-eight states to be admitted, changing American attitudes about immigration.

New Mexico

20. In 1921, the U.S. set _____ to control the number of immigrants in the U.S. from different parts of the world.

quotas

21. The U.S. yearly issues _____ visas to legal immigrants.

675,000

22. _____ _____ is the exodus of talented people from LDCs to places with more opportunities and more lucrative job offers.

Brain drain

23. Since the 1960's, five-sixths of all immigrants come from _____._____.and _____.

Latin America, Asia

24. People who arrive in the U.S. without the consent of the U.S. government are called _____ _____.

undocumented immigrants

25. A person who, for a price, helps Mexicans enter the U.S. illegally is called a _____.

coyote

26. The border between the U.S. and _____ extends over 2,000 miles, and is witness to a large amount of illegal immigration.

Mexico

27. People who migrate to Europe and Middle Eastern countries to work, but do not receive citizenship are known as _____ _____.

guest workers

28. The _____ _____ receives many immigrants from countries that are its former colonies.

United Kingdom

29. A person who moves from one place to another within the same region is an _____ _____.

intraregional migrant

30. Since the 1790 U.S. Census, the geographic center of the U.S. population has continually moved mostly _____ and slightly _____ of its original position.

west, south

31. During the last one-hundred years, African-Americans in the U.S. have migrated from the _____ to northern cities such as New York, Detroit, and Chicago.

South

32. _____ constructed a new capital in the interior of the country to facilitate settlement of the interior.

Brazil

33. Migration from rural to _____ areas has skyrocketed in recent years in Asia, Latin America, and Africa.

urban

34. Overcrowding and lack of housing causes many people in Brazil and elsewhere to live in favelas or _____.

slums

35. The most significant _____ _____ are no longer natural boundaries, but acquiring the necessary official documentation..

intervening obstacles

36. _____ have been most successful at taking advantage of U.S. immigration law by establishing a family member in the U.S. and bringing the rest of the family through _____ _____.

Asians

chain migration

37. The Mariel Boatlift brought emigrants from _____ to the U.S..

Cuba

CHAPTER 4

FOLK AND POPULAR CULTURE

People interact with the environments in which they live. Humans establish routines and belief systems to give reinforce their world view. Groups of people interact in ways that become characteristic for the entire group. Meaningful actions are repeated by more of the group and the actions become customs. The routine becomes meaningful and there is a yearly cycle of events and actions. The relationship between social customs and the cultural landscape is one facet of cultural geography. People change the natural environment and create landscapes, or built environments, to suit their needs and/or preferences. Distinct cultural differences arise when a group of people receives all of their stimuli from within the group and from their local environment. Regional differences are diminishing with modern technology and communication. As communication and transportation becomes faster and more widely spread, there are few areas in the world which remain completely isolated. English replaces indigenous languages. Levi's replace traditional dress, and Latin American rhythms are heard around the world.

Folk and Popular Culture: Culture combines values, material artifacts, and political institutions. Culture is affected by migration. Material culture derives from basic needs--food, clothing, and shelter. Leisure activities, arts and recreation, are another element of culture. Individuals, as lovers of routine, form *habits,* or repetitive acts. *Customs* are repetitive acts of a group performed to the extent that it becomes characteristic of the group. A *custom* is a habit that a group of people has widely adopted. People in a group manifest the feeling of the group as *culture*, the body of customary beliefs, social forms, and material traits of a group of people.

Social customs can be divided into two categories. *Folk culture* is traditionally practiced by small, homogeneous groups living in isolated areas. A group develops distinctive customs from experiencing local, social, and physical conditions in isolation from other groups. Groups living in proximity may generate a variety of folk customs in a limited geographic area because of limited communication. *Popular culture* is found in large, heterogeneous societies that share certain habits despite differences in other personal characteristics. Geographers are interested in *where* folk and popular cultures are located, their spatial distribution, diffusion, and integration with other social characteristics. Geographers also study the relation between material culture and the physical environment. The amount of integration between groups explains *why* cultural characteristics changes across space. Popular customs are diffused quickly through media, communication, and rapid transportation networks. Globalization of customs and culture is affecting local diversity in the world. Popular customs threaten the environment through a lack of sensitivity to particularly fragile or unique ecosystems.

Key Issue 1: Where Do Folk and Popular Cultures Originate and Diffuse? (121)

Origin of Folk and Popular Customs (121-122): Social customs originate at a *hearth*, or place of origin. Folk customs often have anonymous, multiple, simultaneous hearths, sources, dates of conception, and originators. Popular customs are generally a product of economically developed countries with a strong and stable infrastructure. Technology and increased leisure time generated by mass production increased the means for acquisition. Leisure time increases when jobs shift from predominantly agricultural (necessary for subsistence living) to service and manufacturing (specialized jobs).

    Origin of Folk Music (122): *Folk songs* are usually anonymous and are orally transmitted. Songs are written about the activities in daily life familiar to the majority of people. They tell stories and transmit information about farming, life-cycle events, mysteries, or beliefs. Themes in folk music are recurrent, and can be traced to multiple hearths. Geographer *George Carney* identified four major hearths for country music in the U.S. based on the birthplaces of people in the field: southern Appalachia, central Tennessee and Kentucky, the Ozark and Ouachita uplands of western Arkansas and eastern Oklahoma, and north-central Texas.

    Origin of Popular Music (123): *Popular music* contrasts significantly with folk music. It is specially written for mass-production and consumption. Popular music, as it is now known in the U.S., began around 1900 when music hall and vaudeville shows were main sources of popular entertainment. *Tin Pan Alley*, along 28th Street between Fifth Avenue and Broadway, grew from the demand for catchy, memorable tunes which were then turned to profits by the sale of mass produced copies of sheet music. Tin Pan Alley disappeared after World War II when recorded music replaced sheet. Popular music was made available during the war for the soldiers and civilians overseas through broadcasts by the Armed Forces Radio Network. English became the international language for music.

Diffusion of Folk and Popular Customs (123-124): Folk songs are communicated orally on a much smaller scale, primarily through migration rather than through electronic communication. Popular customs are diffused following a process of *hierarchical diffusion* from *hearths* or *nodes of innovation*. Hollywood, CA and New York City are strong nodes of innovation, both for ideas and for means of communication. Folk culture spreads through relocation diffusion as migration.

    The Amish: Relocation Diffusion of Folk Culture (124): The *Amish* began as followers of a Swiss Mennonite Bishop named Jakob Amman. He established a group of followers and that became known as the Amish. They migrated from three areas: Bern, Switzerland; Alsace, France; and the Palatinate region of Germany. The European Amish eventually merged with the common culture. In the 1700s, Amish from Bern and the Palatinate settled in Pennsylvania. A second group, encouraged to migrate by promises of cheap land, followed in the early 1800s and settled in Ohio, Illinois, Iowa and Ontario. Relying on less advanced technology and traditional customs, they have influenced the landscape of the U.S. Folk customs dictate every son must receive his own farm. Because of high land prices, a single farm in Pennsylvania could be sold and the revenue would buy enough land for the entire family in places like southwestern Kentucky.

Sports: Example of Hierarchical Diffusion:

Folk Culture Origin and Globalization of Soccer (124-126): *Soccer* has grown to be one of the most popular game in the world. It began as a folk custom in England in the eleventh century when the head of a Danish soldier was found which they began to kick. Boys got the idea of inflating a cow bladder. Early games were played by a mob between villages. The winning village was the one who got the ball to the center of the rival village. In the twelfth century "*football*" was confined to a vacant lot and the rules were standardized. King Henry II outlawed the game in the late 1100's, and it was legalized again by King James I in 1603. It became a popular culture with the game's increased skill of the players and the support of clubs in the 1800s. People began to have time to participate in spectator sports. In 1863 the Football Association was formed to organize professional leagues and to formalize the structure of the sport. *Rugby* was a spin-off, formed when a player at Rugby College picked up the ball and ran with it in 1823. Soccer was exported to continental Europe and onward through contact with English players. The British Empire was a vehicle for diffusion, there being Englishmen migrating around the globe. Russia received the game when a factory near Moscow advertised in London for soccer playing workers. They were absorbed into the culture and Moscow's Dynamo team is the country's most famous. Soccer has never reached the same height of popularity in the U.S. as it has other places. A game was played in the U.S. and, instead of adopting soccer rules, Rugby rules were adopted. The game has evolved into a completely new game–American *football*.

Other Sports (126): Every country and culture has its favored game. Organized spectator sports are now a part of popular custom. The common element is people's willingness to pay for the privilege of watching a game. The soccer World Cup final match is the single most watched historical event.

Key Issue 2: Why Is Folk Culture Clustered?

Isolation Promotes Cultural Diversity (126):

Himalayan Art (126-128): Geographers *P. Karan* and *Cotton Mather* investigated a narrow corridor of 2,500 km in the Himalayan Mountains of Bhutan, Nepal and northern India. They contain four religious groups: Tibetan Buddhists, Hindus, Muslims, and Southeast Asian Animists. Limited interaction and spatial proximity included, there are four distinctive folk customs reflected in artwork, based on beliefs about the world around them as well as the proximate natural environment.

Influence of the Physical Environment (128): Folk culture may reflect conditions of the natural environment or folk culture may ignore the environment. Food and shelter demonstrate the influence of cultural values on folk culture.

Distinctive Food Preferences (128): People adapt their food preferences to conditions in the environment. What isn't available can't be eaten. *Soybeans* are widely grown in Asia. They have to be processed as they are toxic in their raw state and indigestible. Fuel is scarce in Asia, so they can't be subjected to a lengthy cooking process. Instead bean sprouts, bean curd, and soy sauce are eaten. Fuel shortages in Italy have created a preference for quick-frying foods. In northern Europe, availability of fuel has developed preferences for slowly stewed and baked foods.

Food Diversity in Transylvania (128-129): Food preferences can develop differently while living in close proximity. Culturally diverse people occupy Transylvania and their soups show distinct traditions. Preferences for ingredients range from vegetables, pork, sauerkraut, to cherry tree twigs, curdled milk, goose and others. Every cultural group has its own recipe. Cooking traditions are often evidence of cultural heritage long after acculturation has rendered people indistinguishable from those of the majority.

Food Attractions and Taboos (129-131): A restriction on behavior imposed by social custom is a *taboo*. Food taboos arise from perceived negative agents or forces in the environment. The Ainus in Japan don't eat otter as it is believed to be a forgetful animal and consumption of it might cause one to become forgetful. *Food attractions* are the opposite. Foods are thought to enhance sought after traits such as love-making, fertility, or strength. Some food taboos may have grown out of a concern for the environment. For example, some types of food or animals may only be consumed by a few people, often of high-rank. Americans won't eat insects despite their nutritional value, relied on in developing countries to supplement diet.

Folk Housing (131): French geographer *Jean Brunhes,* a major contributor to human geography's cultural landscape tradition, views the house as being among the essential facts of human geography.

Distinctive Building Materials (131): *Houses* are the products of both cultural tradition and natural conditions. They are built using available materials, the most common are wood and brick, although stone, grass, sod, and skins are also used. Wood is generally preferred as it is easy to work with. In hot, dry climates, *adobe* bricks are made by baking wet mud in the sun. Stone is used as a primary building material as well as for decoration. Social factors influence choices. People may import preferred materials or find less expensive ways of creating the same effect.

Distinctive House Form and Orientation (131): House form and orientation may result from customary beliefs or environmental factors. Religious and cultural values are reflected in housing. Sacred walls, arrangement of furniture, sacred corners, number and direction of doors, orientation of the house, sleeping patterns, and subsequent buildings all influence the form a house takes. Many skyscrapers do not number the thirteenth floor.

Housing and Environment (131-132): Houses are built to protect humans from the natural environment. In snowy and wet areas, roofs are pitched to facilitate runoff. It may be necessary to avoid the sun or use its energy as much as possible.

Areas with similar climates and building materials do not necessarily share ideas about housing. *R. W. McColl's* comparison of four relatively isolated villages in dry, northern and western China yielded four distinct house types, all of which served as protection from the extreme hot and cold temperatures.

      U.S. Folk House Forms (132-135): Houses built across the United States reflect the popular house types of the time and place from which settlers came. Three *hearths* for house types have been identified by *Fred Kniffen,* who considered the house a good reflection of cultural heritage, current fashion, functional needs and the impact of environment: *New England, Middle Atlantic*, and *Lower Chesapeake. New England* is the place of origin for four major types of houses, popular in the 1700s and early 1800s: the *Saltbox, Two Chimney, Cape Cod*, and *Front Gable* and *Wing*. These house types, along with their builders, settled in a band along the northern U.S.. The people in the *Middle Atlantic* region constructed the *"I"-house* which became the most extensive style in the eastern half of the U.S. and the Midwest. *Lower Chesapeake* houses diffused along the southeast coast. With a quick lesson in architecture, a trained eye can still spot the original patterns of settlement across the United States. Modern regional distinctions are no longer as prominent because rapid communication and transportation systems mobilize ideas and people.

Key Issue 3: Why Is Popular Culture Widely Distributed?

Diffusion of Popular Housing, Clothing, and Food (135):

      Popular Housing Styles (135): Modern technology has influenced the shapes, materials, detailing, and other aspects of housing. Houses built since the 1940s show different trends in building. *Fashion* is the major influence, rather than cultural heritage, changing housing from a *folk custom* to a *popular custom*.

      Modern House Styles (1945-1960) (135): *Modern house styles* were most popular between 1945 and 1960 and included the dominant type, *minimal traditional*, as well as *ranch houses, split-level houses, contemporary* and *shed style houses*. *Ranch* houses are of interest as these single level houses took up a larger lot and encouraged *urban sprawl*.

      Neo-Eclectic House Styles (Since 1960) (135-136): The first style was the *mansard* style, as well as *Neo-Tudor, Neo-French,* and *Neo-colonial* styles. These styles incorporate a large central "great room" into the scheme of things, replacing family and living rooms and making room for the television. Regional differences still exist to some extent in noticeable tendencies. Color, style, floor coverings, garages, porches, and decks all vary regionally.

      Rapid Diffusion of Clothing Styles (136-138): Clothing is distributed across the U.S. landscape with little regard for distinctive physical features. Occupation will affect clothing styles a great deal in the more developed countries. Income is a second major influence, with relatively affluent people disregarding and replacing entire wardrobes for the season's latest fashion trends. Mass produced copies of designer clothes are instantly available to the general public. People in more developed countries can travel either in person or from an armchair to see the folk cultures and their dress around the world. Many ideas and items of clothing have come into general usage in more developed countries.

Jeans (138): *Jeans* acquired an image of youthful independence in the 1960s in the U.S., as young people adopted a style of clothing previously associated with low-status manual laborers and farmers. Jeans have become a world wide phenomenon, fetching unbelievable prices on the black market. Regional preferences for particular styles of jeans have developed--button or zipper fly.

Popular Food Customs:

Alcohol and Fresh Produce (138-139): Consumption of large quantities of alcoholic beverages and fresh produce are characteristic of the food customs of popular societies. In the U.S. consumption of alcohol types tends to be greatest around the area of production. Alcohol consumption is relatively low in areas populated by Mormons and Baptists. Consumption increases with advertising and is relatively high in Nevada, due to gambling and resort activities. Regional variations in produce consumption include Southerners eating okra and other warm-weather crops while folks in California and the Northeast consume large amounts of cooler-weather crops. Consumption of alcohol and produce depend on income and advertising. Other regional variations exist which are inexplicable.

Wine Production (139-140): Grapes can be grown in a variety of locations, though today wine is made primarily in locations where people like to drink it, have a tradition of excellence in making it, and have the money to purchase it. Wines are generally named for the region of production and dated. American wines are named after the grape variety. Monasteries preserved the art of wine making during its decline which paralleled that of the Roman Empire. Wine production has increased in popularity around the world except where religions dominate which prohibit the consumption of alcohol.

Role of Television in Diffusing Popular Culture:

Diffusion of Television (140-141): Television is the most popular leisure activity in relatively developed countries throughout the world. It is also the most important mechanism by which knowledge of popular customs is rapidly diffused around the world. Television ownership skyrocketed after 1945. By the mid 1950s more than 75% of all households in America owned televisions, 85% of the world's 37 million sets. Different levels of television service today fall into four categories: countries where nearly every household has a set (North America, Europe, Australia, New Zealand, and Japan); countries where ownership is common though not universal (wealthier Latin America and poorer European states); countries where televisions exist though not extensively due to cost (Africa, Asia and poorer Latin America); and, finally, about 30 countries (mostly very poor African and Asian) that have relatively few sets.

Government Control of Television (141): Control of television falls to the private sector's corporations, making a profit by selling advertising time. Private ownership of television companies occurs in America and other Western Hemisphere countries. Most governments control television companies in order to control and censor information distribution.

Reduced Government Control (143): Governments are loosing their tenuous grip on the control of television information. Satellite dishes receive hundreds of channels. Television has been a force for political unrest rather than stability, contrary to *George Orwell's* expectations in his 1949 book 1984.

Key Issue 4: Why Does Globalization of Popular Culture Cause Problems?

Threat To Folk Culture (143):

Loss of Traditional Values (143-144): The loss of folk customs is symbolic of the loss of traditional cultural values and cultural dominance by Western perspectives. Folk modes of dress are being replaced by preferences for and the availability of a more developed country's mode of dress. The business suit has become the international dress for businessmen and politicians.

Change in Traditional Role of Women (144): Women's roles are also changing. Many cultures have a folk tradition which places women in roles subservient to men. Women have had limited access to education and have been victimized, which limits their advancement. Popular cultures have brought some concepts of legal equality as well as economic and social opportunities outside of the home. Prostitution has increased and is supported in some countries as a major source of income.

Threat of Foreign Media Imperialism (144): Lesser developed countries fear the loss of independence through increased infusion of popular customs. The U.S., the United Kingdom and Japan dominate the television industry in most LDCs. Leaders view television as a new method for economic and cultural imperialism. Many characteristically American beliefs conflict with and threaten to drive out traditional social customs.

Western Control of News Media (145): The news gathering capabilities and the network of gathering and distributing the news is more feared than the entertainment function of televisions. The Associated Press (AP) and Reuters are the dominant world news distributor, American and British owned. The AP and Reuters provide stories for newspapers and radio stations around the world. Visnew Ltd. and Worldwide Television News Corporation (WTN)–British-American owned– supply most of the world's television news video. This external news process is threatening, especially to governments which control the media.

Environmental Impact of Popular Culture (145):

Modifying Nature (145): Popular customs disregard the natural environment, imposing structures on the environment, rather than working within it.

Diffusion of Golf (145-146): Golf has become a very popular leisure time activity and, with its increased popularity, hundreds of golf courses have been created. Golf courses restructure and recreate the landscape so that every hole of the course is perfect. Golf has regional variability in the U.S.

Uniform Landscapes (146-147): Popular customs can be seen across the U.S.. Promoters of popular customs want a uniform appearance, to generate "product recognition" and greater consumption. There are several chains of restaurants, quick stops, grocery stores, department stores, and motels which recur from coast to coast. Fast-food restaurants are standard. They look alike, smell alike, the food tastes the same, and they all have uncomfortable chairs and stools. They are attractive because they are convenient , affordable, and familiar.

Global Diffusion of the Uniform Landscape (147): The landscape around the world is becoming more uniform as popular customs diffuse in the form of stores, restaurants, and other consumer products, and other consumer products. Japanese-style cars dominate consumer preferences around the world. Other auto makers are following the lead by producing cars which are similar in appearance and performance.

Negative Environmental Impact:

Increased Demand for Natural Resources (147-148): Increased consumption requires the increased use of natural resources for production and transportation. Natural resources are being overly consumed, especially petroleum. Animals have become endangered and pushed to extinction. Preference for and means of obtaining increasing amounts of meat have not pushed domestic animals into extinction, rather they are raised in ever larger numbers.

Pollution (148): With consumption of resources comes pollution of the air, soil, and water--the natural environment. Most items produced for popular customs are discarded rather than recycled. Mass production of goods also means mass production of pollution such as solids, liquids, gases, heat, noise, and light.

Summary: Isolation maintains and encourages diversity. The people of the world come in contact with each other more today than ever in the past. Many own a pair of jeans or have, at the very least, seen them. Tourism is encouraged by less developed countries (LDCs) to infuse much needed capital into struggling economies. Contact with people from more developed countries (MDCs) is coupled with the spread of popular cultures which threaten the unique customs of the many diverse peoples of the world.

CHAPTER 4
KEY TERMS AND CONCEPTS

Habit: Repetitive act performed by an individual.

Custom: Repetitive acts of a group performed to the extent that they become characteristic of the group. A custom is a habit that a group of people has widely adopted.

Culture: The body of customary beliefs, social forms, and material traits of a group of people.

Folk Culture: Traditionally practiced primarily by small, homogenous groups living in isolated rural areas. They vary more from place to place at a given time.

Popular Culture: Found in large, heterogeneous societies that share certain habits despite differences in other personal characteristics. Most Americans wear jeans fairly regularly.

Hearth: Place of origin for a custom, idea, language, or group of people.

Folk Songs: Songs written about daily activities that are anonymous and orally transmitted, often sharing information necessary for life.

George Carney: A geographer who identified four hearths for country music in the U.S.

Popular Music: Music written specifically for mass distribution and personal gain with a known origin. U.S. Popular Music traditions began in the early 1900's.

Tin Pan Alley: The hearth for early popular music culture, creating massive amounts of sheet music for sale, and for use in vaudeville shows.

Hierarchical Diffusion: Diffusion which occurs from a very strong hearth or node of innovation. U.S. movies are diffused from Hollywood, California.

Amish: A belief system and lifestyle begun in Switzerland in the 1600s by Jakob Amman. The Amish migrated to the Americas in the 1700s and the 1800s. They have had a distinct impact on the landscape.

Soccer: A game diffused from England which has gained immense worldwide popularity and become a popular custom. It is played on a field by two opposing teams which may not touch the ball with their arms nor their hands.

Rugby: Invented in 1823 when a player at Rugby College picked up a soccer ball and ran with it. It has since developed into a separate game and is the precursor for American football.

Football: The name for soccer in other countries. American football is a more physical version of Rugby, developed and popularized by American colleges and universities.

P. Karan & Cotton Mather: Geographers who studied the peoples of a part of the Himalayan Mountains, who found distinct cultural groups which were apparent in their respective forms of artwork.

Soybeans: A crop grown because of its nutritional value. It must be processed and has come to be processed differently depending on availability of fuels.

Taboo: A restriction on behavior imposed by social custom.

Food attractions: Foods consumed because of belief in some inherent trait or substance which will enhance the consumer.

Jean Brunhes: Geographer whose work contributed much to human geography's cultural landscape tradition, studying housing.

House: Structures built to protect people from the natural environment. They are the products of both cultural tradition and natural conditions.

Adobe: A building material made from baking mud in the sun, used in dry, hot areas.

R. W. McColl: Studied four villages in China living in isolation from one another. They developed four distinctly different house types.

Fred Kniffen: Studied the folk house forms of the U.S. and identified three hearths for early house types reflected in subsequent settlement across the country.

Urban Sprawl: A function of people taking up larger and larger areas for houses and properties, rather than using tiny lots and building things very close together.

Jeans: An interesting phenomena in the diffusion of popular culture. They are viewed by some as a symbol for freedom, affluence, America, or the meeting of the masses.

CHAPTER 4
PROGRESSIVE REVIEW

1. _____ culture is dependent on time and changes and diffuses very rapidly.   Popular

2. Folk and popular culture derive from the _____ and _____ activities of daily life.   survival, leisure

3. _____ _____ is often anonymous, having multiple hearths and originators while _____ _____ has a known origin and creator.   Folk culture
popular culture

4. _____ _____ transmit information orally that is important to a group of people.   Folk songs

5. Popular music began in the early 1900s with _____.   vaudeville

6. The music industry was based in New York in _____ _____ Alley, which was a collection of people devoted to writing, printing, and selling massive amounts of sheet music.   Tin Pan

7. Popular music started to diffuse during World War II when the _____ _____ _____ _____ transmitted American music overseas.   Armed Forces
Radio Network

8. _____ _____ _____ and _____, _____ are examples of strong nodes of innovation.   New York City
Hollywood, CA

9. The _____ have made a distinct mark on the American landscape because of their traditional farming techniques and architectural styles.   Amish

10. Some of the original Amish settlements in _____ are being sold to buy property elsewhere to provide _____ for the _____.   Pennsylvania,
farms, sons

11. _____ is the most popular sport in the world.   Soccer

12. _____ and then American _____ were derived from the game of soccer.   Rugby, football

13. People living in _____ tend to develop distinct cultural traits and folk customs.   isolation

14. _____ are a food crop high in protein requiring a great deal of processing to enable digestion.   soybeans

15. Traditions in _____ are evident long after people have been acculturated into a larger group.   cooking or food

16. Food _____ and _____ are beliefs about food discouraging and encouraging consumption.   taboos, attractions

17. _____ _____ views the house as being among the essential objects for the study of human geography.   Jean Brunhes

18. Three hearths for house types in the U.S. are _____ _____, _____ Atlantic, and _____ Chesapeake.   New England, Middle, Lower

19. _____ are a readily recognized and widespread symbol of popular culture.   Jeans

20. Wines are grown world wide and are named by _____ _____ in the U.S. and by _____ in the rest of the world.   grape variety, region

21. The _____ is the most important tool for spreading information, including popular culture.   television

22. Many folk cultures are being infused by ideas from _____ _____ which have the potential of altering, if not destroying, them.   popular cultures

23. The world television industry is dominated by three MDC countries: _____, _____, and _____.   U.S., Japan, United Kingdom

24. Fast food restaurants, motels, and department stores look alike to produce _____ _____.   product recognition

25. Production of goods results in many different types of environmental _____.   pollution

CHAPTER 5

LANGUAGE

Languages are integral to people, enabling them to converse with one another. Language is a component of culture and individual identity, along with religion and ethnicity. English is a particularly interesting case study for language because of its familiarity to the reader. Having an extensive written history, there is much to examine to help understand the evolution of English. All languages change and evolve with the peoples who use them. Moving from place to place, country to country, or continent to continent, people take their languages with them and new languages evolve from the marriage of cultures. Today, English is spoken around the world. It is spoken differently in America, England, South Africa, India, and other places because of different influences in each place. Americans have lived in relative isolation from England, allowing the two to evolve differently. The same is true of cultures and languages around the world, giving rise to unique language families, branches, groups, and dialects.

Language (155): *Language* is a system of written and/or verbal communication. *Speech* is a collection of sounds that a group of people understands to have the same meaning. The written version of a language is called a *literary tradition,* which may or may not exist alongside the *verbal language*, or a spoken language.

Key Issue 1: Where Are Different Languages Distributed?

Language Families (155-156): Languages are related to one another and can be described by their family, branch, group, and dialect. A *language family* includes individual languages related through a common ancestor that existed before recorded history. The Indo-European family contains 50% of the world's population, Sino-Tibetan contains 20 %, and 20% in four families–Austronesian, Afro-Asiatic, Niger-Congo, and Dravidian. The remaining 10% of the population speaks a variety of other languages. A *language branch* includes languages that share a common origin but have further evolved into individual languages. A *language group* is a group of languages within a branch that share a common origin in the relatively recent past and display relatively few differences in grammar and vocabulary. A *dialect* is a form of a language spoken in a local area. The *official language* is the dialect of a language used for government, business, education, and mass communication. Figures 5-1, 5-2, and 5-3 are extremely important reference tools for understanding this discussion of language origination, evolution, and diffusion.

Indo-European Languages (156-157): More than 2.5 billion people, half the world's population, speak an Indo-European language as their first language, and 0.5 billion people have an Indo-European language as their second language.

Germanic Language Branch (157):

West Germanic Group: English and German (157-159): High German evolved into modern standard German. English developed from the Low Germanic group, as well as did Dutch (of the Netherlands), Flemish (northern Belgium) and Afrikaans (South Africa), Frisian (northeastern Netherlands), and a German dialect spoken in the northern lowlands of Germany.

North Germanic Group: Scandinavian Languages (159): The four Scandinavian languages all evolved from Old Norse--*Swedish, Danish, Norwegian,* and *Icelandic.* Migration and political changes contributed to these languages becoming distinct from one another.

Romance Language Branch (159): The Latin language used by the Romans 2000 years ago was diffused by the Roman Empire's forces and has become *Spanish, Portuguese, French,* and *Italian.* The languages are roughly contained by the modern countries whose borders follow physical boundaries which serve as intervening obstacles between peoples. *Romanian* is spoken in Romania and Moldova and is separated from other Romance-speaking European countries by Slavic-speaking countries.

Indo-Iranian Language Branch (159): The largest of the Indo-European language families with more than 100 individual languages and 1 billion speakers.

Indic (Eastern) Group of Indo-Iranian Language Branch (159-161): *Indic* languages comprise the world's second largest language group. This branch encompasses the most widely used languages of India, Pakistan, and Bangladesh. One third of *Indians* speak *Hindi,* which can be spoken in many ways though there is only one official way to write the language—using a script called *Devanagari,* used since the seventh century AD. The written language remained consistent for all Hindi speakers because few people could read or write, while the spoken language evolved in different locals. *Pakistan* uses *Urdu* which is like Hindi, though written using the *Arabic alphabet.* Most Pakistanis are Muslims and the Quran is written in Arabic. *Hindustani* is the basis for both languages. Hindi was the dialect from New Delhi and was encouraged in the nineteenth century by the British for use in India's government. India's 1 billion people speak many different languages and since independence in 1947, the constitution has been amended to recognize 18 official languages—13 Indo-European, 4 Dravidian, and one Sino-Tibetan language. English is an "associate" language though few can speak it. It is often employed by Indians who can't otherwise communicate.

Iranian (Western) Group of Indo-Iranian Language Branch (161): The *Iranian* languages are spoken in Iran and neighboring countries in southwestern Asia. The main languages include *Persian* in Iran, *Pashto* in eastern Afghanistan and western Pakistan, and *Kurdish* of the Kurds of western Iran, northern Iraq, and eastern Turkey. All are written with the *Arabic alphabet.*

Balto-Slavic Language Branch of Indo-European (161, 163): *Slavic* was a single language that branched off in the seventh century when Slavs migrated from Asia to Eastern Europe creating East, West, and South Slavic groups and a Baltic group. Slavic languages are not easily differentiated as differences are relatively small. They are generally mutually intelligible, though differences are a source of pride and are being preserved and in some cases accentuated in recent independence movements.

East Slavic and Baltic Groups of Balto-Slavic Language Branch (162): *Eastern Slavic* languages are the most widely used Slavic languages. Russian is one of the six official languages of the United Nations. More than 80% of Russians speak the language. It is the lingua franca for people of the former Soviet Union. Russian was taught as a second language to encourage unity. *Ukrainian* and *Belorusian* are the next most wide-spread East Slavic languages and have been established as the official languages in Ukraine and Belarus. The two principal Baltic languages are *Latvian* and *Lithuanian*, official languages of Latvia and Lithuania. *Estonian*, the official language of Estonia, is an *Uralic* language unrelated to the Indo-European family.

West and South Slavic Groups of Balto-Slavic Language Branch (162-163): *Polish*, followed by *Czech* and *Slovak,* are the most commonly spoken *West Slavic* languages. During the Communist era, Czechoslovakia contained twice as many Czechs as Slovaks and tried to balance the use of the two languages, which are mutually understandable. In 1993 Slovakia ceded from the Czech Republic, renewing feelings of resentment of perceived Czech dominance of the country's culture. *South Slavic* languages include *Serbo-Croatian* and *Bulgarian.* Serbs and Croats speak the same language; the former writing with the *Cyrillic alphabet* and the Croats using the *Roman alphabet.* *Slovene* is the official language of Slovenia, while *Macedonian* is used in the former Yugoslav republic of Macedonia.

Other Language Families (163): Half the world's population speaks an Indo-European Language, a quarter speaks a Sino-Tibetan language, and the rest speak another language (Figures 5-1 and 5-2).

Sino-Tibetan Language Family (163-164): In the People's Republic of China, with over 1 billion people, the languages are generally Sinitic branch of the Sino-Tibetan language family. Smaller countries in Southeast Asia also speak Sino-Tibetan languages.

Sinitic Branch (164): *Mandarin*, meaning common speech, is the most common language in the world, spoken by three-fourths of the Chinese people. It is an official language of the United Nations and the official language of both the People's Republic of China and Taiwan. Four other Chinese languages are *Cantonese, Wu, Min,* and *Hakka*, though the government imposes Mandarin. All use a consistent written form, and the small number of languages contribute to a sense of unity. The Chinese spoken languages are based on 420 one-syllable words, more different sounds than humans are able to make. Each actual spoken sound denotes more than one thing, and meaning is inferred from *context* in the sentence and the *tone of voice* used by the speaker. Multiple-syllable words are created meaning is inferred. The 4,000 year old written language uses thousands of characters, some of which represent sounds. Most are *ideograms* which represent ideas or concepts rather than pronunciations.

Austro-Thai and Tibeto-Burman Branches of Sino-Tibetan Family (164): The major language of the *Austro-Thai branch* is *Thai*, spoken in Laos, Thailand, and parts of Vietnam. *Lao* is considered by some to be a separate language. The principal language of the *Tibeto-Burman branch* is *Burmese* spoken in Myanmar (Burma).

Other East and Southeast Asian Language Families (164): Japanese and Korean both form distinctive language families because of their relative isolation-- Japan is an island and Korea is a peninsular state.

Japanese (164-165): The *Japanese* received their original writing system from the Chinese. The language structure differs from Chinese. Japanese uses two systems of *phonetic symbols* either in place of the ideograms or alongside them.

Korean (165): *Korean* is classed separately though it may be related to Japanese and the Altaic languages of central Asia. Korean is written using *hankul*, in which each letter represents a sound. More than half the vocabulary is Chinese and Japanese and Chinese are the principal sources for new words.

Austro-Asiatic (165): *Austro-Asiatic* languages include *Vietnamese*, the dominant tongue of the Southeast Asian language family. It is written using the *Roman alphabet,* with many *diacritical marks* above the vowels. The system was developed in the seventh century by Roman Catholic missionaries.

Afro-Asiatic Language Family (165): This family includes *Arabic* and *Hebrew* and a number of languages spoken in northern Africa and southwestern Asia. It is the fourth largest language family. Languages of this family were used to write the holiest books of three world religions, the Judeo-Christian Bible and the Islamic Quran. Arabic is the major Afro-Asiatic language, the official language of several countries in North Africa and southwestern Asia. About 230 million people speak Arabic and more have knowledge of the language because Muslims become familiar with the Quran. It is the sixth official language of the United Nations.

Altaic and Uralic Language Families (165): The two families are similar in word formation, grammatical endings, and other structural elements. They are believed to have separate origins. The *Altaic* family is thought to have come from the steppes bordering the Qilian Shan and Altai mountains between Tibet and China, or it may be a conglomeration of many languages.

Altaic Languages (165-166): Altaic languages are spoken in an 8,000-km band of Asia between Turkey and Mongolia and China. *Turkish* is the most widely spoken Altaic language. It is now written with the Latin alphabet, a change from Arabic ordered in 1928 by the Turkish government, led by *Kemal Ataturk* to help modernize the economy and culture of Turkey. At least one million Altaic language speakers include Azerbaijani, Bashkir, Chuvash, Kazakh, Kyrgyz, Mongolian, Tartar, Turkmen, Uighur, and Uzbek. The Soviet Union suppressed the use of these languages, and forced the use of the *Russian Cyrillic alphabet* on a population familiar with the Arabic alphabet. With the fall of the Soviet Union, many of these languages have been recognized by the newly independent countries of Azerbaijan, Kazakhstan, Kyrgyzstan, Turkmenistan, and Uzbekistan. New countries don't always follow cultural boundaries, dividing speakers of such Altaic languages as *Bashkir, Chuvash, Tatar,* and *Uighur.*

Uralic Languages (166): Proto-Uralic was first used 7,000 years ago by people living in the Ural Mountains, north of the Kurgan homeland. Migrants took the language to Estonia, Finland and Siberia. A second branch took the language to Hungary.

African Language Families (166-167): Africa has nearly 1,000 documented languages and several thousand named dialects. People lived in relative isolation for at least 5,000 years. Each group of people developed its own language, religion, and other cultural traditions. Only ten African languages are spoken by more than 10 million people. Few have a written tradition aside from the documentation done by missionaries in using either Latin or Arabic alphabets. Language distribution is more distinct in northern Africa and more complex in sub-Saharan Africa.

Niger-Congo Language Family (167): The *Niger-Congo* family has six branches that include more than 95% of sub-Saharan African speakers. The remaining 5% speak languages in the *Koisan* or *Nilo-Saharan* families. Several million South Africans speak either *English* or *Afrikaans*--a language evolved from Dutch colonial time. The largest branch is *Benue-Congo*, dominated by *Swahili*, the official language only of Tanzania. It is the lingua franca for much of eastern Africa. It is a mixture derived from African groups coming in contact with Arab traders. It is unique in its extensive literary tradition.

Nilo-Saharan Language Family (167): These families are spoken in north central Africa by a few million people. There are six branches: *Fur*, *Koma*, *Maba*, *Saharan*, *Songhai*, and *Chari-Nile* which is further broken up into four groups *Berta*, *Kunama*, *East Sudanic*, and *Central Sudanic*--divided into ten subgroups.

Khoisan Language Family (167): The *Khoisan* family is in southwest Africa; they employ clicking sounds.

Austronesian Language Family (167-168): About 6 percent of the world speaks an *Austronesian* language, most frequently is *Malay-Indonesian* of Indonesia, the world's most populous country. Austronesian languages are spoken on islands in the South Pacific. The people of Madagascar speak *Malagasy* even though they are separated by 3,000 km from any Austronesian language speaking people. It is believed people sailed in small boats to Madagascar approximately 2,000 years ago.

Nigeria: Conflict Among Speakers of Different Languages (168): Nigeria has had continuous problems dealing with the presence of many languages. More than 200 distinct languages are used, none by a majority of the population. *Hausa* is spoken in the north by approximately 25% of the total population. *Ibo* is spoken in the southeast as well as *Efik* and *Ijaw*. In the southwest, *Yoruba* and *Edo* are of importance. English, the official language, is spoken by 2% of the population, a residual from colonial times.

Key Issue 2: Why Do People in Different Locations Speak Similar Languages? (168): Global distribution of languages happens because of interaction and isolation. As people migrate, languages are redistributed. If the groups maintain close ties, the language in both places will remain very similar.

Without contact the language in the two locations will evolve into separate languages.

Origin and Diffusion of English (168): English is spoken by one-half billion people, second to Mandarin. English speakers are distributed around the world. English is the official language in 42 countries, which comprise 2 billion people, even if they don't speak the language.

    English Colonies (168-169): Figure 8-4 shows the location of former British colonies; English is the official language of most of them. English diffused from England to North America in the seventeenth century. England dominated the North American colonies after a battle with France making English the principal language of North America. The British took control of Ireland, South Asia, the South Pacific, and southern Africa. The U.S. has diffused English to the Philippines.

    Origin of English in England (169): The Celts were the original inhabitants of the British Isles, arriving around 2000 BC, and speaking Celtic. Tribes invaded from Europe around 450 AD and pushed the Celts into Cornwall, Scotland, and Wales.

    German Invasion (169-170): Three tribes invaded--the Jutes from northern Denmark, the Angles from southern Denmark, and the Saxons from northwestern Germany--often called the Anglo-Saxons, the two larger tribes. Modern English evolved from their languages which were all very similar. The tribes came from the northern lowlands so English is classified as a Low Germanic language within the West Germanic group. Comparing modern German and English with dispersed, isolated Germanic groups gives clues about their historical development. Vikings, defeated in their effort to conquer the islands, stayed and subsequently enriched the language with new words.

    Norman Invasion (170): In 1066 the Normans invaded England and established French as the official language for the next 150 years. In 1024 England lost control of Normandy. Fewer people wanted to speak French, English regained dominance, and in 1362 Parliament enacted the Statute of Pleading making English the official language for court business. The common Germanic language and French spoken by leaders mixed and became modern English.

Origin and Diffusion of Romance Languages (170): Spanish, Portuguese, French, Italian, and Romanian are all Romance languages because they developed from Latin, the "Roman's language." The rise of the Roman empire 2,000 years ago diffused the Latin language.

    Role of Roman Empire (170-171): At its height in the second century AD, the Roman Empire extended from the Atlantic Ocean, to the Black Sea--all the lands bordering the Mediterranean Sea. The Roman armies brought Latin with them and native languages were either extinguished or suppressed. Latin had regional variations because the empire grew over a period of several hundred years taking Latin (at a different point of development) and incorporating elements of the local languages. *Vulgar Latin*, the language of the people, was different than the standard literary form. Soldiers spread Vulgar Latin to the provinces.

Collapse of Roman Empire (171): The Roman Empire collapsed in the fifth century and communication amongst the former provinces declined, isolating them from one another and from the source of the Latin language. By the eighth century, the provinces had developed distinct languages.

Origin and Diffusion of Indo-European (171): Germanic, Romance, Balto-Slavic, and Indo-Iranian languages are theoretically descended from a single language, called Proto-Indo-European, but no clear evidence exists because of the lack of written records or recorded history.

Evidence of Common Origin of Indo-European Languages (171): Evidence of a common ancestor comes from the analysis of common words across the various languages. Common root words indicate "relatedness" between languages. Though it is not known who the people were who spoke the Indo-European language.

Two Theories of Origin and Diffusion (171): The Proto-Indo-European language is thought to have originated in different locations and diffused either through warfare and conquest, or through peaceful sharing of food.

Theory 1: Kurgan Origin (171): *Marija Gimbutas* proposed the Kurgan people of the steppes near the border between present-day Russia and Kazakhstan. These nomadic herders with horses conquered much of Europe and south Asia between 3500 and 2500 BC.

Theory 2: Origin in Anatolia (171-173): Archaeologist *Colin Renfrew* proposes eastern Anatolia, part of modern Turkey, as the place of origin and they lived approximately 2,000 years before the Kurgans. He believes affluence from agricultural practices enabled the growing prosperity to travel northward, eastward, westward, and either directly along the southern coasts of the Black and Caspian seas, or indirectly (by way of Russia) north of the seas. Language diffused because its speakers were more numerous and prosperous because they grew their own food.

Isolated Languages (173): An *isolated language* is unrelated to any other and therefore not attached to any language family. They develop through lack of interaction with speakers of other languages.

A Pre-Indo-European Survivor: Basque (173): The isolation of the Basques in the Pyrenees Mountains of northern Spain and southwestern France has helped preserve this pre-Indo-European language. Approximately 1 million Basque speakers live in the Pyrenees Mountains between France and Spain. No attempt to link it to the Indo-European languages has been successful. Their isolation helps preserve the language.

An Unchanging Language: Icelandic (173-174): Icelandic is related to the North Germanic Languages, though it has changed the least since colonization by Norwegians in 874 AD. Their island location has kept the people isolated and the lack of contact has maintained the language for a thousand years.

Key Issue 3: Why Is Our Language Spoken Differently in Different Locations? (174): When people in two locations maintain contact, the language may not evolve into distinct languages, but may develop differences so each becomes a *dialect*. Dialects reflect the relationship between culture and the landscape. They develop distinctive distribution through various social processes-- *migration, interaction,* and *isolation.*

Dialects of English (174): English has a wide variety of dialects because of the large number of English speakers and the language's world wide distribution. There are differences in pronunciation, spelling, and meaning of particular words. In a language with multiple dialects, one may be recognized as the *standard language* which is well-established recognized for government, business, education, and mass communication. *British Received Pronunciation (BRP)*, spoken by upper-class Britons in London has become well known because of politicians, broadcasters, and actors.

    Dialects in England (174-175): The three invading tribes settled in different parts of Britain: the Angles in the north, the Jutes in the southeast, and the Saxons in the south and west. The regional dialects of Old English depended on the settlers: *Kentish* in the southeast, *West Saxon* in the southwest, *Mercian* in the center of the island, and *Northumbrian* in the north. After the Norman invasion of 1066 and English reemerged, five major regional dialects had developed roughly following the pattern before the Norman invasion: Northern, East Midland, West Midland, Southwestern, and Southeastern or Kentish. The dialect from London, Cambridge, and Oxford emerged as the standard through the use of the printing press (introduced in 1476)–grammar and spelling books were written based on the London dialect.

    Current Dialect Difference in England (175-176): Dialectic differences are especially strong in rural areas. Regional dialects can be grouped into three main ones: Northern, Midland, and Southern. Pronunciation differences are especially strong.

    English in North America (176): The English spoken in modern America owes most of its attributes to the earliest colonists. Other language speakers were acculturated and spoke English and contributed significantly to the language.

    Differences Between British and American English (176): Isolation provided the means for independent growth of the two which now differ in *vocabulary, spelling,* and *pronunciation.* In the U.S. new objects, features and places were often given names borrowed from Native Americans. New inventions were named differently in the two places. Spelling diverged due to *Noah Webster*, the author of the first comprehensive American dictionaries and grammar books. He wrote hoping to develop a unique American dialect of English to increase internal unity while reducing ties to England. Pronunciation differs for many reasons, including isolation, and differences in class background. Speech patterns changed more in England than America.

    Dialects in the United States (177): The original thirteen colonies along the Atlantic Coast can be organized into three areas: New England, Middle Atlantic, and

Southeastern. Speech patterns of the original settlers were adopted by new arrivals so the dialects were perpetuated.

Settlement in the East (177): The original thirteen colonies along the Atlantic Coast can be grouped into three areas: New England, Middle Atlantic, and Southeastern. New England was composed mainly of Puritans from southeastern England and a few from northern England. The Middle Atlantic was settled by a diverse group including Quakers from north England, Scots, Irish, Germans, Dutch, and Swedes. The Southeastern area was settled by people from the southeast of England with a multitude of socioeconomic backgrounds.

Current Dialect Differences in the East (177-178): Individual dialects still exist in the eastern U.S., though distinctions diminish with increased communication and transportation. An *isogloss*, the geographic boundary for the extent of word usage, helps in the study of dialects. Isoglosses are more difficult to draw for pronunciation than for word usage. The boundary lines overlap and delineate regions. Mobility and mass media have created more uniform language usage.

Pronunciation Differences (178): Regional pronunciations are distinct in the U.S. The Southern and New England dialects are fairly well known. Diffusion of dialects from the east occurred with the westward movement of colonists. Most people who settled the American West came from the Middle Atlantic states rather than New England and the southern states. The area south of the Ohio River was settled by colonists from Virginia and other southern states. People from the Middle Atlantic states settled the area north of the Ohio River, and some New Englanders settled the Great Lakes area. Readily available, fast means of transportation created a more uniform dialect in the West.

Romance Language Dialects (178-179): The dominant dialect, or the standard language, is often that spoken by upper-class residents of the capital city, or those with the political or economic strength.

Dialects in France (179): The French dialect *Francien* from around Paris became the official language in the sixteenth century after which many local dialects disappeared. There are still significant differences between the northern and southern dialects. There is a province in southwestern France where the dialect is called *Languedoc*, the southern dialect is called *Occitan*, and about 3 million people speak a form of Occitan known as *Provençal*.

Worldwide Diffusion of Spanish and Portuguese (179-180): Spain also had many dialects during the Middle Ages. *Castilian* is from the north-central part of the country in Old Castile during the ninth century. It spread across the country to its current extent during the fifteenth century when it became the official language for the entire country. Many regional dialects survive in isolated areas. Spanish and Portuguese have diffused to North, Central, and South America. Approximately 90% of the speakers of these languages live outside Europe, mostly in the Americas. Spanish is the official language of 18 Latin American states and Portuguese is the official language of Brazil. The languages were brought by the Spaniards and Portuguese who settled and explored the Americas. As in the case with English, Spanish and Portuguese evolved in the Americas in ways different from the ways they evolved in their places of origin. Portugal, Brazil, and several countries in Africa have all agreed to standardize the Portuguese language in order to increase interaction between these large and diverse groups of people.

Key Issue 4: Why Do People Preserve Local Languages? (180): Language displays the two trends of globalization and local diversity. English has become the principal language for the world, endangering local languages.

Preserving Language Diversity (180): Thousands of languages are *extinct languages* and are no longer spoken or read in daily activities by anyone in the world. Gothic belonged to the East Germanic group of the Germanic branch of Indo-European languages. Gothic and the entire East Germanic group is extinct. The language, spoken in the Crimea in Russia in the sixteenth century, died because its speakers switched to other languages. Most switched to Latin after their conversion to Christianity. Endangered languages are now being preserved. The European Union established the European Bureau of Lesser Used Languages to aid their preservation, especially the Celtic languages.

Hebrew: Reviving Extinct Languages (180-181): *Hebrew* is a modern language revived after it died out in the fourth century. It was only used for Jewish religious services. The Old Testament was written in Hebrew (a small part was written in the Afro-Asiatic language, *Aramaic*). Hebrew is the official language of *Israel*, a country created in 1948. The language is used to unite the Jewish population gathered from around the world. *Eliezer Ben-Yehuda* initiated the revival of Hebrew, creating words, writing the first modern Hebrew dictionary, and refusing to speak any other language.

Celtic: Preserving Endangered Languages (181): The Celtic branch of Indo-European was spoken in the British Isles before the invasion of the Angles, Jutes, and Saxons. Celtic languages were spoken in present-day Germany, France, and northern Italy as well. The Celtic languages survive only in Scotland, Wales, Ireland, and the Brittany peninsula of France.

Celtic Groups (181-182): There are two groups, *Goidelic* (Gaelic) and *Brythonic*. The two surviving Goidelic languages are *Irish Gaelic* with 75,000 exclusive speakers and *Scottish Gaelic* with 80,000 exclusive speakers. The Brythonic speakers fled to Wales, Cornwall, and into Brittany. Welsh dominated Wales, was conquered by the English in 1283, survived, and in the nineteenth century English speakers moved in to work in coal mines and factories. Welsh survives and dominates more isolated communities. Cornish died out in 1777, was revived, and now has several hundred speakers. It is taught in grade schools and adult evening classes. In Brittany, 50,000 people still speak *Breton* which includes more French words than the other Celtic languages. Language survival depends on the military and political strength of its speakers. The Celts lost much territory and power to the Angles, Jutes, and Saxons. In Ireland, Irish Gaelic was forbidden and children were encouraged to speak English.

Revival of Celtic Languages (182): Celtic Languages have enjoyed a recent resurgence. Welsh schools must teach the Welsh language, and folk history and music have been added to the curriculum. There is an increasing number of fluent

Irish Gaelic and Cornish. Road signs are posted in Welsh. The BBC produces Welsh-language programs. Folk and rock singers bring attention to the Gaelic languages.

Multilingual States (182): Boundaries between languages don't necessarily follow country boundaries.

Belgium (182): Southern Belgians, Walloons, speak French and northern Belgians, Flemings, speak a dialect of Dutch called Flemish. The country is divided into two regions. Walloons have dominated Belgium's economy and politics. Because of the dominance of the Walloons and French, the country was divided into two independent regions with their own regional governments. Brussels, the country's capital is officially bilingual and tax revenues to the regional governments. Conflicts have arisen because of language usage.

Switzerland (183): Switzerland peacefully exists with multiple languages. There are four official languages and a decentralized government--German (65 percent), French (18 percent), Italian (12 percent), and Romansh (1 percent).

Global Dominance of English (183): English has become the international language for communication and encourages globalization.

English: An Example of a Lingua Franca (183-184): English has become the *lingua franca* for much of the world--a language of international communication. It is used in communication, business, schools, research, and medicine; it is seen in pop culture; and it is necessary for smaller countries that want to participate more fully in world affairs. People may also learn a simplified form, called a *pidgin language*. Speakers may learn a few grammar rules and words of a lingua franca and thereby be able to communicate. A pidgin language has no native speakers. Swahili is the lingua franca in East Africa, Hindustani in south Asia, and Russian in the former Soviet Union. Approximately 200 million people speak English as their second language while an unknown number have a working knowledge of the language.

Expansion Diffusion of English (184): Historically languages became the lingua franca through migration and conquest. English's usage has grown through expansion diffusion, the spread of a trait through the snowballing effect of an idea. English is changing through diffusion of new vocabulary, spelling, and pronunciation, as well as by fusing with other languages.

New Vocabulary, Spelling, and Pronunciation (184-185): Language must continue to evolve, adding new words and usage to deal with new situations and concepts. Most changes to English have come from common usage and ethnic dialects. The African-American dialect has roots in the forced migration of African natives for the slave trade. A distinct dialect was preserved so that they could speak without being understood by their white masters. Many African-Americans migrated to the cities of the north, retaining their dialect called *Ebonics*, a combination of *ebony* and *phonics*. Today, the dialect is preserved, playing a central role as an identifying factor of a distinct culture.

Diffusion to Other Languages (185): English words are increasingly integrated into other languages.

Franglais (185): The French language is a source of pride and unity for France. French is the official language in 26 countries and was the lingua franca for international diplomats. The French don't like the infiltration of English words called *franglais*, a combination of the French words *francais* and *anglais*. The French Academy has been the arbiter of French since 1635 to protect the language.

Spanglish (185): English is diffusion into the Spanish spoken by 17 million people in the United States, and called *Spanglish*. In Miami with its large population from Cuba, it sometimes called *Cubonics*. As with franglais, Spanglish involves converting English word forms to Spanish. It is richer than borrowing words; it is a creation of new words.

Summary: Language is integral to human beings. Communication exists because people have found, through time, common representations for thoughts, expressions, objects, and actions. Language can be as widespread as English or as isolated as Basque but its importance does not change. People move and take culture (and language) with them where it either remains relatively intact or changes reflecting new influences from other people, environments, or experiences. Approximately five-sixths of the material on the Internet is in English, reinforcing English as world's lingua franca. The reader of the present Study Guide can participate in this learning experience owing to a common language–English.

CHAPTER 5
KEY TERMS AND CONCEPTS

Language: A system of communication through speech, a collection of sounds that a group of people understands to have the same or similar meaning. Language may be written, verbal, or visual.

Speech: A collection of sounds that a group of people understands to have the same meaning.

Literary Tradition: A written version of a language. A language may or may not have a written form.

Verbal Language: A language which is spoken and heard; speech. Many languages only exist in a verbal form with history passed down in stories which must be remembered.

Language Family: Includes individual languages related through a common ancestor that existed before recorded history. There are six main language families, with numerous other languages in either very small families or which are independently classifiable.

Language Branch: Includes languages that share a common origin, but have further evolved into individual languages.

Language Group: Comprises individual languages within a branch that share a common origin in the relatively recent past, and display relatively few differences in grammar and vocabulary.

Dialect: Form of a language spoken in a local area. There can be countless dialects which are all part of a given language.

Official Language: The dialect of a language which is used for government, business, education, and mass communication.

Place of Origin: The place or area from which a given language family, branch, group, or dialect stems. American English can trace its origins back to England.

Diffusion: The spreading of a concept across the landscape, usually accompanied by the movement of people.

Official Language: A language or dialect of a language adopted for use by a government.

Standard Language: The dialect or language used for official government business, education, and mass communications.

Indo-European Language Family: A language family with nearly three billion speakers; important artistic and literary traditions. The family of languages which includes Germanic, Romance, Balto-Slavic, and Indo-Iranian language branches. There is, theoretically, a Proto-Indo-European language from which the various groups have descended.

Germanic Languages: The Germanic branch of the Indo-European family includes West, North, and East Germanic groups. The original Germanic language has been lost though speakers lived at least across central and northern Europe.

West Germanic Group: Comprised of High and Low Germanic languages from the south and north of present day Germany. High Germanic has evolved into modern German, while Low Germanic has evolved into English (an official language of the United Nations) and the Low German dialects—Dutch, Flemish, and Frisian.

North Germanic Group: Old Norse is the language which has evolved into the Scandinavian languages of Swedish, Danish, Norwegian, and Icelandic.

East Germanic Group: Gothic, now extinct, was spoken by the Goths in eastern and northern Europe.

Romance Language Branch: Evolved from the dispersal of Roman soldiers during the reign of the Roman Empire. Contains two of the official languages of the United Nations, Spanish and French, as well as Portuguese, Italian, and Romanian of Romania and Moldova, as well as other less prolific languages. This branch is most familiar to English speakers.

Indo-Iranian Language Branch: The most prolific of the Indo-European language branches with more than 100 individual languages, more than one billion people, and two main groups—Indic and Iranian.

Indic Language Group: Second largest language group in world, encompassing language of India, Pakistan and Bangladesh. Hindi and Urdu are the most important languages, though there are many others.

Devanagari: The script used since the seventh century to write the multitude of Hindi dialects. Few people write the language, which has kept it from evolving as has the verbal language.

Arabic Alphabet: The script generally used by Muslims or in countries which have come in contact with Islam. The script used to write the Quran, the holy book of Islam.

Hindustani: The original language that evolved into Urdu and Hindi.

Iranian Language Group: Includes languages spoken in Iran and neighboring countries in southwestern Asia. All are written with the Arabic alphabet

Balto-Slavic Language Branch: Originally Slavic, the group contains closely related languages of Asia and central Europe.

Baltic Group: Latvian and Lithuanian are the principle languages of this group, spoken primarily around the Baltic Sea.

East Slavic Group: Contains Russian, one of the official languages of the United Nations. The lingua franca for the countries of the former Soviet Union.

West Slavic Group: Polish is the most widely spoken language, followed by Czech and Slovak. Differences in the latter two have been cause for a great deal of unrest in former Czechoslovakia.

South Slavic: Examples include Bulgarian as well as Serbo-Croatian, essentially the same language with different literary traditions being written with the Cyrillic and Roman alphabets, respectively.

Cyrillic Alphabet: An alphabet using some of the characters from the Grecian's ancient form of writing. It is a phonetic alphabet, each symbol representing a spoken sound.

Roman Alphabet: The alphabet used by the ancient Romans to write Latin. It has evolved into the script now being read. It is a phonetic alphabet as well.

Sino-Tibetan Language Family: The People's Republic of China and smaller countries in southeast Asia have languages in this family. There are three branches: Sinitic, Austro-Thai and Tibetan-Burman.

Sinitic Branch: The main languages of China fall into this branch. Mandarin is spoken by 75% of the population and is an official language of the UN, China, and Taiwan. The languages are composed of 420 one-syllable words, and meaning is inferred from context in sentences and the tone of voice of the speaker.

Context and Tone of Voice: Some words have meaning from their context--their relative position with other words. Some meaning is conveyed by the tone of voice, or the way something is spoken. Chinese relies heavily on context and tone of voice for word meanings.

Ideograms: Written symbols which represent ideas or concepts rather than pronunciation.

Austro-Thai Branch: Mainly the Thai language of Laos, Thailand, and parts of Vietnam.

Tibeto-Burman Branch: The principal language is Burmese used in Myanmar.

Japanese Language Family: The island location of Japan has allowed the language to evolve into a language structurally different from those of China, despite the introduction of cultural traits. It is written using both ideograms and phonetic symbols.

Korean Language Family: Separate language family, though related to both Japanese and the Altaic languages. More than half the vocabulary is Chinese.

Hankul: The writing system for Korean; each letter represents a sound.

Austro-Asiatic Language Family: Languages spoken in Southeast Asia. Vietnamese is the dominant language and is written with the Roman alphabet with diacritical marks above the vowels.

Diacritical Marks: Marks placed above letters to show different pronunciations in a written language.

Afro-Asiatic Language Family: This family includes Arabic, Hebrew, Aramaic, and others. It is the language family used for the holy books of three major world religions–the Judeo-Christian Bible and the Islamic Quran.

Arabic: The dominant language of the Afro-Asiatic language family with over 200 million native speakers. It is an official language of the United Nations. It is relatively standardized due to the Quran.

Altaic Language Family: Is used in a band 8,000 km long in Asia between Turkey and Mongolia and China. Turkish is the main language though there are several others in this area as well.

Uralic Language Family: An ancient language with relatively known origins; it is now spoken in Estonia, Finland, Siberia, and Hungary.

African Language Families: There are nearly 1,000 different African languages and thousands of dialects. Only ten are spoken by more than 5 million people, due to people's isolation from one another.

Niger-Congo Language Family: Has six branches which encompass more than 95% of Sub-Saharan speakers.

Nilo-Saharan Language Family: Languages spoken in north central Africa by a few million people. There are six branches.

Khoisan Language Family: Language found in southwest Africa which uses clicking sounds.

Austronesian Language Family: Languages spoken on islands in the South Pacific and on Madagascar.

Swahili: The strongest language of eastern Africa. Used as the lingua franca for the diverse peoples of this area.

Angles, Jutes, and Saxons: The three tribes who came into the British islands-- the Jutes from northern Denmark, the Angles from southern Denmark, and the Saxons from northwestern Germany. The languages were Low, West German languages and evolved into English.

Vulgar Latin: The form of Latin spoken by "the masses" of the populace as well as being the version spoken by Roman soldiers, which was then transmitted to the provinces. The dialects that arose through time differences and different regional languages have evolved even further to become separate and distinct languages.

Proto-Indo-European Language: The precursor to the Indo-European Language family, with at least two theories for location of the hearth.

Marija Gimbutas: One of the people investigating the Proto-Indo-European Language who says the language diffused through conquest.

Colin Renfrew: An archaeologist investigating the Proto-Indo-European Language who says the language diffused because of increased affluence and status of agriculturally based peoples.

Isolated Languages: Languages which are unrelated to any other language and are, therefore, not attached to any language family.

Basque: An anomalous survivor from before Indo-European languages. It is believed to be completely unrelated to Indo-European languages.

British Received Pronunciation (BRP): The dialect of English associated with the upper-class Britons living in the London area, and now considered standard in the United Kingdom.

Noah Webster: Promoted the use of American English to unify the people of the Americas as separate from England.

Isogloss: A boundary separating regions in which different language usage predominates.

Extinct Language: A language which is no longer spoken or read in daily activities by anyone in the world.

Hebrew: It is a modern language revived in the twentieth century after it died out in the fourth century. It is the official language of Israel, reinstated to bring unity to the varied Jewish population.

Eliezer Ben-Yehuda: The father of modern Hebrew. He wrote modern grammar rules, invented many words, and wrote the first modern Hebrew dictionary.

Endangered Language: A language in danger of becoming an extinct language.

Celtic Branch: The languages of most of Europe, northern Europe and the British Isles from about 2000 years ago. It now exists in two groups, Goidelic and Brythonic which have become Irish Gaelic, Scottish Gaelic, and Breton.

Lingua Franca: A language mutually understood and commonly used in trade by people who have different native languages.

Pidgin Language: A form of speech with no native speakers that adopts a simplified grammar and limited vocabulary of a lingua franca, used for communications among speakers of two different languages.

Creolized Language: A language resulting from the mixing often of a colonizer's language with the indigenous language of the people being dominated.

CHAPTER 5
PROGRESSIVE REVIEW

1. The written version of a language is called a _____ tradition.

literary

2. Language relatedness can be broken down into a hierarchy: _____, _____, _____, _____, and _____.

families, branches, groups, languages, dialects

3. The _____-_____ language family contains 50% of the speakers of the world.

Indo-European

4. The second most important language family is the _____-_____, with 20% of the world's population.

Sino-Tibetan

5. Another 20% speak languages in the Austronesian, _____-_____, _____-_____, and Dravidian language families.

Afro-Asiatic, Niger-Congo

6. Language diffuses through _____.

migration

7. English has become the world's main _____ _____, used in business, commerce, government and other world matters.

lingua franca

8. The six official language of the United Nations are _____, _____, _____, _____, _____, and _____.

Spanish, French, English, Russian, Mandarin Chinese, Arabic

9. England was invaded in 450 AD by the _____, _____, and _____ whose language became modern English.

Angles, Jutes, Saxons

10. English is a _____ _____ (group) language.

Low Germanic

11. The first known occupants of the British Isles from around 2000 BC were the _____.

Celts

12. Swedish, Danish, Norwegian, and Icelandic are all North Germanic languages, stemming from _____ _____, their common ancestor.

Old Norse

13. Of the Scandinavian languages, isoiation maintained _____, making it an interesting language to study.

Icelandic

14. _____, an East Germanic group language, is now an _____ _____ meaning it is no longer used or spoken in day to day life by anyone.

Gothic, extinct language

15. The Indo-European language family consists of eight language branches, the four most significant have a total of 1.6 billion speakers: _____, _____, _____-_____, and Indo-Iranian as well as the Albanian, Armenian, Greek and Celtic branches.

Germanic, Romance, Balto-Slavic

16. The Romance language branch stems from the _____ spoken by the ancient Romans.

Latin

17. In an effort to unify the Roman Empire, other languages were _____ or _____ in favor of Latin.

suppressed, extinguished

18. _____ _____ is the form of the language spoken by the Roman soldiers who occupied the provinces.

Vulgar Latin

19. In the fifth century the collapse of the _____ _____ cut off communication between the various provinces, which left them isolated from one another.

Roman Empire

20. Romance languages are the group most familiar to English speakers, the four most widely used modern languages being _____, _____, _____, and _____.

Spanish, Portuguese, French, Italian

21. Isolation across Europe is due mostly to intervening obstacles, _____ _____, which make communication and travel difficult.

natural boundaries

22. _____ is the language unrelated to other European languages and isolated in a region between Spain and France.

Basque

23. Speakers of Portuguese are attempting to _____ the language to enable communication and the exchange of such things as movies, television programs, music and literature.

standardize

24. A _____ _____ can be constructed using a lingua franca as a base and adding elements of the native language.

pidgin language

25. A _____ _____ is a mixing of an indigenous language with that of a conquering people.

creole language

26. The _____-_____ language branch is the largest of the Indo-European family and its _____ group is the second largest language group in the world.

Indo-Iranian, Indic

27. _____ is a collection of languages from India.

Hindi

28. There are numerous written scripts including, though certainly not limited to _____, _____, _____, _____, ideograms, hankel, and phonetic alphabets.

Latin, Arabic, Devanagari, Cyrillic

29. India has _____ established official languages recognized by the government.

18

30. The _____-_____ language branch has relatively few differences between languages, and has a common ancestor of _____.

Balto-Slavic Slavic

31. The most widely used language of the above branch is _____, one of the six official languages of the UN. It has become the lingua franca for the republics formed in the post Communist era.

Russian

32. The West Slavic Group is dominated by speakers of _____, followed by _____ and _____ who, while united in one country, tried to balance the use of the two languages. They are now separated into the two countries of the _____ _____ and _____.

Polish, Czech, Slovak

Czech Republic, Slovakia

33. The South Slavic languages include Serbo-Croatian and Bulgarian, the former being a language spoken by Serbs and Croats, the difference being their written language, using the _____ and _____ alphabets.

Cyrillic, Roman

34. There are two proposed _____, or places of origin, for the Indo-European languages: _____ and _____.

hearths, Kurgan, Anatolia

35. There are many languages unrelated to any other nor attached to a language family, such as Basque a pre-Indo-European language, which are called _____ languages.

isolated

36. _____ is the Chinese language spoken by 75% of its population and adopted as an official language of the United Nations.

Mandarin

37. Their 4,000 year old written language uses thousands of _____ most of which are _____, representing ideas or concepts.

characters
ideograms

38. _____ and _____ are two language families which have developed in relative geographic isolation from other cultures.

Japanese,
Korean

39. Afro-Asiatic languages were used to write the holy books of three major world religions: _____, _____, and _____.

Judaism,
Christianity, Islam

40. _____ is the dominant language of the Afro-Asiatic language family with 200 million native speakers and the Quran (which serves as the language standard), and is an official language of the United Nations.

Arabic

41. Hebrew is a revived _____ language, essentially recreated by _____ _____-_____ to unify the populace of Israel.

extinct, Eliezer
Ben-Yehuda

42. Africa has nearly _____ distinct languages and several thousand dialects. Language history of Africa is difficult to trace due to a lack of much _____ _____.

1,000

written tradition

43. Nigeria is plagued by problems which arise from a great deal of cultural diversity seen in the _____ distinct languages used, the most wide spread of which is _____.

200
Hausa

44. _____ is an anomalous African language with an extensive body of literature and is the lingua franca for eastern Africa.

Swahili

45. _____ _____, the father of American English, started the now long upheld tradition of the Webster's American Dictionary.

Noah Webster

CHAPTER 6

RELIGION

Religions have a hearth, they diffused across the landscapes of the world, they have unique distributions, and they exhibit distinct characteristics. Geography helps us understand the spread of religions around the earth and the changes they bring to human culture and architecture. Sometimes adherents to religions compete for territory and constituents, which has often led to conflict. Chapter Six investigates many aspects of religion including how different people have come to accept religion.

Religion: Geographers ask *where* and *why* religions are distributed around the world the way they are. They ask *where* religions originated and *where* they are currently prevalent. They ask *why* distributions vary and have changed with time. They also ask *how* religion affects the landscape and relations between people. *Globalization* and *local diversity* create religious tension because cultural world views and local belief systems come into conflict with more prevalent belief systems with a different structure and different appeal.

Key Issue 1: Where Are Religions Distributed?

Universalizing Religions (195): Religions that attempt to be global and to appeal to all people with no specific ties to culture or location are *universalizing religions*. About 58 percent of the world's population adheres to a universal religion, 23 percent to an ethnic religion, and 19 percent to no religion. Religions can be generally divided into three levels, the largest of which is a *branch*. A branch is divided into a *denomination* and further divided into *sects*--relatively small denominational groups which have broken away from the established church.

     Christianity (195): *Christianity* has the largest number of adherents (about 2 billion) and the most widespread distribution. It is the primary religion in North America, South America, Australia, and Europe. It also has a presence in Africa and Asia.

     Branches of Christianity (195-197): Christianity has three major branches: Roman Catholic (50 percent of Christians), Protestant (24 percent), and Eastern Orthodox (11 percent) with 14 percent of Christians belonging to a variety of other churches. The distribution of the branches of Christianity in Europe is shown in Figure 6-2. Roman Catholics dominate in the southeast and southwest, Protestants are strong in the northwest, and Eastern Orthodox are common in the east and southeast of Europe.

Christianity in the Western Hemisphere (197-198): Roman Catholics dominate Latin America (90 percent) and the Canadian province of Quebec. Protestants are the majority in the remaining parts of the U.S. and Canada with pockets of strong Catholic influence (30 percent of North America). Among Protestants in the U.S., Baptists dominate the old South of the U.S., Methodists and Lutherans dominate the upper Midwest, and Latter-Day Saints in Utah. Pentecostal, Presbyterian, and Episcopal churches are also present. The dominant religions of areas within the U.S. can frequently be traced to the European homelands of the migrants who settled those areas.

Other Branches of Christianity (198-199): There are a few, relatively small Christian churches that have survived in Egypt, Syria, Armenia, Lebanon, Azerbaijan, and Ethiopia.

Islam (199): North Africa to Central Asia is dominated by *Islam*; the religion has more than 1 billion followers. Bangladesh and Indonesia are the major concentrations outside the main region. The word *Islam* means *submission to the will of God*, called *Allah* by Muslims. A Muslim is a practitioner of Islam. Muslims believe in one God, as do Christians, and they believe in the *five pillars*, which are the fundamental manifestations which a Muslim should fulfill in order to remain devout.

Branches of Islam (199-200): There are two branches of Islam: *Sunni* (Arabic for orthodox) which comprises 83 percent of Muslims and *Shiite* (sectarian). Iran is dominated by Sunnis. Most Shiites (70 percent) live in Iran or Iraq (where they are twice as numerous as Sunnis). Shiites outnumber Sunnis in Azerbaijan, Lebanon, and Bahrain. The majority of the remaining Shiites live in Yemen and Afghanistan.

Nation of Islam in the United States (200): In 1930, *Elijah Muhammad* founded the *Nation of Islam* in Detroit. Black Muslims lived austerely and wanted an autonomous nation within the U.S.. *Malcolm X* broke off from Nation of Islam in 1963, after he made a pilgrimage to Makkah and converted to the orthodox Muslim religion. Two years later he was assassinated; many people suspect the Nation of Islam of murdering Malcolm X. After Elijah Muhammad's death in 1975, his son Wallace took the movement closer to the orthodox church. However, splinter groups adopted the original name, Nation of Islam, and continue to follow the separatist teachings of Elijah Muhammad..

Buddhism (200): *Buddhism* is the third universalizing religions with over 300 million followers (Figure 6-1) located primarily in China and Southeast Asia. Buddhists follow the Four Noble Truths as their guidance to clean living.

Branches of Buddhism (200): Like Christianity and Islam, Buddhism has multiple branches, with two main branches. *Theravada* Buddhists, located mostly in Southeast Asia, believe that, in order to be a good Buddhist, one must become a monk and study full time in order to become enlightened. *Mahayana* is a emphasizes helping others and teaching others, rather than self-introspection, and this branch predominates farther north in Asia (China, Japan, Korea, Mongolia, and Tibet). Many Buddhists (especially in China and Japan) believe simultaneously in other religions.

Ethnic Religions (200): An *ethnic religion* appeals primarily to one group of people living in one place. About 23 percent of the world's population belongs to an ethnic religion. Ethnic religions *may* be based on the physical characteristics of a place and may be more provincial in scope due to their limited appeal.

Hinduism (200): The largest ethnic religion in the world is *Hinduism* with *700 million* followers. Approximately 97 percent of Hindus are concentrated in India and 2 percent in Nepal. Hindus believe there is more than one path to reach God. Hinduism allows people to worship gods in very personal, unique ways; there is no rule book that dictates a universal technique. Three approaches have the most followers and are geographically concentrated--Shiva and Shakti in the north, Shakti and Vishnu in the east, Vishnu in the west, and Shiva along with some Vishnu in the south.

Other Ethnic Religions (200-201):

Confucianism (201): The teaching and philosophy of Confucius has became a religion in China. *Confucianism* is described as ethical principles for leading a good, orderly life. It is primarily important to the Chinese people.

Taoism (201): *Taoism,* originates from the writings of *Lao-Zi,* a contemporary of Confucius. His writings emphasized the mystical and magical aspects of life, rather than public service emphasized by the writings of Confucius. Today, Taoism is practiced in China and Taiwan.

Shintoism (201): Since ancient times the distinct ethnic religion of Japan has been *Shintoism.* Shintoists consider forces of nature such as rocks, rivers, mountains, and trees to be divine. Under the Japanese Emperor Meiji Shintoism became the official state religion; the emperor was considered divine making Shintoism both a political and religious institution. Many people in Japan believe both in Buddhism and Shintoism though the Emperor is no longer considered divine.

Judaism (201-202): *Judaism* is an ethnic religion which originated along the eastern Mediterranean Sea. Abraham is considered the father of Judaism, though the name comes from Judah, one of Jacob's sons which also one of the last surviving tribes of Hebrews. The roots of Christianity and Islam are found in Judaism; Jesus and Abraham were both Jews. Today, 6 million of the 18 million Jews worldwide live in the U.S., 4 million live in Israel, and 2 million live in the former Soviet Union Republics.

Judaism is the first recorded *monotheistic* religion, belief there is one god, which contrasts with *polytheism*, or worship of a collection of gods.

Ethnic African Religions (202): Many African people, about 10 percent of Africans, are *animists*, believing that inanimate objects such as rocks and plants as well as thunderstorms and earthquakes are animated and have spirits and conscious life. Animist beliefs are adapted monotheist systems with a hierarchy of divinities below the supreme god. Many Africans are now primarily Christian (50 percent) and Muslim (40 percent).

Key Issue 2: Why do Religions Have Different Distributions?

Origin of Religions

Origin of Christianity (202-203): Christianity is based upon the teachings of *Jesus*, a Jew born in Bethlehem who preached the gospel of God. Due to the faith his followers he was given the name *Christ*, the Greek word for *messiah* which means *anointed*. He was betrayed and put to death as an agitator. Christianity has three primary branches: Roman Catholic, Eastern Orthodox, and Protestant. Each branch has unique rituals.

Roman Catholics believe in the teachings in the Bible as they are interpreted by the church hierarchy, headed by the *Pope* in Rome. Eastern Orthodox and Roman Catholics believe in the seven sacraments which are rituals that convey God's grace to humanity.

The *Eastern Orthodox* church split with Rome in the fifth century, the split becoming final in 1054. Eastern Orthodox Christians reject the doctrines of the Roman Catholics added since the eighth century. The Eastern Orthodox Church doesn't accept the Pope as the leader of the church.

Protestantism was begun by *Martin Luther*, a German, in 1517 when he posted his ninety-five theses on a church door; they said a person should communicate directly to God, rather than perform sacraments. Grace is achieved through faith rather than the sacraments.

Origin of Islam (203): Muslims trace their religion, along with Jews and Christians, to the children of Abraham. Jews and Christians follow Sarah and her son Isaac; Muslims trace Abraham's second wife Hagar and their son, Ishmael, as their ancestors. Islam was founded by its Prophet, *Muhammad,* who was born in *Makkah*. The Angel Gabriel gave Muhammad the elements of the gospel and he, in turn, put them into the holy book of Islam, the *Quran (Koran)*. After being unsuccessful in preaching his gospel in his home city of *Makkah*, Muhammad migrated to *Madina,* where people listened to and adopted his declarations. By Muhammad's death in 632, he had converted most of present day Saudi Arabia to Islam.

The main conflict between the two main branches, *Sunni* and *Shiite*, is over the line of succession from Muhammad. The successor determines the divine interpreter of the Quran. The Shiites dominate Iraq and Iran. The Shah of Iran and the Ayatollah Khomeni competed for the leadership of the Shiite branch until the Ayatollah won, due to his stricter adherence to the Islamic statutes.

Origin of Buddhism (203-204): *Siddhartha Gautauma* founded Buddhism in 563 BC in what is modern day Nepal, near India. Although he was privileged due to his status as the son of a lord, he one day realized that he could no longer enjoy his amenities because other people were suffering. After spending six years in a forest, Siddhartha emerged as the *Buddha*, or the *enlightened one*. Theravada Buddhism is the older branch and supports the belief that Buddhism is a full-time occupation requiring renunciation of the world and becoming a monk. Mahayana Buddhism split from Theravada 2,000 years ago and emphasizes self-help, solitary introspection, teaching, and helping others.

Origin of Hinduism, an Ethnic Religion (204): Hinduism is a pre-historic religion; the earliest documents relating to it date back to 1500 BC. Hinduism was brought to India in 1400 BC by invading Aryan tribes from Central Asia. The Aryans first settled the Punjab area of northern India. Intermingling for centuries with the native Dravidian populations did modify the religious beliefs of the Aryans. *Hinduism* means *the religious system of India.*

Diffusion of Religions

Diffusion of Universalizing Religions (204-205): The three universalizing religions all have *hearths,* or places of origin. All three hearths are in Asia-- Christianity and Islam in Southwest Asia and Buddhism in South Asia. Followers diffused their beliefs along distinct paths around the globe (Figure 6-4).

There are two processes of *diffusion--relocation* (migration) and *expansion.* Expansion is divided into *hierarchical* (diffusion through key leaders) and *contagious* (widespread diffusion).

Diffusion of Christianity (205-206): Christianity's hearth is in Palestine, and it has spread through relocation diffusion and contagious diffusion. *Missionaries* are individuals who help transmit a universalizing religion through relocation diffusion. Missionaries helped spread the Christianity through relocation diffusion. A famous missionary in Christianity, *Paul,* took Christianity to many parts of the Roman Empire. Believers who had daily contact with pagan non-believers also spread Christianity (contagious diffusion). *Pagan* is a word that was once used to describe a follower of a polytheistic religion and is Latin for *countryside.*

The Roman Empire further increased the dominance through hierarchical diffusion because Emperor Constantine embraced Christianity in 313. Colonization by and migration of Europeans further spread Christianity to North, Central, and South America, Australia, and New Zealand. Catholicism and Protestantism in the western hemisphere can be traced to the migrating Europeans who settled in various areas.

Diffusion of Islam (206): Muslim armies took over portions of northern Africa, Asia (including India), and southern Europe and converted many non-Arabs, often through intermarriage. While the hearth of Islam is Southwest Asia, relocation diffusion of missionaries and traders spread the religion.

Diffusion of Buddhism (206-207): Buddhism did not rapidly expand much beyond its hearth in northeastern India. A converted emperor named Asoka attempted to establish the social principles of Buddhism into his empire (273-232 BC). Descendants of Asoka sent missionaries to outside territories and gained strong footholds in China, Southeast Asia, and Japan. Ironically, during the same period, Buddhism lost much of its support in India.

Lack of Diffusion of Ethnic Religions:

Mingling of Ethnic and Universalizing Religions (207-208): Universalizing religions supplant or mingle with ethnic religions. Many African religions have mixed with Christianity to create unique churches. In East Asia, Buddhism and Shintoism have been transformed into a single belief system. Most Japanese embrace both religions. Ethnic religions diffuse if their followers migrate. Mauritius' inhabitants are Hindu, Christian, and Muslim the religions of the island settlers.

Judaism, an Exception (208): The hearth of Judaism is the Eastern Mediterranean from which the Jews were expelled, called the *diaspora*. Jews have lived in Europe, North Africa, and Asia maintaining their religion while adopting local languages and other cultural characteristics. Historically, Jews were forced to live in *ghettos* in the less desirable parts of European cities. Ghettos are a city neighborhood set up by law to be inhabited only by Jews, the term first being used in Venice, Italy during the sixteenth century. During the 1930's and early 1940's many European Jews were killed or forced to emigrate, with many immigrating to the U.S.

Holy Places:

Holy Places in Universalizing Religions (209): Buddhism and Islam emphasize shrines because of their importance in the life of Buddha and Muhammad.

Buddhist Shrines (209-210): There are eight holy Buddhist shrines (Figure 6-9). The four most important are in northeastern India and southern Nepal where the great events of Buddha's life took place--where he was born, received enlightenment, gave his first sermon, and died. The other four Buddhist sites are important because they were the locations of Buddha's principle miracles.

Holy Places in Islam (210): The holiest cities are associated with the life of the Prophet Muhammad. *Makkah* and *Madina* are the two most important places. In Makkah, Muhammad was born; in Madinah he first successfully converted non-believers. Muslims are expected to make a pilgrimage, a *hajj*, to Makkah. The hajj attracts one million Muslims from countries other than Saudi Arabia--from the Middle East and northern Africa and Asian countries.

Holy Places in Ethnic Religions (210-211): Ethnic religions are closely tied to the physical geography of a particular place, and followers make pilgrimages to these locations.

Holy Places in Hinduism (211, 213): A Hindu pilgrimage is a *tirtha*, an act of purification. Many of the holy places are riverbanks are coastlines. The Ganges is the holiest river in India because of its association with Shiva, a primary god. Mountains are also considered holy if the Hindi god Shiva is thought to have visited there. The remoteness of many of the revered locations makes pilgrimages costly, time consuming, and difficult. Better transportation with technology have increased the capacity of people to make pilgrimages to their respective holy places.

Cosmogony in Ethnic Religions (213): A set of beliefs concerning the origin of the universe is *cosmogony*. Daoism and Confucianism believe that all things are made up of two dynamic, opposing forces: *Yin* and *Yang*. The principles of yin and yang are responsible for all events, and are ever-changing. Christianity and Islam, however, believe that God created the universe for humans to inhabit. Christians view their presence as more of a partnership with God, whereas Muslims believe God bears the responsibility for the Earth's creation. Some people believe that natural disasters such as floods are the actions of God, yet Christians believe their efforts can help to minimize the effects of such tragic events. Adherents of ethnic religions do not attempt to transform the environment to such an extent.

The Calendar:
    The Calendar in Ethnic Religions (213): Many ethnic religions around the world have calendars based on agricultural events. Rituals are performed to pray for favorable environmental conditions and to give thanks for past success. The *Bontok* people of the Philippines celebrate similar points in their agricultural cycle and call them *obaya*.
    The Jewish Calendar (213-214): Judaism's holiest days, *Rosh Hashanah* and *Yom Kippur*, occur in autumn when people traditionally have prayed for enough rain to nourish and sustain their crops. *Passover* is the time when Jews have offered God the first fruits of the Spring harvest. *Shavuot* (Feast of Weeks) is at the end of the grain harvest.
    In the Christian world the solar calendar, with twelve months, is used for daily events. However, the Jews and Muslims of the world adhere to the lunar calendar, in which months are only twenty-nine days long. Consequently, the Jewish lunar calendar must be supplemented with an additional month every few years.
    The Solstice (214): The *solstices* (the longest and shortest days of the year) played major roles in pagan religions of history. For example Stonehenge, an astronomical and worshipping place of the Druids, was set up to have geometric alignments with the Summer and Winter solstices.
    The Calendar in Universalizing Religions (214): Universalizing tend to celebrate important events in the lives of the religious founders.
    Christian Holidays (214-215): The birthday of Jesus, *Christmas*, and the day Jesus died, *Good Friday*, are very important days in the Christian Calendar. *Easter* is observed on different days. Protestants and Roman Catholics calculate the date using the Gregorian calendar while the Eastern Orthodox Church uses the Julian calendar. Easter is a celebration of the season--harvest or planting depending on location.
    Muslim Calendar (215): Muslims maintain a strict lunar calendar, therefore their holidays fall in different seasons with different generations. *Ramadan* is the month in which Muslims fast and try to make the hajj.
    Buddhist Holidays (215): Buddhists celebrate Buddha's birth, Enlightenment, and death, though they observe them on different days of the year.

Key Issue 3: Why and How do Religions Organize Space?

Places of Worship: *Sacred structures* are physical anchors of religion, though the structures may play different roles.
    Christian Churches (215-216): The *church* is the place to which Christians come to worship God. Christian landscapes have a high density of churches because regular, collective worship is very important to their religion. Churches require considerable expenses and much wealth has been invested in the construction and maintenance of churches.
    Church Architecture (216): Early churches were modeled after the Roman building for public assembly, the *basilica*. The Eastern Orthodox and Roman

Catholic churches tend to be more elaborate while Protestant churches, especially in North America, are typically more modest in their architecture.

Places of Worship in Other Religions:

Muslim Mosques (216): Muslims pray in *mosques*; unlike churches, mosques are not sanctified, but act as a location for communities to come together to pray. *Minarets* are towers which are features of mosques where a *muzzan* summons people to pray.

Hindu Temples (216): Hindus pray in *temples* which are dimly lit and possess images of one or more of the deities to whom it is dedicated. Temples are typically small places as Hindus worship individually, not in congregations.

Buddhist and Shintoist Pagodas (216): *Pagodas* are temples built to enshrine part of Buddha's body or clothing; they are not intended for congregational worship. Individual prayer is usually undertaken elsewhere.

Sacred Space (216-217):
The most significant sacred use of space is for disposing of the dead.

Disposing of the Dead (217): Christians, Muslims, and Jews normally bury their dead in plots of land called *cemeteries*. Some Christians bury their dead with the feet pointed toward Jerusalem, so they may rise toward God at the second coming of Christ. Mandan Indians of the northern plains pointed the feet of their dead toward the Southeast, for they believed their ancestors originated there. Cemeteries may consume large amounts of space so they are used as parks in some densely populated areas of the world. In some places like China, where productive farm land is scarce, cemeteries are burdensome to local agricultural output; the government encourages people to cremate. Hindus prefer to burn their dead in *cremation* ceremonies that use substantial amounts of wood. They believe cremation frees the soul from the body. Zoroastrians would expose their dead to scavenging birds and animals to prevent corpses from polluting the elements. In Micronesia, some societies dispose of their dead by burying them at sea.

Religious Settlements (218): A *utopian settlement* is a settlement that is built around a religious or other idealistic way of life. For example, New Harmony, Indiana and Bethlehem, Pennsylvania were set up by people who wanted the perfect religious society. Salt Lake City, based on the plans of Zion by Joseph Smith, was founded and developed as a utopian city. Church-related buildings are strategically located throughout the city. Most utopian experiments have long since died out or are no longer inhabited by people of the original denomination.

Religious Placenames (218): Religious *toponyms* are found in many parts of the U.S., especially where the Catholic Church is present; many cities are named after saints. St. Louis (the French version) and San Diego (the Spanish version) are examples of religious toponyms.

Administration of Space (218):
Some religious communities are highly *autonomous,* or *self-governed*. Interaction between groups is rather low. The other extreme are highly-organized *hierarchical religions*.

Hierarchical Religions (218-219): A *hierarchical religion* has a well-defined geographic structure and organizes territory into local administrative units

Roman Catholic Hierarchy (219-221): Roman Catholicism is a very hierarchical religion. It is headed by the *Pope* who delegates geographic provinces to the authority of *archbishops*, who in turn oversee *bishops*. Each Bishop oversees a *diocese*, a group of *parishes*. Each parish is headed by a *priest*. The layout of the Catholic Church is not unlike that of a national government, although the boundaries may cross national borders. The number of people and the amount of space represented by each church unit varies.

Latter-Day Saints (221): The Mormons also exercise a very structured self-government with its largest core in Salt Lake City. Its common level of government is the *ward;* wards are combined into *stakes.* All are administered by the church's *president* and *board* in Salt Lake City. Boundaries are frequently redrawn to maintain an ideal size of 5,000 people per stake.

Locally Autonomous Religions (221): *Autonomous religions* are self-sufficient and communities loosely cooperate with each other.

Local Autonomy in Islam (221-222): Of the three universal religions, Islam provides the most local autonomy. In the Muslim place of worship everyone is suppose to participate equally in their devotion to God. Strong Islamic ties are facilitated by high degrees of communication and migration.

Protestant Denominations (222): Among Protestant churches Baptists are very unstructured, as are various groups of the United Church of Christ. However, the Lutheran, Methodist, and Episcopalian churches have hierarchies, not very much different from the Roman Catholic Church.

Ethnic Religions (222): Judaism and Hinduism are relatively unstructured with no centralized religious authority. Ideas are shared through writings, pilgrimages, and tradition.

Key Issue 4: Why do Territorial Conflicts Arise Among Religious Groups?
(222): Recent religious conflicts are due to religious *fundamentalism*--a literal interpretation and a strict and intense adherence to basic principles of a religion. Religious fundamentalism is difficult to adhere to and embrace because of the increasing importance of the world economy and world community. Fundamentalist religions are exclusionary and have difficulty integrating changing values, economic activities, and different people.

Religion vs. Government Policies (222-223): Christianity, Buddhism, Islam, and Hinduism have all come into conflict with government action and international policies.

Religion vs. Social Change (223): Christian dominated regions like Europe and North America, are more amenable to embracing social changes.

Hinduism v. Social Equality (223): When the Aryans invaded India, bringing with them their Hindu religion, they also brought a *caste system.* All people were divided into four castes. In order of most prominence to least, they are: Brahmans (priests and top administrators), the *Kshatriyas* (warriors), the *Vaisyas* (merchants), and the *Shudra* (farm workers). Below all of these were the *untouchables* caste which had few legal rights until recently. Because one was born into a caste there was no accepted way of moving into a better class. Theoretically, the untouchables were the indigenous people of India who were conquered by the Aryans. Hinduism later survived conquests by the Muslims, as well as the Christian British, and is a cultural trait shared by the majority of Indians.

Religion vs. Communism (223): Communism in Eastern Europe and Asia affected Eastern Orthodox Christianity, Islam, and Buddhism.

Eastern Orthodox Christianity and Islam vs. the Soviet Union (223-224): In 1721, Czar Peter the Great made the Russian Orthodox Church part of the government. The Bolshevik revolution (1917) brought the communist government and antireligious programs. *Karl Marx* and *V.I. Lenin* viewed religion as a threat to communist government policies. Church ties to the government were severed and the church was discouraged and repressed. Religion is enjoying a resurgence in post-Soviet Union countries. Roman Catholic, Orthodox, and Islamic followers are rediscovering their religion and rewriting government policy and law to conform with religious ideals and doctrines.

Buddhism vs. Southeast Asian Countries (224): Vietnamese governments and French and American presence during the Vietnam War were not sympathetic to Buddhists. Current communist governments discourage religious activities.

Religion vs. Religion (224): Conflicts are likely along the boundaries of religiously dominated areas.

Religious Wars in the Middle East (224): Since Judaism, Christianity, and Islam all have similar roots, they consider the eastern Mediterranean as their Holy Lands. As a result, competition for control of this land has been a constant source of conflict for militant adherents of each of these religions.

Judaism considered the territory the Promised Land and many customs and rituals acquired meaning from the agricultural life of the ancient Hebrew tribe. Jerusalem was the location of the Temple, the traditional center of worship which was destroyed, rebuilt, and destroyed again. Christians consider Palestine holy because Jesus spent his life there, spreading the gospel. Jerusalem is the third holiest city of Islam because the rock upon which Muhammad is thought to have ascended to heaven is located there in the Dome of the Rock. The Western (Wailing) Wall is the last remaining portion of the Jewish Second Temple.

Christians vs. Muslims (224-225): Muslims controlled most of the Middle East between the seventh century and 1917. The Arab army moved into North Africa and Europe in the eighth century, but were stopped in France. Europe is dominated by Christians except in portions of present-day Spain. The Arab army also advanced east into Constantinople and into Southeast Europe where civil wars (with an historical religious component) continue. During the Crusades, Christians captured Jerusalem a few times, but never held it for a prolonged period of time.

Jews vs. Muslims (225-226): The Jews dominated in Palestine before they were expelled by the Romans in AD 70, not to return in large numbers until 1948, when the state of Israel was created. Great Britain took control over Palestine after it helped to defeat the Ottoman Empire in 1917. Since the inception of the Israeli state in 1948, it has been involved in four official wars; they occurred in 1949, 1956, 1967, and 1973. During its wars with Arab neighbors, Israel acquired territories such as the Golan Heights, the Sinai Peninsula, and the West Bank. Israel has withdrawn from some of the territory though Jerusalem remains an area of conflict because of religious significance to both Jews and Muslims.

Religious Wars in Ireland (226-227): Northern Ireland is an example of hostile religious conflict. *Ireland* was a British colony until, in 1937, it was granted independence. It became a republic in 1949. However, the people in its six northern colonies, being mostly Protestant like Great Britain, voted to remain in the United Kingdom. The minority status of the Catholics made them into second-class citizens who are excluded from the best jobs and schools in the six counties. The *Irish Republican Army (IRA)* worked to bring unity to Ireland by means of force. A Protestant equivalent, the *Ulster Defense Force (UDF),* worked to retain the ties with Great Britain by the same means of force, except they targeted Catholics instead of Protestants.

Summary: Interestingly, the hearths of Judaism, Christianity, and Islam are in the same geographic region of the Middle East. Although all three religions are very much related in their ancient roots, there are today seemingly endless conflicts among all three faiths. It is pertinent to note how the dominions of each religion has evolved, expanded, and contracted throughout history.

CHAPTER 6
KEY TERMS AND CONCEPTS

Universalizing Religions: A religion that attempts to appeal to all people, not just those living in a particular location. Islam, Christianity, and Buddhism are universalizing religions.

Branch: A large and fundamental division within a religion. For example, Protestantism and Roman Catholicism are branches of the Christian faith.

Denomination: A division within a branch of a religion. For example, Baptists and Methodists are denominations of the Protestant branch of Christianity.

Sect: A relatively small denominational group that has broken away from an established church. Sometimes sects are ostracized by more orthodox church members.

Christianity: One of the world's dominating religions. It is a monotheistic belief system based on the teachings of Christ, Greek for *messiah* which means anointed. There are three major branches of Christianity: Roman Catholic, Protestant, and Eastern Orthodox, along with other minor branches. An adherent is called a Christian

Islam: Second largest number of belief systems in the world. The word means submission to the will of Allah (God). Follow the five pillars of faith, and the Quaran (Koran) as written by Muhammad. There are two main branches of Islam. Sunni is the dominant branch and is more orthodox. Shiite is a sectarian branch. An adherent to Islam is called a Muslim, or Moslem. Because most Muslims are located in the Middle East where Islam dominates, they are called Arabs, though Arab denotes their geographic origins and culture, not religion.

Buddhism: Third and third largest universalizing religion in the world. Buddhists follow the Four Noble Truths, as founded by Siddhartha Gautama and his emergence enlightened as the Buddha. There are two main branches. Theravada Buddhists believe a monastic lifestyle is the path to enlightenment while Mahayana Buddhists emphasize teaching and helping others.

Martin Luther: German who started **Protestantism**, a branch of Christianity, in 1517 when he wrote 95 theses saying a person should communicate directly to God, rather than perform sacraments.

Ethnic Religion: A religion with a relatively concentrated spatial distribution whose principles are likely to be based on the physical characteristics of the particular location in which its adherents are concentrated. These religions are harder-pressed to serve global constituents.

Monotheism: The doctrine or belief in only one God. Christianity, Judaism, and Islam all believe in a single, all-powerful God.

Polytheism: The doctrine or belief in more than one God. Hindus, Ancient Greeks, and Romans all believed in more than one God.

Animism: Belief that objects (such as plants and stones), or natural events (like thunderstorms and earthquakes), have a discrete spirit and conscious life. This was prevalent in many of the tribes of Africa, though less so now than in the past because of the influence of Islamic and Christian missionaries.

Hinduism: Name means *the religions system of India*. A broad belief system in which people are encouraged to personalize their method for worshiping gods. There are several main gods, found in areas dominated by the primary worship of specific gods: Shiva, Shakti, and Vishnu.

Hearth: Place of origin for. All three universalizing religions have hearths in Asia.

Missionary: An individual who helps to diffuse a universalizing religion. The recruitment of new members is important to the growth of many religions.

Pagan: The follower of a polytheistic religion or one who is irreligious. The Latin word for *countryside*.

Ghetto: During the Middle Ages, a neighborhood in a city set up by law to be inhabited only by Jews. Now used to denote a section of a city in which members of any minority group dominates (because of social, legal, or economic pressure).

Pilgrimage: A journey to a place considered sacred for religious purposes. For example, Muslims travel to Makkah for their pilgrimage and call it a *hajj*. Hindus call a pilgrimage a *tirtha* and is an act of purification.

Cosmogony: A set of religious beliefs concerning the origin of the universe. Judaism, Islam, and Christianity believe that God created the universe.

Solstice: The time of year that the sunlight is the shortest (winter solstice) or the longest (summer solstice). It was a very important date for many ancient religions.

Sacred Structures: The physical anchors of a religion, though the role it plays in the religion may be different.

Church: The place to which Christians come to worship, and is considered sanctified. The history and architecture of churches is important to understanding the role a church plays in its community.

Mosque: Place where Muslims come to pray, often as a community. The prayers are said by a *muzzan* from a *minaret*, or tower.

Temple: Small intimate places in which Hindus come to say their own prayers, though not a place for large groups of people to worship at one time. Contain images, artifacts, and items of the deity to which the temple is dedicated.

Pagoda: The tall, many sided towers that are used by Buddhists and Shintoists for containment of religious articles, often things associated with the Buddha.

Cemetery: Place where the dead are buried. Different religions have rules, or etiquette, for burials.

Cremation: The burning of the dead body, some believe to free the soul from the body.

Catacombs: Underground passages used to bury dead Christians when Roman statutes prohibited their religion. After Christianity became legal, the dead were buried in yards near churches.

Utopian Settlement: Settlement built around a religious or idealistic way of life. Salt Lake City is a modern city planned and built to be oriented toward access to a religious way of life.

Autonomous Religion: A religion that does not have a central authority but shares ideas and cooperates informally. There is little administrative structure in these religions.

Hierarchical Religions: A religion in which a central authority exercises a high degree of control. The Pope and organization of the Roman Catholic church seems a clear example.

Roman Catholic Hierarchy: Very structured, hierarchical religion, headed by the Pope who oversees archbishops and they, in turn, bishops. A Bishop oversees a diocese, a group of parishes, each headed by a priest.

Fundamentalism: Literal interpretation and strict adherence to basic principles of a religion, often leading to intolerant policies between religious groups.

Caste: The class or distinct hereditary order into which a Hindu is assigned according to religious law. The lowest caste is the untouchables and the highest caste is the Brahmans.

CHAPTER 6
PROGRESSIVE REVIEW

1. The locales from which religions expand are known as _____.

hearths

2. Religions that appeal to a wide range of people are called _____ religions.

universalizing

3. A relatively small group which has broken away from a denomination is a _____.

sect

4. Christianity was founded on the teachings of _____.

Jesus

5. _____ spread a religion by traveling and gaining converts.

Missionaries

6. The followers of polytheistic religions are known by monotheists as _____.

pagans

7. Eastern Orthodox is one of three branches of the _____ religion.

Christian

8. Latin America is dominated by the _____ _____ branch of the _____ religion.

Roman Catholic, Christian

9. The militant organization, the Irish Republican Army, targets _____ in Northern Ireland.

Protestants

10. In Northern Ireland, _____ _____ are a minority of the population.

Roman Catholics

11. Followers of the _____ church cluster around the state of Utah.

Mormon

12. The prophet of _____ is Muhammad.

Islam

13. Islam's holiest city is _____, to which all Muslims who are capable are expected to make a _____ some time in their lifetime.

Makkah
pilgrimage or hajj

14. A devout Muslim lives by the _____ _____ of Islam.

five pillars

15. _____ and _____ are the two main branches of Islam.

Sunni, Shiite

16. In the U.S., The Nation of Islam, was formed in 1930 by _____ _____.   Elijah Muhammad

17. The third-largest universalizing religion, _____ was   Buddhism
founded in present-day _____ by Siddhartha Gautama.   Nepal

18. Today, most Buddhists live in the East Asian countries of   China, Japan
_____ and _____.

19. The largest ethnic religion in the world is _____, with over   Hinduism, 700
_____ million believers.

20. Nearly all Hindus reside in _____.   India

21. Systematic division of Indians into classes is known as   caste,
the _____ system, in which the _____ represent the lowest   untouchables
level.

22. Confucianism originated in _____ in the fifth century BC.   China

23. The modern Jewish state of _____ has existed since   Israel, 1948
_____.

24. The sequestering of Jews in certain neighborhoods   ghettos
known as _____ occurred in many European cities during the
middle ages.

25. Today, there are about _____ million Jews living   18
throughout the world.

26. _____ virtually disappeared from Persia after Islam was   Zoroastrianism
introduced by invaders.

27. The longest and shortest days of the year, known as the
summer and winter _____, were sacred for ancient pagans   solstices
and have significance in many religious calendars.

28. The _____ is the most important waterway for Hindus.   Ganges

29. Muslims call their pilgrimages to Makkah a _____ and the   hajj
Hindus call their pilgrimages a _____.   tirtha

30. _____ religions have very structured governing bodies   Hierarchical
and geographic provinces.

31. Structures can have meaning; Muslims pray in _____, Christians worship in _____, Hindus pray in _____, and Buddhists don't generally pray in _____.

Mosques, churches, temples, pagodas

32. Martin Luther's theses established the _____ branch of Christianity.

Protestant

33. In Japan, _____ and _____ are practiced simultaneously by many people.

Buddhism, Shintoism

34. People dispose of their dead by burying them in _____ or by destroying the bodies through _____ or _____.

cemeteries cremation, exposure

35. The holiest Islamic place in Jerusalem is the _____ of the _____.

Dome, Rock

36. Many of the conflicts in the _____ _____ are brought about because Christianity, Judaism, and Islam all have roots in the area.

Middle East

CHAPTER 7

ETHNICITY

Ethnicity is growing in importance as people all over the world embrace their cultural heritage. Personal and group identity is important and ethnicity is likely to remain diverse even with the globalization of religions, language, economics, and politics. Ethnic groups sometimes organize and become nationalities. Some nationalities have self-determination and self-rule. A nation-state is a country where the boundaries correspond to those of an ethnic group. Conflict often arises where boundaries do not correspond and countries fight for control of territory. Chapter Seven explains the nuances between ethnicity and nationality and lays the basis for understanding the complex nature of Political Geography in Chapter Eight.

Ethnicity: *Ethnicity* is identity with a group of people who share the cultural traditions of a particular homeland or hearth. Geographers study where various ethnicities are located. Ethnicity is tied to place because the cultural traits of the group of people are tied to the area from having lived in the same are as their ancestors. Why ethnicities are distinct comes from their interaction with and isolation from other groups. Migration is the force through which cultural groups move around and relocate around the globe. *Local diversity* is closely tied to ethnicity because people are tied to their ethnicity in language practice and religious beliefs. *Globalization* is affected by ethnicity though no ethnic group seeks dominance of the earth, though ethnic groups do fight to gain control of territory. Ethnic diversity will remain in the world even if globalization diminishes language and religious diversity.

Key Issue 1: Where Are Ethnicities Distributed?:

Distribution of Ethnicities in the United States (231): The United States' population is comprised of about 12 percent African-Americans, 9 percent Hispanics or Latinos, 3 percent Asian-Americans, and 1 percent American Indians (Native Americans).

Clustering of Ethnicities (231):

Regional Concentrations of Ethnicities (231): African-Americans are clustered in the Southeast—Alabama, Georgia, Louisiana, South Carolina, and Mississippi. There are strikingly few in Maine, New Hampshire, and Vermont, Idaho, Montana, North Dakota, South Dakota, Utah and Wyoming. The terms describing Hispanics and Latin Americans vary, and, depending on country of origin, their *self-identification* is more important. Most Hispanic and Latino populations come from Mexico (64 percent), Puerto Rico (11 percent), and Cuba (4 percent). Hispanics are clustered in Arizona, California, New Mexico, and Texas. There are also significant populations in Florida and New York while there are few in 11 states, mostly in the Southeast. Asian Americans come from China (25 percent), Philippines (20 percent), Japan (12 percent), India (12 percent), and Vietnam (12 percent). The largest concentrations are in Hawaii and California. American Indians (Native Americans) and Alaska Natives are located mostly in the Southwest and Plains states.

Concentration of Ethnicities in Cities (232-233): African-Americans are clustered in cities. About one-fourth of all Americans live in cities, whereas more than one-half of African-Americans live in cities. Most African-Americans in Michigan live in Detroit and in Illinois most live in Chicago while in New York most Hispanics live in New York City. In California some Hispanics are clustered in Los Angeles though the rest of the state contains approximately the same proportion of Hispanics as the whole state. In Texas, most of the state has Texas' average proportion of Hispanics with concentrations in El Paso and San Antonio. Around the turn of the century there were many ethnic neighborhoods formed by immigrants from all over the world—especially from European countries. Many cities today have large African-American and Hispanic neighborhoods. These neighborhoods have come into conflict with the majority population as they did in Los Angeles in 1992 after the _Rodney King_ trial which acquitted white police officers accused of beating an African-American.

African-American Migration Patterns (233): Investigating migrational patterns helps geographers explain regular distribution of language, religion, and ethnicities. There are three migration flows that explain the distribution of African-Americans in the United States.

Forced Migration from Africa (233): _Slavery_ is a system under which one person owns another person like a piece of property and can force that slave to work for the owner's benefit. Africans were forced to migrate from Africa as slaves and were first brought to Jamestown, Virginia on a Dutch ship in 1619. In the eighteenth century more than 400,000 Africans were brought to the U.S. colonies. In 1808 importing slaves was banned, though 250,000 were illegally imported in the next 50 years. Romans had slaves 2,000 years ago. The European _feudal system_ had serfs (laborers) working the land and were not free to migrate. In the 1700s at least 10 million Africans were brought to the Western Hemisphere. The European powers brought slaves from different regions in Africa to different regions in the Western Hemisphere. The _triangular slave trade_ developed; it was an efficient triangular trading pattern where ships left Europe with trade goods to buy slaves, shipped slaves and gold from Africa to the Caribbean islands, and returned to Europe with sugar and molasses. Families where separated when stronger and younger villagers were seized. Approximately one-fourth of the Africans died crossing the Atlantic. In America, they were forced to work and were used on large plantations in the Southeast. The Civil War was fought to keep 11 pro-slavery states from seceding from the Union. _Abraham Lincoln_ issued the _Emancipation Proclamation_, freeing slaves, and the _Thirteenth Amendment to the Constitution_ outlawed slavery. Freed slaves could work as _sharecroppers_; they rented the fields from a landowner and paid rent with a share of the crops. Acquiring necessary goods and supplies financially burdened African-Americans and forced them to grow cash crops rather than food.

Immigration to the North (236-237): Farm machinery reduced the need for agricultural laborers and forced sharecroppers off the land. They were pulled to the city by job prospects resulting from growing industrialization in the North. Four main routes were used—along U.S. Route 1 to the Northeastern cities, north along U.S. Route 25 to Detroit and U.S. Route 21 to Cleveland, and northwest along U.S. Routes 61 and 66 to Chicago and St. Louis, and West to Texas and California along U.S. Routes 80 and 90. There were two waves: in the 1910s and 1920s around World War I, and in the 1940s and 1950s around World War II. These migrations drastically changed the ethnic composition of destination cities.

Expansion of the Ghetto (237): African Americans sought out areas in cities with other African-Americans. The areas became known as *ghettos* after the Jewish neighborhoods formed in the Middle Ages. They were comparatively densely settle areas with drastic shortages of housing. Many buildings lacked sanitation, heating, and kitchen. They spread into adjacent areas in the 1950s and 1960s.

Differentiating Ethnicity and Race (237-238): *Race* is identity with a group of people who share a biological ancestor, and is distinct from ethnicity. In the U.S., Asians are a race and Asian-Americans encompass basically the same ethnic group of people, though Asian-American is a broad grouping for people from diverse Asian backgrounds. African-American and black can be both race and ethnic identifiers, though some African-Americans descend from regions other than Africa. African-American describes an ethnic group while black describes people with dark skin. Hispanic or Latino is not considered a race, so ethnic Hispanics or Latinos can choose any race—white, black, or Asian—to identify themselves. Racial traits are genetically transmitted from parents to children and are seen in biological features, though genetic variability for all humans is so great that any pre-judged classification is inappropriate and meaningless. *Racism* is the belief that race is the primary determinant of human traits and capacities and that racial differences produce an inherent superiority of a particular race. A *racist* is a person who believes in racism. In geography, ethnicity can be studied because ethnicity has a base in a particular location. The biological functioning of humans is not significantly different, though skin color is the most fundamental basis by which people in many societies groups themselves.

Race in the Untied States (238-239): The U.S. Census Bureau asks people to self-identify themselves every 10 years. They use 6 races and people can check more than one box—white, black or African-American, Asian, American Indian or Alaska Native, Native Hawaiian or Pacific Islander, or other race. The U.S. in 1990 was 80 percent white, 12 percent black, 3 percent Asian, 1 percent American Indian or Alaska Native, 0.1 percent Native Hawaiian or Pacific Islander, and 4 percent other race.

"Separate But Equal" Doctrine (239): The 1896 U.S. Supreme Court ruling on *Plessy v. Ferguson* upheld Louisiana's law requiring black and white passengers to ride in separate railway cars. *Separate but equal* doctrines was taken to mean everyone had access to the same things, though people didn't necessarily care to socialize with each other. *Segregation* was the separation of blacks from whites as much as possible in transit systems, shops, restaurants, hotels, and schools. Housing *covenants*, rules agreed to by neighborhoods of people, restricted the selling of property so that blacks, and sometimes Jews and Catholics, couldn't buy property in some places.

"White Flight" (239-240): Segregation was abolished in the 1950s and 1960s with the U.S. Supreme Court decision in *Brown v. Board of Education of Topeka, Kansas* ruling separate schools were unconstitutional. Schools were desegregated. Black ghetto expansion of the 1950s in cities pushed whites out. *Block-busting* occurred where real estate agents convinced white homeowners living near a black area to sell their houses at low prices, preying on their fears that black families would cause property values to decline. Block-busting exacerbated white flight and fortunes were made reselling property to black families. Segregation and inequality still remain.

Division by Race in South Africa (240-241): Segregation in South Africa grew as segregation in the U.S. decreased. *Apartheid* was the legal system enforcing the physical separation of different races into separate geographic areas. Apartheid was repealed in the 1990s though it will take years for all the effects to disappear.

Apartheid System (241): Babies were classified as black, white, colored (mixed), or Asian. Each had a different status and determined where each would live. Blacks could only have certain jobs, lower wages, could not vote, or be elected to national office. The British took South Africa in 1795. Slaves freed in 1833 went northeast and gold and diamonds were found in the Transval, the British took over the area. In 1948 Afrikaners and the Nationalist party won elections and resisted the local blacks by creating apartheid laws. Most countries cut off relations to South Africa in the 1970s and 1980s. Poorer neighboring countries maintained economic ties. The South African government established *homelands* to keep blacks geographically separated from whites. The white government expected blacks to become a citizen of a homeland and move there. The homeland plan was never fully executed.

Dismantling of Apartheid (241) In 1991 apartheid laws were repealed by the white-dominated government. The *African National Congress* was legalized and *Nelson Mandela* was released from jail. In 1994 he was elected the first black president in the first election where blacks were allowed to vote. South Africa is now ruled by a black majority; blacks are still much poorer than whites.

Key Issue 2: Where Have Ethnicities Been Transformed into Nationalities? (241-242): *Nationality* is identity with a group of people who share legal attachment and personal allegiance to a particular country. A *nation* or *nationality* is a group of people tied together to a particular place through legal status and cultural traditions. Ethnicity describes cultural identity while nationality describes political ties and ideas about voting, passports, and civic duties. American is a nationality, Hispanic-American or African-American are ethnicities, and race is the genetic heritage with skin color being most visible trait. The distinctions in other parts of the world are more difficult to identify.

Rise of Nationalities (242-243): Immigrants to the U.S. now identify themselves by ethnicity, though immigration records were organized by nationality. The United States became, for many, their nationality because of shared values.

    Nation-States (243): When an ethnic group desires self-rule and that desire is a shared value, the group becomes a *nationality*. The right to govern oneself is called *self-determination*. A *nation-state* is a state whose territory corresponds to the territory of a nationality.

    Nation-States in Europe (243): During the nineteenth century most European ethnicities became nationalities. By around 1900 Europe consisted of nation-states. Disagreements about territory grew in Africa and Asia where boundaries ignored ethnicities. After World War 1 the Ottoman and Austro-Hungarian empires were dismantled and European boundaries were redrawn to accommodate nation-states. In the 1930s the *German National Socialists (Nazis)* wanted all German-speaking parts of Europe to be a part on one state. After taking control of other German speaking countries and then invading Poland, World War II began when England and France moved to defend themselves.

    Denmark: There are No Perfect Nation-States (243): The boundaries of Denmark follow those of the Danish ethnicity which is more than 1,000 years old. The boundary between Denmark and Germany doesn't precisely divide the two nationalities. Areas in the region lost to Germany during the war voted to determine which country they would belong to which left some German speakers in Denmark and some Danish speakers in Germany. Denmark controls the Faeroe Islands and Greenland. Greenland is 50 times the size of Denmark and contains 14 percent Danes; the rest are native Greenlanders and Inuits. Greenland got more authority over themselves in 1979.

    Nationalism (243-244): *Nationalism* is loyalty and devotion to a nationality. Nationalism promotes one nationality and culture above that of other nations. Mass media is used by some states to foster nationalism while other states control the media believing it to be a risk to the government. Most countries control or regulate communication media. States promote nationalism with flags, songs, symbols, and holidays, often those of the dominant ethnicity. Negative images or *propaganda* about another country are sometimes used to bring a sense of unity to a nation-state. *Centripetal force* is an attitude that tends to unify people and enhance support for a state. Most nation-states gain support by emphasizing the shared attitudes of its people.

Nationalities in Former Colonies (244): Many nationalities were created in the 1940s and 1950s when colonies became independent countries. Boundaries were often drawn to separate ethnicities, though boundaries don't completely separate people are forced to migrate.

    Creating Nationalities in South Asia (244): In 1947 the British ended colonial rule of the Indian subcontinent and created India and Pakistan. East Pakistan became Bangladesh in 1971. The boundaries originally divided Hindus from Muslims. Fighting for territory in the area has a long history. Muslims gained area in the Punjab area and grew in number after two invasions, in 1000 AD and in the thirteenth century. Hindus, Muslims, and the British began fighting in the 1800s. After World War II Muslims and Hindus fought over the territory and *Mahatma Gandhi* led the Hindus as an advocate of nonviolence and reconciliation. He was assassinated in 1948, ending possibilities of a single, peaceful state.

Migration in South Asia (243): After people ended up on the "wrong" side of the border, people migrated to areas dominated by their ethnic group. In India and Pakistan, many people were killed trying to get to the other country.

Ethnic Disputes in Kashmir (243): The border was never agreed upon in Kashmir and guerrilla wars have caused between India and Pakistan. India blames Pakistan for the unrest because Kashmir is mostly Muslim. Pakistan wants the area to vote, confident Kashmir would choose to become a part of Pakistan. India also has 17 million Sikhs with a religion combining Islam and Hinduism. They would like to have their own state and have a majority in Punjab.

Converting Ethnicities to Nationalities in Africa (245-246): The boundaries of African countries are mostly the result of the division of Africa amongst colonial powers. There are several thousand ethnicities. Some of these tribes are divided between states or are grouped with dissimilar tribes.

Pre-European States in Africa (246-247): Africa originally relied on the tribe rather than on a politically and economically organized states. Some countries in West Africa organized in the Middle Ages into larger kingdoms.

Impact of European Colonization (247): Between the 1800s and 1914 (World War I) European colonial powers divided the area to control natural resources and transportation routes. When African countries gained independence after World War II, the current boundaries often matched the colonial boundaries. Most states contain many different ethnicities and the historic homelands of many different people.

Revival of Ethnic Identity (247): Ethnicity remains very important to Africans, often more important than nationality, and has become, once again, an important part of people's identities in much of Europe.

Ethnicity and Communism (247-248): From 1945 until the early 1990s, communism and economic cooperation were more important in parts of Europe than nation-states. The communist leaders of the former Soviet Union used centripetal forces to discourage ethnic identity. The Russian language was used to promote "socialist realism" and communist economic and political values. Religion was suppressed and Russian language taught in schools. The structure of the Soviet Union and Czechoslovakia and Yugoslavia recognized ethnic groups. The 15 republics of the Soviet Union were organized along ethnic boundaries and sub-units granted some autonomy to smaller ethnicities.

Rebirth of Nationalism in Eastern Europe (248): In the 1990s ethnic identity has become a driving force in the politics of the area. Many have organized into nation-states, though there are still many ethnicities that are minorities in other states. Bulgaria's Turkish minority has pushed for more rights. Communism has been replaced by an ideology encouraging ethnic identity through language and religion. Minorities in the Soviet Union, Yugoslavia, and Czechoslovakia contributed to the dismantling of the countries, asking for representation and self-determination in smaller, independent nation-states. It is a peaceful transition when ethnic boundaries are clearly definable. Yugoslavia has become separate nation-states. Slovenia is dominated by Slovenes and has been a relatively peaceful transition.

Key Issue 3: Why Do Ethnicities Clash? (248-249): A *multi-ethnic state* is a state containing more than one ethnicity. Sometimes multiple ethnicities contribute to one nationality, as is the case with Belgium. *Multinational states* contain two or more ethnic groups with traditions of self-determination that agree to coexist peacefully by recognizing each other as distinct nationalities, as is the case with the United Kingdom—England, Scotland, Wales, and Northern Ireland. England conquered Wales in 1282 and united with England through the *Act of Union of 1536*. Wales became a local government and now the Welsh language is being preserved. Scotland was independent until 1603 when it was united with England. The *Act of Union of 1707* united the two. Great Britain contains England, Wales, and Scotland and British describes their combined nationality. Ireland was ruled by the British and the *Act of Union of 1801* created the United Kingdom of Great Britain and Ireland. In the 1920s, Ireland became a separate country and Northern Ireland, dominated by Protestants, remained British. National soccer teams is the greatest visible effect of the separate nationalities.

Ethnic Competition to Dominate Nationality (242-243): There are many conflicts in the Horn of Africa and in Sri Lanka.

Horn of Africa (249):

Ethiopia and Eritrea (249): The Italians ruled Eritrea along the Red Sea. It had been an independent country for 2,000 years. Ethiopia took control and gained independence from Italy and changed the name to Ethiopia. The Eritreans have become the minority. Many Eritreans fled to Sudan. Eritrea became independent in 1993 and is north of Ethiopia, along the Red Sea. Ethiopia is a multi-ethnic state with Christian Amharas, Muslim Oromos, and Ethiopian Orthodox Tigres. In eastern Ethiopia in Ogaden, Ethiopians moved Somalis to Somalia and they remain along the border or wandering in Somalia.

Sudan (250): The Arab-Muslims in the north have fought the southern black Christians and animists in the south since the 1980s. The southern groups have resisted becoming Muslims. Gender segregation laws have been enacted and women have strict laws they must follow. Women may not dress or act provocatively though they may wear traditional, colorful *tobes* and don't have to wear veils. Sudanese have been forced to migrate within the country and many have fled to Ethiopia.

Somalia (250): Somalis are Sunni Muslims and speak Somali making Somalia a nation-state. There are 6 major ethnic groups (clans) with many sub-clans with regional ties to different parts of Somalia. Splits within clans in Somalia has changed the geographic divisions. Somaliland in the north is ruled by the Isaak clan and has declared itself a separate state. Fighting between clans for power and famine and warfare brought U.S. troops in 1992 to protect food deliveries and reduce the number of guns. The U.S. left in 1994.

Buddhists vs. Hindus in Sri Lanka (250-251): Sri Lanka has Sinhalese (Buddhists speaking an Indo-European language) and Tamils (Hindus speaking a Dravidian language). Sinhalese are 74 percent of the 19 million population. Sri Lanka is a world center for Buddhism. Tamils are mostly migrants from India and share a language with 60 percent of Indians. India is 80 kilometers from Sri Lanka and has sent troops to protect the Tamils.

Overlapping of Ethnicities and Nationalities (251): The Middle East has three religious groups and emerging strong nationalities.

Conflict over the Holy Land (251): Jerusalem is important to Jews, Christians, and Muslims. Israel is dominated by Jews and its border states are Muslim. Israel captured the West Bank, the Golan Heights, the Gaza Strip, and the Sinai peninsula. A peace treaty was signed in 1979 returning the Sinai Peninsula to Egypt in exchange for formal recognition. Territories occupied by Israel are still under debate and .

Palestinians: Conflict Between an Ethnicity and a Nationality (251-253): Israel's neighboring countries have all come to peace with Israel. The Palestinian nationality emerged in the 1960s and are comprised of a wide group of people. Israel turned the Gaza and West Bank to Palestinians and the *Palestine Liberation Organization (PLO)* became the governing organization. Palestine can not decide if the territory is sufficient or if they want the whole territory that is Israel. Some Israelis would like to retain the Palestinian territory and some would like to have peace.

Lebanon: Conflicts Among Several Nationalities and Ethnicities (253): Lebanon contains a large number of Europeans. Lebanon contains 17 ethnicities and 3.4 million people. Civil war broke out in the mid 1970s.

Lebanon's Ethnic Diversity (253): Lebanon is estimated to have 7.1 percent Druze, 37.6 percent Christians, 21.3 percent Sunnis, and 34 percent Shiites. The Christian minority is 60 percent Maronites, 5 percent Greek Orthodox, and Greek Catholics, Armenians, Syrian Orthodox (Jacobites), and Caldeans (Assyrians). Lebanese Muslims are 36 percent Shiites, with Mitwali and Hezbollah sects, and Sunnis. Druze combines Islam and Christianity. The different groups live in different regions.

Lebanon's Constitution (254-255): Lebanon's constitution (1943) preserves the identity of the groups through mandatory representation, though there are unwritten conventions about the religious affiliation of the heads of state. As Muslims gained the majority, the government was unable to accommodate changes.

Lebanon's Civil War (255-256): Refugees from the 1967 Arab-Israeli War and the PLO controlling southern Lebanon upset the balance. Each religious group formed its own military to protect its territory. Syria has assumed control of Lebanon and established a cease-fire. A 1990 constitution and a round of elections brought peace, a reorganization of power, and a Muslim majority as Christians boycotted the elections. Most of Lebanon, especially Beirut still lies in ruins.

Key Issue 4: Why Does Ethnic Cleansing Occur? (256): The largest ethnic cleansing occurred in Europe around World War II with the deportation and extermination of Jews, gypsies, and other ethnic groups. After the war Germans, Poles, and Russians relocated to the newly drawn areas which were dominated by their ethnic group.

Defining Ethnic Cleansing (257): *Ethnic cleansing* is a new tem describing the process in which a more powerful ethnic group forcibly removes a less powerful one in order to create an ethnically homogeneous region. Ethnic cleansing occurs where one group wants to rid an area of another group. Bosnian Serbs "cleansed" the area of Bosnian Muslims in Bosnia and Herzegovina. Bosnian Muslims were forced to join the Bosnian Serb army or health insurance and social benefits were removed from their village's Bosnian Muslims. Strong, able bodied Bosnian Muslims were often killed or deported in order to protect their villages, while women, children, and the elderly could receive international relief in open refugee camps.

Ethnic Cleansing in Former Yugoslavia (257): The Balkan Mountain (the Balkans) countries include Albania, Bulgaria, Greece, Romania, and countries from former Yugoslavia.

Creation of Multi-Ethnic Yugoslavia (257-258): The Balkan Peninsula has a complex collection of ethnicities and were historically ruled by the Austria-Hungary Empire in the north, the Ottomans in the South. There were Muslims in the southern areas. Yugoslavia was created to unite ethnicities speaking similar South Slavic languages and included Serbs, Croats, Slovenes, Macedonians, and Montenegrens.

Ethnic Diversity in the Former Yugoslavia (258): Yugoslavia had seven neighbors and separated democracies and communists. The six republics had a great deal of local autonomy. Five of the republics were the country's recognized nationalities. There were four official languages, three major religions, and two alphabets. There was one unit of currency, the dinar.

Destruction of Multi-Ethnic Yugoslavia (258-259): Rivalries reemerged in the 1980s after more thirty years of peace and rule by *Josip Broz Tito*. The country broke up in the 1990s and Bosnia, Herzegovina, Croatia, Macedonia, and Slovenia were created with two republics remaining in Yugoslavia. Fighting over territory in the area happened only after separate countries emerged. Serbs and Croats fought over Krajina, and Albanians fought in Kosova to free themselves from Serbia.

Complexity in Bosnia-Herzegovina (259-260): Bosnian Muslims were considered an ethnicity rather than a nationality in Bosnia and Herzegovina. In both countries there are Bosnian Muslims (40 percent), Serbs (32 percent), and Croats (18 percent). Serbs and Croats want to unite with Serbia and Croatia and engaged in ethnic cleansing of Bosnian Muslims. Bosnian Serbs worked to clear Bosnian Muslims living between them and Serbia. Bosnia and Herzegovina were divided into three regions with the Bosnian Croat and Muslim regions combining into a federation and the Bosnian Serbs getting nearly half the territory with only one-third of the population.

Balkanization (260-261): *Balkanized* is used to describe an area that could not be organized into one or more stable states because of ethnic antagonism. *Balkanization* is used to describe the breakdown of a state through internal disputes among its different nationalities. Balkanization led to World War I because of ally involvement, and there is speculation about another large-scale war because of ally involvement in the present conflicts.

Summary: The way people identify themselves comes from their place of origin, their folk and popular culture, language, and religion. Ethnicity is the set of cultural traditions people have. The labels people use to describe themselves can include their ethnic heritage, race, and nationality. The United States has a large number of ethnicities and one nationality—American. There can be multi-national and multi-ethnic states. Multi-national states can have difficulty if national groups have a desire for self-determination. When state or regional borders separate ethnicities or nationalities often there will be conflict. Ethnic cleansing is a tragic result of nationalities coming into conflict.

CHAPTER 7
KEY TERMS AND CONCEPTS

Ethnicity: Identity with a group of people who share the cultural traditions of a particular homeland or hearth. Ethnicity is not the same as race; it is much less stable.

Self-Identification: The descriptors people use to identify themselves. They may have a multi-ethnic, multi-racial, linguistic, or religious background that contributes to their identity.

Rodney King: African-American man who was allegedly beaten by white police officers while the affair was captured on video tape. The accused officers were acquitted and Los Angeles erupted in conflict as a result of the court decision.

Slavery: System whereby one person owns another person like a piece of property and can force that slave to work for the owner's benefit. Slavery has been abolished in the United States.

Feudal System: European system in the Middle Ages where lords owned pieces of property and had serfs who had to work the land and were not free to relocate.

Triangular Slave Trade: System used by Europeans to take goods from Europe to Africa, slaves and gold to the Americas, and sugar and molasses back to Europe.

Abraham Lincoln: President who read the **Emancipation Proclamation** freeing slaves at the close of the American Civil War.

Thirteenth Amendment to the Constitution: Officially outlawed slavery in the United States.

Ghettos: The word originates from the neighborhoods Jews were forced to live in cities in Europe. In American cities, the term gained usage for areas dominated by African-Americans and Hispanics and often lacked basic sanitation and kitchens and were over crowded.

Race: Identity with a group of people who share a biological ancestor. Skin color is the most visible trait of race.

Racism: The *belief* that race is the primary determinant of human traits and capacities and that racial differences produce an inherent superiority of a particular race. Given the genetic variability of all humans, it is inappropriate and meaningless for judgmental classification of people.

Racist: A person who subscribes to the ideas of racism.

Plessy v. Ferguson: A court case started in Louisiana and upheld by the U.S. Supreme Court requiring black and white passengers to ride in separate railway cars.

Separate But Equal: Doctrines saying that as long as people had access to the same services, it was allowable for people to have separate services.

Segregation: The separation of blacks from whites as much as possible. Segregation can also be the separation of religious groups, racial groups, or ethnic groups.

Covenants: A set of rules agreed to by a neighborhood limiting people's actions so that the neighborhood remains essentially the same. Often covenants limited people's ability to sell property to blacks, Jews, or Catholics.

Brown v. Board of Education of Topeka, Kansas: The U.S. Supreme Court ruled that separate schools were unconstitutional and schools were promptly desegregated.

Block-Busting: A process in which real estate agents convince white property owners in neighborhoods adjacent to black areas to sell their property as quickly as possible. The agents would then sell the properties to blacks at a significant profit. Contributed to white people moving from the central city areas.

White Flight: The phenomenon of white people leaving central city areas because of fears about having black neighbors, or adjacent black neighborhoods.

Apartheid: Laws (no longer in effect) in South Africa that physically separated different races into different geographic areas. In 1991, apartheid in South Africa ceased to legally exist.

Homelands: A program established by the apartheid government of South Africa where homelands were established and blacks were encouraged to declare citizenship of a homeland and move there. The goal was to keep blacks and whites geographically separated and the plan was never fully instituted.

Nelson Mandela: The leader of the South African **African National Congress** party which fought for black representation in the government. He was elected the first black president in 1994.

Nationality: Identity with a group of people who share legal attachment and personal allegiance to a particular country. An ethnicity can become a nationality when they develop a desire for self-rule that is shared.

Self-Determination: Concept that people have the right to govern themselves. This increasingly becomes a factor when states have many nationalities within their borders.

Nation-State: A state whose territory corresponds to that occupied by a particular nation. Denmark is an example.

German National Socialists (Nazis): The group of people who tried to unite all German speakers into one state and invoked World War II after invading Poland and France and England moved to defend themselves.

Nationalism: Attitude of the people in a nation in support of the existence and growth of a particular state. It is the loyalty and devotion to a nationality. Nazi Germany greatly emphasized nationalism.

Centripetal Forces: Attitudes that tend to unify a people and enhance support for the state. Forces that bring people together around their core.

Mahatma Gandhi: Advocate of nonviolence and reconciliation and tried to unite Muslims and Hindus in a peaceful state. He was assassinated in 1948.

Multi-Ethnic State: State containing more than one ethnicity.

Multinational State: State containing more multiple ethnic groups with traditions of self-determination that agree to coexist peacefully by recognizing each other as distinct nationalities.

Act of Union: Acts created in the United Kingdom uniting with England Wales, Scotland, and Northern Ireland.

Palestine Liberation Organization (PLO): The governing organization of Palestine and its territories.

Ethnic Cleansing: The process in which a more powerful ethnic group forcibly removes a less powerful one in order to create an ethnically homogeneous region. Often, ethnic cleansing takes the form of forcibly removing or killing other ethnic groups.

Josip Broz Tito: The leader of Yugoslavia that maintained peace for thirty years in the multi-ethnic Yugoslavia.

Balkanized: Small geographic area that can not be successfully organized into one or more stable states because it is inhabited by many nationalities with complex, long-standing antagonisms toward each other.

Balkanization: Process by which a state breaks down through conflicts among its nationalities. The former USSR is a good example.

CHAPTER 7
PROGRESSIVE REVIEW

1. The U.S. is comprised of _____ main groups of ethnicities. 4

2. African-Americans are clustered in the _____ region, Hispanics in the _____ region, and American Indians (Native Americans) in the _____ and _____ states.

   Southeast,
   Southwest
   Southwest, Plains

3. About _____ (proportion) of all Americans live in cities, and more than _____ of the African-Americans live in cities.

   ¼
   ½

4. At the turn of the century there were many ethnic neighborhoods in cities though now the dominant ethnic neighborhoods in most American cities are _____ _____ and _____.

   African American
   Latino/Hispanic

5. _____ _____ is the way people describe themselves and the groups they associate with.

   self-identification

6. The _____ _____ was active in the Middle Ages in Europe and had serfs and land owners.

   feudal system

7. More than _____ million Africans were brought to the Western Hemisphere.

   11

8. _____ happens when one group of people forces another to work for them, takes away their human rights, and owns them like property.

   Slavery

9. Approximately _____ of the people taken from Africa died on the ships crossing the Atlantic.

   ¼

10. Two major documents freed slaves in the U.S.: _____ _____, and _____ _____ _____ _____ _____.

    Emancipation
    Proclamation,
    Thirteenth
    Amendment to
    the Constitution

11. Much of the black migration from the north followed major _____ and the destinations were _____.

    highways, cities

12. Areas in a city dominated by an ethnic group are called _____.

    ghettos

13. _____ is different than ethnicity and there are essentially three main types, white, black, and Asian, though the U.S. Census Bureau uses six. race

14. The _____ _____ of human beings is so great that judgements based on it are inappropriate and meaningless. genetic diversity

15. _____ _____ _____ was taken to mean that as long as people had access to services and schools, there could be different ones for different people. Separate but equal

16. _____ was outlawed in the U.S. and then grew in support in South Africa. Segregation

17. Block-busting significantly contributed to _____ _____. white flight

18. The legal system separating people by race is called _____. apartheid

19. _____ were legally discriminated against in South Africa and segregated into separate areas. Blacks

20. The _____ system was never fully implemented because of a change of government in South Africa. homeland

21. _____ _____ became the first black president in _____. Nelson Mandela 1994

22. When people have a high degree of loyalty and devotion to their state they are said to possess a high degree of _____. nationalism

23. The concept that nationalities have the right to govern themselves is _____ _____. self-determination

24. A _____ is a collection of people who share a common culture and history who may live in more than one country. nation

25. The boundaries of states _____ correspond completely to the boundaries of nations. rarely

26. _____ and _____ were created by the British to separate religious groups. India, Pakistan

27. The main groups in South Asia are _____ and _____. Muslims, Hindus

28. _____ is a region in northern India which has conflict because of religious ethnic groups.

Kashmir

29. Much of the conflict in Africa happens because there are several thousand _____.

ethnicities

30. Physical separation of people based on race was called _____ in South Africa.

apartheid

31. Feelings of nationalism are especially heated in the former Soviet Union region of _____ _____.

Eastern Europe

32. The Soviet Union used the _____ language to promote economic and political values and required it be taught in schools.

Russian

33. A _____-_____ state may contain multiple ethnicities that all contribute to one _____.

multi-ethnic
nationality

34. A _____ state, depending on the nationalistic traditions of the people, may be mostly peaceful, as is the case with the United Kingdom.

multinational

35. In the United Kingdom, _____ is the most visible remaining show of the separate nationalities.

soccer

36. In the Horn of Africa, _____, _____, and _____ all have conflicts that have grown out of the desire for ethnic and religious groups to have self-determination

Ethiopia, Sudan, Somalia

37. Off the southeast coast of India, _____ _____ has conflicts arising from differences of religion, language, and history of the Sinhalese and Tamils.

Sri Lanka

38. _____ is the only country in the Middle East with a significant Christian population, though the majority of people are Muslim with a Druze minority.

Lebanon

39. Many ethnicities have to _____ to a country with a similar ethnic group dominating the state when boundaries have been created which divide their territory.

migrate

40. _____ _____ occurs when one group wants to remove another group from an area.

Ethnic cleansing.

CHAPTER 8

POLITICAL GEOGRAPHY

With today's global economy and instantaneous communication, people are constantly being given information about places located around the planet. In order to understand this information it is imperative to know about the nations that cover the surface of Earth. Chapter Eight explains the foundations of Political Geography and imparts an understanding of the cultural and physical factors that determine how states fare individually and in regional and worldwide governments.

Political Geography: Political boundaries are very real, though they cannot be seen on the ground. Geographers are interested in *why* the division of the world is changing. *Globalization*, for political geography, is the trend whereby countries transfer military, economic, and political authority to regional and worldwide authorities. The major superpowers of the Cold War no longer exist so countries are organizing into groups to cooperate in order to compete economically with other regions. *Local diversity* has actually increased as people demand more control over themselves and independence from other governments.

Key Issue 1: Where Are States Located?: The number of defined countries has increased from 50 approximately fifty years ago to nearly 200 hundred today (Figure 8-1).

Defining States (267): A *state* is an area organized into a political unit and ruled by an established government that has control over its internal and foreign affairs, a different idea than the 50 states of the United States. A state has territory and a permanent population. *Sovereignty* is independent control over its affairs. A state has to have *sovereignty*, the ability of that country to rule its internal and external affairs without the interference of a second country.

Problems of Defining States (267): There is debate about number of sovereign states in the world.

Korea: One State or Two? (267): After World War II, Korea was divided into two states along the 38° north latitude, each with a separate and conflicting philosophy on government. Today, although each believes Korea is a nation incomplete without its corresponding half, most of the world acknowledges that two sovereign nations occupy the Korean Peninsula. In 1992, both were admitted to the United Nations as separate countries.

China and Taiwan: One State or Two? (267-268): Taiwan and China have a similar relationship. After a civil war in the late 1940s, one group claiming to be the legitimate rulers of China fled to Taiwan. Each claims to have legitimate rule on the entire nation, however the United Nations voted to transfer the ownership of China's seat at the UN from Taiwan (and the Nationalists) to China (and the Communists) in 1971.

Antarctica (268): A unique territorial dispute is found in the remote, polar continent of Antarctica. Many nations lay claim to this frozen land, but the U.S., Russia, and other states believe no country has authority over this land mass. There are research stations on Antarctica though there are no permanent settlements.

Varying Size of States (269, 271): The state with the largest land area is Russia with 11 percent of the world's entire land area. China, Canada, United States, Brazil and Australia also cover large areas of land. *Microstates* are states with very small land areas. The smallest is Monaco and other small states are Andorra, Antigua and Barbuda, Bahrain, Barbados, Dominica, Grenada, Liechtenstein, Maldives, Malta, Micronesia, Palau, St. Kitts and Nevis, St. Lucia, San Marino, St. Vincent and the Grenadines, São Tomé e Príncipe, the Seychelles, and Singapore, many of which are islands.

Development of the State Concept (237-238): Before the 1800's much of the Earth's land was unorganized territory.

    Ancient and Medieval States (271-272):

Ancient States (271-272): However, early in human history there were a few ancient nations. There were many city-states in the Fertile Crescent that stretched from Persia to the Mediterranean. A *city-state* is a sovereign state consisting of a town and the surrounding countryside from which most of its food was derived; walls often clearly marked the area of a city. The ancient state of Egypt was situated in the Nile River valley from 3000 BC until it was annexed by the Roman Empire in the fourth century BC.

Early European States (272): The *Roman Empire* was the largest ancient nation. It controlled most of Europe, North Africa, and Southwest Asia at its peak. However, it collapsed in the fifth century AD. Beginning in 1100 AD, a few kingdoms had emerged in Europe that would become the modern nations of Great Britain, Spain, and France.

    Colonies (272): Territory that is legally tied to a sovereign state (rather than being independent) is a *colony*.

Colonialism (272, 274): The policy by countries to enlarge their territory through the establishment of colonies is named *colonialism*. European powers sought to establish colonies in other parts of the world in order to spread Christianity, gain wealth and resources, and increase their political influence. The colonial era began in the 1400s when European explorers found other lands. Most colonies have gained independence. The mainland colonies in the Americas rejected foreign rule between 1776 and 1824 in a series of revolutions. Afterward, the European colonial powers led by Britain and France concentrated their efforts on Africa and Asian land. After World War II most of the colonies on these two continents declared their independence. *Imperialism* is control of territory already occupied and organized by an indigenous society, whereas colonialism is control of a previously uninhabited or sparsely inhabited land.

Colonial Practices (274-275): France attempted to assimilate its colonies into French culture. Many former French colonies have retained close ties with France. The British used government structures and policies to protect their colonies' diverse cultures, local customs, and educational systems. Most African and Asian colonies have gained independence and most of their current boundaries follow colonial boundaries.

The Few Remaining Colonies (275): Most remaining colonies are islands in the Pacific Ocean or the Caribbean Sea. The most populous remaining colony in the world was Hong Kong. In 1997 rule over Hong Kong passed into the hands of the Chinese from the British. Puerto Rico is now the most populous colony and is part of the Commonwealth of the United Sates. The smallest colony in the world is Pitcairn Island which is less than two square miles in area and has less than sixty-five people.

Key Issue 2: Where Are Boundaries Drawn Between States? (276): States are separated by *boundaries*, invisible lines marking the extent of a state's territory. They result from physical and cultural features. Boundary selection interests geographers because selecting them is very difficult and can become a point of conflict between neighbors.

Shapes of States (276): The shape of a state is a part of its identity which is recognized universally. Shapes also contribute to economic and militaristic strategies.

Five Basic Shapes (276):

Compact States: Efficient (276): States where the distance from the center of the country to their perimeter does not vary significantly are *compact states*. These states allow for efficient internal communication. Hungary and Poland are compact states.

Prorupted States: Access or Disruption (276): *Prorupted states* are like compact states except they have a projecting extension that interrupts linkages between other countries or provides access to some resource such as water. There are many examples of states formed with intentional proruptions, especially in Africa.

Elongated States: Potential Isolation (276-277): *Elongated states* are very long countries which have some parts that are relatively isolated from others. Chile is the best example of the elongated state. Internal communication is difficult in this form of state

Fragmented States: Problematic (277-278): *Fragmented states* are nations with noncontiguous territory, such as countries made up of islands. The Philippines and Japan exhibit these traits. Panama is also fragmented by the Canal Zone that bisects it. Fragmented states suffer from poorer communication and poorer integration than other states.

Perforated States: South Africa (278): A nation which completely surrounds another one is a *perforated state*. South Africa completely engulfs the state of

Lesotho. Often the surrounding state has tremendous influence on its internal neighbor.

Landlocked States (278-279): A *landlocked state* lacks a direct outlet to the sea because it is completely surrounded by several other countries. They are common in Africa where 14 of 54 states are landlocked. This is a geographical legacy from the colonial era when borders were not designed for the advantage the African countries but for the aims of their European occupants. Being landlocked is an economic hindrance because a country has much more difficulty conducting international trade with other countries because it lacks ports.

Landlocked States in Southern Africa (279): Zimbabwe in southern Africa faced a problem in its export/import sector when it attempted to bypass South Africa's railroad lines to facilitate international trade. The alternate railroad lines were quite difficult to use because of wars in the country of Mozambique. Distant seaports were also unreliable because of the civil war. Zimbabwe has to ship through the seaport of Durban.

Types of Boundaries (279-280): Historically, frontiers have separated states. A *frontier* is a zone where no state exercises complete political control—a neutral zone. Frontiers were utilized so that two countries would be less likely to have a direct conflict. Frontiers remain only in Antarctica and the Arabian Peninsula. Today, frontiers have been replaced by *boundaries* which are precise linear divisions that separate countries. Boundaries are divided between *physical* and *cultural*.

Physical Boundaries (280): *Physical boundaries* exist where natural features of the Earth serve as borders between two regions.

Mountain Boundaries (280): *Mountain* borders can be effective borders if they are difficult to cross. The Andes and the Himalayas both serve as international boundaries.

Desert Boundaries (280): *Deserts* can also serve to separate states. Like mountains, deserts are difficult and troublesome to cross. The Sahara in northern Africa is a desert boundary.

Water Boundaries (280-281): *Water*—rivers, lakes, and oceans—serves as the most common physical boundaries. Unfortunately, water boundaries change over time. Rivers can meander and change locations. Oceanic boundaries are difficult because perceptions differ as to the extent of possession of water beyond a country's coast. The law of the sea gives countries twelve nautical miles of ocean as their exclusive territory. Countries separated by less than 400 miles of sea must negotiate boundaries for exclusive fishing rights.

Cultural Boundaries (281): *Cultural boundaries* exist where there are differences such as language and religion.

Geometric Boundaries (281): Sometimes, these boundaries are drawn according to *geometric* configurations. For example, the U.S.-Canadian border has a large straight segment 1,300 miles long which runs on the 49 degree North parallel. This line was drawn by compromise. Straight lines are also common in Africa where the European colonial powers carved up the continent.

Religious Boundaries (281-282): Differences in *religion* are used to determine boundary locations. Northern Ireland and South Asia are good examples of this type of division where Catholics were disconnected from Protestants and Hindus were isolated from Muslims.

Language Boundaries (282): After World War I, *language* was the main criterion used to designate new countries in post-war Europe. These changes lasted, for the most part, until the 1990's when ethnic conflicts devastated the geographical boundaries of Eastern Europe.

Key Issue 3: Why Do Boundaries Between States Cause Problems? (282):

A nation-state exists when the boundaries of a state match the boundaries of the territory inhabited by an ethnic group. Problems exist when the boundaries do not match. There are two problems: either one states contains more than one ethnic group, or one ethnic group is divided among more than one state.

One State with Many Nationalities (282-283): A *multinational state* contains two or more nationalities with traditions of self determination.

Cyprus: Unfriendly Division of an Island (283): Cyprus is the third largest island in the Mediterranean; it is divided between Turkish and Greek residents. In 1974 a move by the Greek majority to unify with Greece brought an invasion by the Turks to protect the Turkish minority. The resulting compromise has divided the island into two parts, one for the Turks and the other for the Greeks. A buffer zone patrolled by UN soldiers assures there is little contact between the two groups.

Former Soviet Union: The Largest Multinational State (283-284): (Refer to Figure 8-14) The early 1990s has been witness to the former Soviet Union's break up. The 15 republics are now independent countries--3 Baltic, 3 European, 5 Central Asian, 3 Caucasus, and Russia.

New Baltic Nation-States (284): The Baltic states of Estonia, Latvia, and Lithuania became independent from Russia because of their historical roots and the fact their culture is different from that of Russians

New European Nation-States (284-285): Belarus, Moldova, and Ukraine are nation-states, each dominated by their respective nationalities of people. Belarusians, Ukrainians, and Russians speak similar East Slavic languages and are predominantly Eastern Orthodox Christians. Belarusians and Ukrainians have been separated from Russia for 500 years of their history due to foreign domination. The Crimean Peninsula, a strategically important location, is part of Ukraine and is populated largely by Russians. When part of the Soviet Union, Russians in the Crimea were comfortable being in the Ukraine, though when Russia and the Ukraine separated, Crimean Russians voted to be independent. Tatars from Central Asia living in the Crimea prefer Ukrainian rule because of suspicion of the Russians. Moldovians are ethnically indistinguishable from Romanians and was part of Romania until the Soviet Union takeover in 1940. Moldovians pushed for reunification with Romania, though Ukrainians and Russians living in Moldova because of the Soviet era boundaries are opposed to reunification.

New Central Asian States (285): There are five states in Central Asia: Kazakhstan, Kyrgyzstan, Tajikistan, Turkmenistan, and Uzbekistan. Turkmenistan and Uzbekistan are dominated by their respective ethic groups. They speak an

Altaic language and are Muslims, as well as do the Kyrgyz and the Kazakhs. Russians are a minority in both countries, while the remaining Uzbeks and Turkmen are spread amongst the other Central Asian states and Russia. Kyrgyzstan is 52 percent Kyrgyz with strong Russian and Uzbek populations. The Kyrgyz resent Russians taking over the best farmland during colonization in the early twentieth century. Kazakhstan is ethnically split between Kazakhs and Russians. Though mostly peaceful, tensions exist which are suppressed because of a depressed economy. Tajikistan is also dominated by Tajiks, though there is a civil war amongst the Tajik people, Muslims speaking an Indic language of the Indo-Iranian branch of Indo-European. The war is between former Communists and Muslim fundamentalists allied with Western-oriented intellectuals.

Russia: Now the Largest Multinational State (285-286): Russia officially recognizes 39 nationalities. There are two principal clusters of Russia's minorities with minor clusters between the Volga River and the Ural Mountains. Independence movements flourish as Russia is less and less willing to suppress these movements. The Chechnyans began fighting a war of independence with the Russians in 1994 after the Russian Army was sent to placate the Chechnyans.

Russians in Other States (286-287): Russians living in countries that were former republics in the Soviet Union are now the minority and have found they are now subject to discrimination. Russia cannot afford to rehouse them, so they have stayed. Other nationalities fear the Russians have been left because the Russians are trying to reassert dominance.

Turmoil in the Caucasus (287-288): The Caucasus region lies between the Black and Caspian seas and is named after the nearby mountains. Three nationalities dominate the area, Azeris, Armenians, and Georgians, and there are other important nationalities—Abkhazians, Chechens, Ingush, Ossetians, Kurds, and Russians. Each nationality would like to create a sovereign nation-state, and none have fully achieved it.

Azeris (288): The Azeris are a group living in this mountainous area. A treaty in 1828 gave half of their territory to Persia and half to Russia. Now twelve million people are split between Iran and the newly formed country of Azerbaijan where Azeris are the dominant nationality. It is a fragmented state with Nakhichevan being located in Armenia.

Armenians (288): Armenians are an ethnic group who populate much of the Caucasus. They were forced to emigrate from Russia and Turkey. The Turks killed hundred of thousands of Armenians during the late 19th and early 20th centuries. Armenia is dominated by Armenians and is the most ethnically homogeneous country in the region. Armenia became an independent country in 1991, and has since been waging a border dispute with Azerbaijan. It is also a fragmented country with Nagorno-Karabakh located inside Azerbaijan.

Georgians (288): Georgia is another new country to rise from the former USSR. Georgians comprise 69 percent of the total population; ethnic diversity has been a source of unrest.

One Nationality in More Than One State (288):

The Kurds (288-289): The *Kurds* are Sunni Muslims who speak an Iranian language of the Indo-Iranian branch of the Indo-European language family. They once lived in Kurdistan but are now divided among several states—mostly Turkey, Iran, and Iraq but also Armenia, Azerbaijan, and Syria. Although the European allies made a state for Kurds following their World War I victory, it was taken over by Turkey soon after. Ever since, Kurds have been suppressed by the Turks. The Kurds have waged a guerrilla war against Turkey since 1984. Kurds have also fared poorly in Iran and Iraq and were unsuccessful in a rebellion in 1991 against Iraq.

Pan-Arab Nation State (289): Arabic is the predominant language and Islam the predominant religion from northern Africa to southwestern Asia. The countries in the region are the result of many colonial powers. Israel is the most prominent exception to the relative homogeneity of the region. Some pan-Arab supporters believe the divisions are superficial and have created a disparity in the distribution of wealth. The *Organization of Petroleum Exporting Countries (OPEC)* was created to control pricing and production of petroleum. The Iran-Iraq war (started in 1980) hurt unity in the area as well as did Iraq's invasion of Kuwait in 1990. The United Nations, led by the United States, launched Desert Storm to expel Iraq from Kuwait. Iraq was defeated but Saddam Hussein remained in power.

Governing Multinational States (Internal Organization of States) (289): States
have restructured their governments to transfer authority from the national government to local governments to appease the demands of local ethnicities.

Unitary and Federal States (289-290): A *unitary state* places power into the hands of a central government. Unitary governments are more common in smaller countries which have few internal differences. Sometimes multinational states use unitary systems where many ethnic groups exist so that one culture may be imposed upon the others. *Federal states* allocate substantial power to smaller units of government within the nation-state. Boundaries can be drawn to correspond with regions inhabited by different ethnicities. The federal system is more accommodating for large states. Most of the world's largest states are federal, including the U.S., Canada, Russia, and Brazil.

Trend Toward Federal Government (290): The recent trend is to decentralize government and establish federal governments.

France: Curbing a Unitary Government (290): France granted more power to its more local departments and communes, allowing them to be responsible for their own internal affairs.

Poland: A New Federal Government (290): Poland has switched to a federalized system of government because the former unitarian regime let buildings, roads, and water systems greatly deteriorate. Poland is now divided into 2,400 municipalities; each is given the option of running various parts of their government or allowing the federal government to do so. Many former government employees were rejected from jobs because of their affiliation with the old communist regime.

Key Issue 4: Why Do States Cooperate With Each Other? (290-291): States suffer from the trend toward local diversity with ethnicities demanding self-determination. Globalization threatens states as they cooperate in regional and worldwide authorities.

Political and Military Cooperation (291): Regional and international organizations have been established to prevent a third world war and to protect countries from invasion.

    The United Nations (291): The largest international organization is the *United Nations* which has grown from 49 states in 1945 to 185 in the early 1990's. Many members were added in 1955 from countries liberated from Nazi Germany, in 1960 from newly independent African countries, and in 1990 from newly emancipated countries from the former USSR. The United Nations has performed many peace-keeping missions in the last few years. The UN has been used to perform this function in the Middle East, Bosnia-Herzegovina, and Somalia during the 1990's.

    Regional Military Alliances (292): Many states joined regional military alliances after World War II.

    Era of Two Superpowers (292-294): During the Napoleonic Wars of the early 1800's, there were eight dominant powers in the world. The same number existed by the outbreak of World War I. When there were so many powerful nations no single state could dominate creating a *balance of power*—a condition of roughly equal strength between opposing alliances. By the end of World War II, the U.S. and Soviet Union were more powerful than all other nations on Earth and became *superpowers*. When allies threatened to tip the scales of power in favor of the other superpower, military intervention often ensued. For example, the Soviet Union sent troops into Czechoslovakia in 1968 and Afghanistan in 1979 to install Soviet-friendly governments. The U.S. has also deployed troops to the Dominican Republic in 1965 and to Panama in 1989 to ensure their governments would remain U.S. allies. Both countries also installed military bases in strategic points around the globe.

    Military Cooperation in Europe (294-295): The *North Atlantic Treaty Organization (NATO)* was formed to create a cohesive military block headed by the U.S., Canada, and 14 democratic European states. The *Warsaw Pact* allied Eastern European countries together to combat any possible invasion. They were designed to balance power in Europe. With a change in the political environment, NATO expanded to include former Warsaw Pact countries. The *Conference on Security and Cooperation in Europe (CSCE)* was founded in 1975 as a forum for all countries interested in ending conflicts in Europe, especially in the Balkans and Caucasus.

    Other Regional Organizations (295): Western Hemisphere countries convene in the *Organization of American States (OAS)*. The OAS promotes social, cultural, political, and economic ties between member countries. In Africa the *Organization for African Unity (OAU)* performs a similar function. Former British colonies are organized into the Commonwealth of Nations. The *Nonaligned Movement* includes nearly every country in Africa and the Middle East.

Economic Cooperation (296): The Soviet Union was disbanded in 1992 ending the era of the superpowers and returning the pattern of the balance of power back to something like

European Union (296): European states have increasingly relied on economic cooperation and have established the *European Union*. This is a common market that increases intraregional trade between member countries by using tariff reduction policies to increase trade in the region. The European Union has also worked to increase living standards in poorer areas such as southern Italy. The European Union has removed most barriers to free trade which has turned Western Europe into the world's wealthiest market.

Former Communist Countries and the European Union (296): Former Warsaw Pact states organized into the *Council for Mutual Economic Assistance (COMECON)* which has since disbanded since the fall of Communism, many of its member countries desire to join the European Union. However, current member countries are hesitant to allow this because the addition of so many poorer countries would likely drain some money from the richer, established countries of the European Union.

German Domination in Western Europe (296-298): The most dominant country in Western Europe is Germany. Even after its defeat in World War II, Germany has emerged as the most populous country with the strongest economy in the European Union. Many of its neighbors worry about Germany's strength, and when history is observed they may have need to be wary.

Summary: A state is a political unit encompassing all peoples within its borders, whereas a nation is a group of people identified by cultural rather than political characteristics who well may reside in part or all of one state or more than one state. Boundaries are drawn because of physical and cultural influences and affect the shape of states and their viability in the global economy. In some parts of the world, such as Western Europe, boundaries have become less important because of economic maturity, while in other places boundaries cause conflict because they divide nationalities. A countries ability to remain healthy and strong and grant power to ethnic and national groups depends on the type of government—either a unitary or federal government. Globalization trends in political geography means countries have transferred power to regional and international authorities or cooperative efforts. Political, military, and economic based regional and international governments are changing the way states deal with each other.

CHAPTER 8
KEY TERMS AND CONCEPTS

Political Globalization: The transference of military, economic, and political power to a regional authority. The European Union is an example of a regional economic authority.

Political Local Diversity: Increases in the number of groups competing for more political control over the states which they populate.

State: An area organized into a political unit and ruled by an established government with control over its internal and foreign affairs. The U.S. as a whole is a state.

Sovereignty: Ability of a state to govern its territory free from control of its internal affairs by other states. When the U.S. broke from Great Britain, it attained sovereignty.

Microstates: States with very small land area. Most are islands.

City-state: A sovereign state that comprises a town and surrounding countryside. San Marino and the Vatican are modern versions of this.

Colony: A territory that is legally tied to a sovereign state rather than completely independent. The U.S. was founded by thirteen original British colonies.

Colonialism: Attempt by one country to establish settlements and to impose its political, economic, and cultural principles in another territory. Great Britain was the largest colonial power in the last three centuries.

Imperialism: Another country's control of territory already occupied and organized by an indigenous society.

Boundary: Invisible line that marks the extent of territory. They are the result of physical and cultural influences.

Compact State: A state in which the distance from the center to any boundary does not vary significantly. Nearly circular shaped states are compact states.

Prorupted State: An otherwise compact state with a large projecting extension. The extension serves either to give access to a geographic feature or to act as a geographical barrier to other states.

Elongated state: A state with a long, narrow shape. Communication and transportation are often difficult.

Fragmented State: A state that includes several discontinuous pieces of territory. The U.S. is such a state because of outlying Alaska and Hawaii.

Perforated State: A state that completely surrounds another one. South Africa completely surrounds Lesotho, making South Africa a perforated state.

Landlocked State: A state which has no outlet to an ocean or a sea. In South America, Paraguay and Bolivia are both landlocked.

Frontier: A zone separating two states in which neither state exercises political control. In the past, such zones were prominent but in today's world they are very rare.

Physical Boundaries: Boundaries between states which exist where natural features of the Earth serve as borders between two regions. Mountains, deserts, and bodies of water are all physical boundaries.

Cultural Boundaries: Boundaries between states which exist where there are cultural differences between people such as language and religion.

Geometric Boundaries: Boundaries drawn according to geometric configurations. The U.S.—Canadian border follows the 49 degree north parallel. Africa was divided amongst European colonial powers using straight lines.

Multinational state: A state that contains more than one nationality. The U.S. is a multinational state.

Organization of Petroleum Exporting Countries (OPEC): A regional organization created to control pricing and production of petroleum.

Unitary State: An internal organization of a state that places most power in the hands of central government officials. The former Soviet Union had this form of government.

Federal State: An internal organization of a state that allocates most powers to units of local government. The U.S. does this in the political sub-units of states, counties, and further sub-divisions.

United Nations: Largest international organization in the world.

Balance of Power: Condition of roughly equal strength between opposing countries or alliances of countries. Today, the U.S. tips any alliance because it is a superpower, far more powerful than any other country on Earth.

Superpowers: The U.S. and Soviet Union were the strongest military and economic powers in the world.

North Atlantic Treaty Organization (NATO): Was formed to create a strong, cohesive military organization between the U.S., Canada, and democratic European states.

Warsaw Pact: Eastern European military oriented regional organization. Most former Warsaw Pact countries have been incorporated into NATO.

Conference on Security and Cooperation in Europe (CSCE): founded in 1975 as a forum for people interested in ending conflicts in Europe, especially in the Balkans and Caucasus.

Organization f American States (OAS): Western Hemisphere regional forum to promote social, cultural, political, and economic ties between member countries.

Organization for African Unity (OAU): Similar to the OAS, though is an African regional organization.

Nonaligned Movement: Africa and Middle Eastern countries have organized into the nonaligned movement.

European Union: Agreement between European countries to increase their collective economic strength and become a cohesive world market.

Council for Mutual Economic Assistance (COMECON): An organization which has dissolved since the fall of Communism. An economically based organization, most of whose members have joined or would like to join the European Union.

CHAPTER 8
PROGRESSIVE REVIEW

1. An area organized into a political unit is called a _____.   state

2. The state in the world with the most _____ is Russia,   area
while China has the largest _____.   population

3. The term *state* is generally used the same as the term
_____.   *country*

4. Political globalization is a trend in which some authority is   regional,
transferred to a _____ and/or _____ authority.   international

5. Individual cultural groups are pressuring governments for
more political power; this trend is called _____ _____.   local diversity

6. Independence from control by another state to control
internal and foreign affairs is _____.   sovereignty

7. _____ was a Japanese colony until it was divided into two   Korea
parts following World War II. The boundary between is a
cultural boundary and is called, in particular, a _____   geometric
boundary.

8. The continent of _____ is territory does not have a   Antarctica
permanent settlement and is not part of a _____ state.   sovereign

9. The nationalists lost a civil war in _____ and left to   China
establish a government of the island of _____.   Taiwan

10. States with a very small land area are called _____ and   microstates
states of this type are mostly islands.

11. The ancient _____ Empire lasted from about 3000 BC   Egyptian
until the fourth century BC, when it was annexed by the
Romans.

12. Great Britain established _____ in many parts of the   colonies
world which added to its _____ base.   economic

13. A *colony* is territory that is tied to a sovereign state and
was previously sparsely or uninhabited while _____ is the   imperialism
control of a terry already occupied and organized by an
indigenous society.

14. The most populous remaining colony in the world was
_____ _____, which reverted to _____ control in 1997, so
now _____ _____ is now the most populous colony. .

Hong Kong,
Chinese
Puerto Rico

15. Most colonial powers were from the continent of _____.

Europe

16. The shape of a state contributes to its _____ and _____
and _____ strengths.

identity
military, economic

17. Territory is limited in extent by _____.

boundaries

18. Due to its shape, Chile is an _____ state.

elongated

19. States which have discontinuous territory are _____
states.

fragmented

20. Lesotho is a _____ state, surrounded by the country of
_____ _____, which is a _____ state

landlocked
South Africa,
perforated

21. The most efficient shape for a state is to be _____ as are
Hungary, Poland, and some island states.

compact

22. _____ states have an area projecting to reach a
resource, such as water for transportation.

Prorupted

23. Zones between states in which no state exercises
complete control are known as _____.

frontiers

24. Three physical elements that act as boundaries are
_____, _____ and _____.

mountain, deserts
water

25. A _____ boundary separates Chile from Argentina in
South America.

mountain

26. After colonial rule ended in most of its countries (shortly
after World War II) _____ was divided by geometric lines with
little attention to cultural boundaries.

Africa

27. _____ _____ is an example of state boundaries drawn
along religious boundaries.

Northern Ireland
or South Asia

28. Three main cultural boundaries are _____, _____, and
_____.

geometric,
religious,
language

29. _____ states contain more than one nationality.
Multinational

30. _____, an island in the Mediterranean Sea, is divided between Greek and _____ nationalities.
Cyprus
Turkish

31. _____, _____, and _____ are new states situated on the shores of the Baltic Sea and were part of the former Soviet Union.
Estonia, Latvia, Lithuania

32. There are _____ states which have been formed from the republics of the former Soviet Union
15

33. The three main regions of new states in the post-Soviet era are _____, _____, and _____ _____.
Baltic, Europe, Central Asia

34. The _____ region is one of the most volatile because of the many ethnic groups and nationalities, and is comprised of three states: _____, _____, and _____.
Caucasus Azerbaijan, Armenia, and Georgia

35. _____ are divided between many states including Turkey, Iran, Iraq, Armenia, Azerbaijan, and Syria.
Kurds

36. _____ states allocate political power to local units of government within a country.
Federal

37. The country of Poland has switched from a _____ form of government to a _____ government since the decline of communism.
unitary federal

38. Equal strength among opposing allies is called a _____ _____ _____.
balance of power

39. The country of _____ has come to dominate the other countries of Western Europe in economic and political power.
Germany

40. _____ _____ include NATO, the Warsaw Pact, OPEC, and the OAU.
Regional governments (organizations)

41. The largest international organization is the _____ _____.
United Nations

42. Most regional governments now have an _____ focus.
economic

CHAPTER 9

DEVELOPMENT

Chapter Nine gives an overview of development and how it has been achieved in different parts of the world. In most of the world's homes, people live without many of the comforts taken for granted in the Western world. People in many places on Earth live without good streets, water systems, education, or health care. Economic, social, and demographic traits mark a country's level of development. In MDCs people tend to have a higher per capita income because they are more apt to work in a more balanced economy in which job yields are higher than in a very restricted economy. Because of higher levels of wealth, people in MDCs can purchase more goods which, in turn, can support more people financially. The populations of MDCs tend to have better health, higher levels of education, more forms of communication, and better infrastructures than countries labeled LDCs. The standard-of-living gap between poorer countries (LDCs) and richer countries (MDCs) continues to grow larger. In an effort to increase their living standards, LDC governments attempt to embrace the concept of economic development. The LDCs have both the highest population growth rates and the highest growth rates in per capita energy consumption.

Development: The world is divided into relatively wealthy and poor regions. The 200 countries in the world have different levels of development. *Development* is the process of improving the material conditions of people through diffusion of knowledge and technology. It is a continuous process. States which have progressed further along the continuum of development are *more developed countries (MDCs)*, also known as *relatively developed* or *developed*. Countries in an early stage of development are *less developed countries (LDCs)*, or *developing countries*. Geographers look at where development occurs and why some regions are more developed than others. *Globalization* of the economy makes for a challenging atmosphere for many countries. Countries rely on their *local diversity* with their own particular skills and resources.

Key Issue 1: Where Are More and Less Developed Countries Distributed?
(305-307): In general, the 30 degree north parallel divides many MDCs to the north from LDCs found to the south; it is known as the *north-south split*. Created by the United Nations, the *human development index (HDI)* is a formula used to indicate the relative level of development based on economic (gross domestic product per capita), social (literacy rate, amount of education), and demographic (life expectancy) indicators. In 1997, Canada ranked first, though Japan, the U.S., and many European countries rank toward the top. Sierra Leone was ranked last and

the 19 lowest-ranking countries were in sub-Saharan Africa. There are nine regions of development (Figure 9-2). Anglo America (U.S. and Canada), Latin America, Western Europe, Eastern Europe, East Asia, South Asia, Southeast Asia, Southwest Asia (combined with North Africa makes up the Middle East), and sub-Saharan Africa. Other important areas are Japan and the South Pacific (primarily Australia and New Zealand).

More Developed Regions (307): Five major areas are considered more developed.

Anglo America (307): HDI = 0.95 Anglo America has less diverse language and religious patterns than elsewhere in the world—95 percent use English as their first language and about 95 percent are Christian. Cultural diversity creates tensions in some areas. The area is rich with minerals and natural resources. The region is the leading consumer market. Globalization pressures have been overcome by being the leading provider of computing, information, and high-tech services as well as many elements of popular culture. Anglo America is the world's most important food exporter and is, paradoxically, home to the world's largest area of unused farm land.

Western Europe (307-308): HDI = 0.93 Most Western Europeans speak an Indo-European language and are Christian. Language and religious diversity is an historical source of conflict. After two world wars, Europe has politically, militarily, economically, and culturally unified. Hindu and Muslim immigrants contribute to local diversity and are responsible for population growth. Western Europe's core area of western Germany, southern Scandinavia, southeastern United Kingdom, Luxembourg, northeastern France, northern Italy, Switzerland, Belgium, and the Netherlands have high development levels while the peripheral areas have comparatively lower standards of living. Western Europeans are trade high-value goods and services in exchange for raw materials. The European Union could make it the largest and richest market.

Eastern Europe (308, 310): HDI = 0.78 Since 1990, this region's HDI is the only one to have decreased. The declining HDI is a residual effect of Communism which divided Eastern Europe from Western Europe. Eastern Europe was controlled for forty-five years following World War II by Soviet-influenced centralized planning. Soviet planners emphasized heavy industry, a spatially dispersed industrial base, and factories located near raw material sources rather than near potential markets. Strong government control of development has made the transition to market economies difficult. The Soviet Union, Czechoslovakia, and Yugoslavia broke up and now have problems because of ethnic conflict, differing economic abilities and strengths, and lack of supporting infrastructure. The region is classified as an MDC; the HDI is low though the region can likely regain economic strength.

Japan (310): HDI = 0.94 Japan has a different cultural tradition than Europe and Anglo America. Japan has intensively farmed land and a high physiological density. They import food and raw materials. They grew through relying on human labor and selling high-quality and high-value products on the market for lower prices.

They created a highly educated and skilled labor force, spending a great deal on research and development.

South Pacific (307): HDI = 0.93 The South Pacific is located on the periphery and has a low population. New Zealand is less well developed and Australia and New Zealand share a cultural heritage with Europe and Anglo America. They export food and resources and the region's economy is tied to Japan and Asian countries.

Less Developed Regions (311): Six regions are less developed.

Latin America (311): HDI = 0.80 Most Latin Americans speak Spanish or Portuguese and are Roman Catholics. Brazil was a colony of Portugal and the rest colonies of Spain. Proportionately more people live in cities, some of which are the largest in the world. People are concentrated along the Atlantic coast and sparse in much of the interior area. Development is high along the South Atlantic coast with high agricultural productivity, exporting wheat and corn. Latin America, interior South America, and the Caribbean islands are less well developed. Unequal income distribution hinders development and many people rely on cash crops grown on large plantations rather than redistributing the land to grow food on.

Southeast Asia (311-312): HDI = 0.67 Indonesia is the most populous country and has 13,667 islands. Java, with the world's highest arithmetic population density, has two-thirds of the population. Warfare and colonialism has weakened the area. The tropical climate limits agriculture because of poor soils and limiting factors of the climate. The physical geography of the area also limits development. Medicine and technology has increased the population. Rice is exported by some countries and imported by others. Many manufacturing products are produced—palm oil, copra, rubber, kapok, and abaca as well as tin and some petroleum. Manufacturing has grown in Thailand, Singapore, Malaysia, and the Philippines. Cheap labor encourages textile manufacturing. The HDI is likely to decline because of economic instability in the 1990s.

Middle East (312-313): HDI = 0.66Most of the Middle East is a desert and most products must be imported. Large oil reserves makes it economically possible with a trade surplus. Petroleum sales makes economic development investments possible. The oil reserves are concentrated in states along the Persian Gulf while others lack reserves. Income disparities causes tensions. Development is limited by or comes into conflict with the region's dominant religion—Islam. Cultural disputes, especially religious disputes, hinders development of the region. Israel, the only Jewish state, suffers from having to maintain military strength rather than investing in development.

East Asia (313): HDI = 0.63 China is the largest country in East Asia and is among the world's poorest countries. The large population may make it a dominant market, though the U.S. will still dominate on a per capita basis. Agriculture is frequently adversely affected and much of the food a farmer produces must pay rent. In 1949 Communists came into power and Nationalist leaders fled to Taiwan. The Communist government seized mot agricultural land and redistributed work and food to each family, selling surplus food to urban dwellers. Strict agricultural control has been loosened and farmers now have a personal incentive to produce food.

The Chinese government controls its citizens' daily lives, though the Chinese people are in a better position than they were before the revolution. Threat of famine has been reduced. China has reduced its natural increase rate so the standard of living can now increase.

South Asia (313): HDI = 0.44 South Asia has the second-highest population and the second-lowest per capita income and includes India, Pakistan, Bangladesh, Sri Lanka, Nepal, and Bhutan. South Asia produces cash crops and exports uranium, bauxite, coal, manganese, iron ore, and chromite. India is a leading producer of rice and wheat, though the regions agricultural productivity depends on climate. It has seasonal monsoons.

Sub-Saharan Africa (314): HDI = 0.35 Sub-Saharan Africa has a low population density and developable resources spread throughout—bauxite, cobalt, copper, iron ore, manganese, petroleum, and uranium. The region has the highest percentage of people living in poverty and suffering from poor health and low education levels. During the colonial era many resources were shipped out of the area. Landlocked areas have difficulty transporting raw materials. Political problems are the result of the many ethnicities. Poor infrastructures, poor leadership, and wide-spread corruption do not increase its chances for economic development. Few countries have a plan for a national economy and a plan for development. The land can not support the growing populations. The tropical and dry climates coupled with intensive agriculture has reduced agricultural output.

Key Issue 2: Why Does Development Vary Among Countries?

Economic Indicators of Development (315):

Gross Domestic Product Per Capita (315-316): The *gross domestic product (GDP)* of a country is the value of its total output of goods and services in a given year. By dividing this value by the population of a country, the *per capita gross domestic product* may be found. In most LDCs the per capita GDP is less than $1,000 per year, while the MDC average is $20,000 annually. The gap in per capita GDP between MDCs and LDCs is expanding. Although per capita GDP is the mean income for a state's population, it can be misleading if the disparity of income within a country is great.

Types of Jobs (316-317): Economies are generally divided into three segments–Primary, Secondary, and Tertiary. *1-Primary sector* includes the harvest of raw materials such as mining, agriculture, fishing, and forestry. *2-Secondary sector* includes manufacturing of raw materials into goods. *3-Tertiary sector* includes the providing of goods and services directly to consumers. In most LDCs agriculture dominates; food consumption is of paramount importance. In more developed countries, agriculture is more efficient so effort can turn to the other two sectors.

Productivity (317): *Productivity* is the value of a particular product compared to the amount of labor needed to make it. *Value added* is the gross value of a product after manufacturing minus the costs of raw materials and energy. Both productivity and value added are much greater in MDCs than in LDCs.

Raw Materials (317): Raw materials are essential to the economic development of a country. Minerals and trees which can be altered with energy from coal, petroleum, uranium, and natural gas help to give an economy a strong base with which to work. European countries ran short of many of these materials, so they sought them by colonizing other places in the world. The U.S. and former Soviet Union evolved into powerful nations in part because they possessed many important resources. Some countries, such as Switzerland and Japan, are very advanced owing to their mastery of international trade.

Consumer Goods (317-318): Some wealth generated by MDCs is used to acquire *essential goods* and services (food, clothing, and shelter) and the remainder for *non-essential goods* and services (cars, telephones, and entertainment). By expanding the number of non-essential goods traded, a country may establish a new niche industry that will compliment and strengthen the existing economy. Non-essential goods are much more prevalent in MDCs than in LDCs. Because of the MDCs higher exposure to urban lifestyles, their members often develop cultural identities which are integrally linked with non-essential goods and services such as telephones, computers, and cars.

Social Indicators of Development (318-319): MDCs invest resources in
education, hospitals, and welfare services.

Education and Literacy (319-320): MDCs tend to have significantly higher levels of education than LDCs. In MDCs students attend school longer, have better access to instructors, and include a higher percentage of females. The *literacy rate* is the percentage of the country's people who can read and write. Literacy rates exceed 95 percent in MDCs but are less than one-third in many LDCs. In LDCs women receive much less education than the men. Education is the key to better jobs and a higher social status in many LDCs.

Health and Welfare (320, 322): Because MDCs can afford more and better health treatments, MDC populations are healthier than populations of LDCs. In many MDCs financial support is given to the sick, elderly, orphaned, and to veterans. However, due to declining economic growth, MDCs are having to cut the amount of available public assistance.

Demographic Indicators of Development (322): The most

Life Expectancy (322): The *life expectancy at birth* is the average number of years a newborn infant can expect to live at current mortality levels. Males are expected to live 9 years longer in MDCs and women to live 13 years longer than in LDCs. The *dependency ratio* is the percentage of young and old people in the population and it is much lower in MDCs.

Infant Mortality Rate (322-323): The *infant mortality rate* is the number of babies who die during their first year of life per 1,000 born. In MDCs this figure is less than 10 per 1,000, but in many developing countries this figure approaches 100 per 1,000 infants born.

Natural Increase Rate (323): The *natural increase rate* is the rate at which a population is growing. Natural increase rates are often higher than two percent in less developed countries, but are ordinarily less than one percent in more developed countries. High rates of natural increase hinder a country from faster per capita economic development.

Crude Birth Rate (323): The *crude birth rate* is total number of live births in a year for every 1,000 people alive in society. Birth rates high enough to induce higher rates of natural increase are more common in LDCs because there is usually more pressure placed on women to have many children and birth control is not as readily available. High birth rates in LDCs contribute to a much younger population than in MDCs.

Key Issue 2: Why Do Less Developed Countries Face Obstacles to Development? (323): LDCs must develop more rapidly which means increasing per capita GDP. LDCs face two problems—adopting development policies and funding development.

Development Through Self-Sufficiency (323-324): Self-sufficient development means balanced growth.

Elements of Self-Sufficiency Approach (324): The *self-sufficiency model* for developing economies suggests a country should spread investment throughout all sectors of its economy, rather than concentrate on sectors perceived to be advantageous. The goal is to achieve a balanced growth in the economy, equalizing growth in urban and rural incomes. Fragile businesses are helped to get established. States that promote a self-sufficiency type of economic policy want to decrease the ability and influence of foreign firms in their countries. Barriers to importing goods are set up and include high taxes on imported goods to protect domestically produced product pricing, establishing quotas to limit import goods, and requiring licenses to restrict the number of legal importers while at the same time limiting export to other countries.

India: Example of the Self-Sufficiency Approach (324): India used many trade barriers—licenses, quotas, and heavy import taxes (*tariffs*). Exports were limited and currency could not be exchanged. Businesses were required to produce domestically needed goods and any modernization, modification, or new products had to be approved. Unsuccessful businesses received government subsidies. The government controlled communication, transportation, energy, and service and high-tech businesses like insurance agencies and automakers.

Problems with the Self-Sufficiency Alternative (324): Due to high costs of goods produced under this policy, self-sufficiency models are becoming less popular as countries reduce tariffs and encourage international trade.

Inefficiency (324): *Inefficiencies* were caused by state firms not having to compete with other firms. The government protects inefficient businesses. Technological advances are ignored because of the lack of competition.

Large Bureaucracy (324): *Costly bureaucracies* are often corrupted and abused by businesses. Entrepreneurs were discouraging so many turned to consulting rather than developing their own ideas.

Development Through International Trade (324): The *international trade model* of development encourages countries to identify and develop their unique assets. Investment in local industries and sale of goods produced provides the initial capital for further development.

  Rostow's Development Model (324-325): *W. W. Rostow*, in the 1950s, developed a five-stage model of economic growth and is a continuum of economic development—traditional society, preconditions for take-off, take-off, drive to maturity, and the age of mass consumption. The steps numbered one (almost void of consumer goods) to five (widely produced consumer goods). MDCs are in stages 4 and/or 5. Countries most exposed to international trade benefit most from the experience by adjusting their economies.

  Examples of International Trade Approach (325): Countries on the Arabian Peninsula along the Persian Gulf and in East and Southeast Asia tried the international trade approach to development.

  Petroleum-Rich Persian Gulf States (325): The petroleum-rich countries of the Persian Gulf have successfully adopted the practices of international trade. The funds received from exporting oil are used to finance economic, communication, housing, highway and school infrastructures. Large amounts of consumer goods from foreign sources are readily available. Islam has been an obstacle to Western business practices, especially restricting women's rights.

  The Four Asian Dragons (325-326): South Korea, Taiwan, Singapore, and Hong Kong are nations successful in adjusting to the international trade environment. They developed manufactured goods industries—clothing and electronics. Their successes have helped them earn the nickname *"The Four Asian Tigers/Dragons."*

  Problems with the International Trade Alternative (326): Even though many states have increased their GDPs by implementing policies encouraging international trade, uneven distribution of resources and frequent market stagnation have blocked continued growth of markets. There are four problems facing LDCs outside the Persian Gulf and the four Asian dragons—uneven resource distribution, market stagnation, and increased dependence on MDCs.

  Recent Triumph of the International Trade Approach (326): Even with the problems of the international trade alternative, it is the preferred method for stimulating development. In the past 25 years, world wealth has doubled and world trade has tripled. India dismantled its self-sufficiency policies and its monopolies on many businesses and services. The competition has increased India's GDP.

Financing Development (326): Many LDCs must rely on MDCs to finance development.

  Loans (326-327): LDCs improve their infrastructure through loans. MDC regional and international organizations (World Bank and International Monetary Fund) provide a method for LDCs to obtain loans. The cumulative LDC debt was $2.1 trillion in 1996 and has ground about $1 trillion every ten years. Many infrastructure projects fail. When LDCs acquire aid through loans, they are often unable to repay the entire principle and the interest on the loan. The populations of

LDCs make up the majority of Earth's population, and they angrily ask for and expect economic equality through funding from MDCs.

Transnational Corporations (327-328): A _transnational corporation_ operates in countries other than the one in which its headquarters are located. They are mostly MDC based—U.S., Japan, Germany, France, and the United Kingdom. International investment has been rapidly increasing though it is unevenly spread around the world. Nearly 65 percent of international investment is from one MDC to another. Eight LDCs received nearly all international investment—China (one-third); South Korea, Malaysia, and Indonesia (one-third) and Thailand, Argentina, Mexico, and Brazil (one-third).

Summary: Development is measured by the attainment of material goods by a state, as reflected by demographic information on education, health, income, and age. In recent years many poor countries in the world very high population growth rates, but their economies have not kept-pace. Poorer countries' main channel toward development lies through borrowing money from MDCs to finance infrastructure improvements. Non-payment on loans has caused considerable tension between MDCs and LDCs.

CHAPTER 9
KEY TERMS AND CONCEPTS

Development: A process of improvement in the material conditions of people through diffusion and application of knowledge and technology. Countries in latter stages of development have more material goods and services than do those in earlier stages.

More Developed Country (Relatively Developed Country, Developed Country, MDC): A country that has progressed along a continuum of economic development. Five regions are more developed—Anglo-America, Western Europe, Eastern Europe, Japan, and South Pacific.

Less Developed Country (Developing Country, LDC): A country that is at a relatively early stage in the process of economic development. LDC regions include Latin America, Southeast Asia, Middle East, East Asia, South Asia, and Sub-Saharan Africa.

North-South Split: The division of the earth at the 30 degree north parallel separating most MDCs (to the north) and LDCs (to the south).

Human Development Index (HDI): A rating system between 0 and 1 which appraises the countries of the world based upon their living standards. Created by the UN to give a relative idea of a country's level of development. Japan had the highest ranking in 1993 and Canada in 1997.

Gross Domestic Product (GDP): The value of the total output of goods and services produced in a country in a given time period, normally one year. MDCs have high GDPs while LDCs have low GDPs.

Per Capita Gross Domestic Product: The GDP divided by the total population of a country. Used as measure of relative wealth. MDCs have high per capita GDPs (average $20,000) while LDCs have low per capita GDPs (average less than $1,000).

Primary Sector: The portion of the economy concerned with the direct extraction of materials from Earth's surface, mostly through agriculture but also through mining, fishing, and forestry. LDCs have large primary sectors.

Secondary Sector: The portion of the economy concerned with manufacturing useful products through processing, transforming, and assembling raw materials. LDCs are becoming more competitive in secondary sectors.

Tertiary Sector: The portion of the economy concerned with transportation, communications, and utilities, sometimes extended to the provision of all goods and services to people in exchange for payment. It is the largest sector in the U.S. and many of the most developed countries. Some models further divide the tertiary sector into a *Quaternary Sector* (the portion of the economy concerned with business services, such as trade, insurance, banking, advertising, and wholesaling) and a *Quinary Sector* (the portion of the economy concerned with health, education, research, government, retailing, tourism, and recreation).

Productivity: The value of a particular product compared to the amount of labor needed to make it. MDCs have much higher productivity than do LDCs because many products in LDCs are labor intensive.

Value Added: The gross value of the product minus the costs of raw materials and energy. Value added is much greater per worker in MDCs than in LDCs.

Essential Goods: The goods and services necessary for survival—food, clothing, and shelter.

Non-essential Goods: Products such as cars, entertainment, and telephones not imperative for survival. However, their production greatly compliments an economy.

Literacy Rate: The percentage of a country's people who can read and write. MDCs develop and retain high rates of literacy in their populations. In LDCs the literacy rate of women is usually much lower than that of men.

Life Expectancy at Birth: The average number of years a newborn infant can expect to live at current mortality levels. LDCs have lower life expectancy rates for both men and women than do MDCs.

Dependency Ratio: The percentage of young and old people in a population that must be supported by the working people.

Infant Mortality Rate: The number of babies born who die during their first year of life per 1,000 born. MDCs have low infant mortality rates and LDCs have high ones.

Natural Increase Rate: The rate at which a population is adding to its population through births and contributed to by people living longer.

Crude Birth Rate: The total number of live births in a year for every 1,000 people alive.

Self-Sufficiency Model: Economic model for development whereby a country isolates itself from imports and exports and supports its businesses so that goods and services used come from within the country. Can be disadvantageous because of the lack of competition with other countries with different levels of technology.

146

Tariffs: Used to describe the taxes places on goods imported into a country. Tariffs are used to deter imports and protect domestically produced goods and services.

International Trade Model: Economic model for development whereby a country identifies and develops their unique assets and opportunities.

W. W. Rostow: Developed a five state model depicting a continuum of economic growth and development from almost void of consumer goods, to widely produced and consumed goods.

Four Asian Tigers/Dragons: Used to describe the Asian countries that have been successful in developing with the international trade model—South Korea, Taiwan, Singapore, and Hong Kong.

Transnational Corporation: Corporation which operates in countries other than the one in which its headquarters are located. Most are based in the U.S., Japan, Germany, France, and the United Kingdom.

CHAPTER 9
PROGRESSIVE REVIEW

1. Most of the world's population lives in relatively _____ countries.

poor

2. In LDCs the _____ gender is universally less educated than their _____ counter parts.

female
male

3. _____ developed countries are home to most of the planet's population, though they economically lag farther and farther behind.

Less

4. _____ is the process of improving the material conditions of people.

Development

5. Developing countries often do not have a large base of _____ resources with which to develop their economies.

natural

6. The global pattern of LDCs and MDCs can be divided by using the _____ degree _____ parallel as a partition.

30, north

7. The _____ sector dominates MDC economies including the U.S..

tertiary

8. Productivity is much greater in _____ developed countries than in _____ developed countries.

more
less

9. Per capita _____ _____ _____ measures the average input into the economy by a country's citizens.

gross domestic
product

10. The countries with the highest average per capita GDP in the world are _____.

MDCs

11. Agriculture, fishing, and mining are part of the _____ sector, which is the strongest sector in _____ developed countries.

primary
less

12. _____ countries colonized overseas areas in the 19th century, and gained access to many raw materials.

European

13. An LDC such as Bangladesh has __ ___ telephones per hundred people than does an MDC such as Britain.

fewer

14. The _____ _____ is the percentage of people in a country capable of reading and writing.

literacy rate

15. Because their populations tend to have many children per family, _____ developed countries also have _____ age structures than do _____ developed countries.

less, younger more

16. The UN's measure of development is called the _____ _____ _____.

Human Development Index

17. _____ has the highest rating in the Human Development Index.

Canada

18. _____ _____ are essential to economic development and are unevenly distributed around the world.

Raw materials

19. Goods necessary for basic living are called _____ _____ while goods that aren't necessary but are highly desirable are called _____ _____.

essential goods non-essential goods

20. Countries trying to develop are implementing the _____ _____ model

international trade

21. _____'s economy was jump-started after World War II by an abundant labor force which manufactured low-end goods cheaper than other countries.

Japan

22. _____ _____ is dominated by Spanish and Portuguese speakers and is an LDC region.

Latin America

23. Most Latin Americans live in _____ rather than _____ areas.

urban or cities, rural

24. In 1949, the _____ won China's civil war and instituted new economic policies.

Communists

25. _____ was the principal beneficiary of the Green Revolution.

India

26. _____ _____ _____ developed a _____-stage model for tracking and plotting economic development through international trade.

W. W. Rostow, five

27. The Four Asian Dragons/Tigers include _____, _____, _____, and _____.

South Korea, Taiwan, Hong Kong, Singapore

28. _____ and _____ tried for many years to implement self-sufficient economic models.

China, India

29. Although self-sufficient economic models are somewhat balanced, they are _____ due to the large _____ which run them.

inefficient, bureaucracies

30. _____ corporations are one of the world's largest sources for investment capital.

Transnational

CHAPTER 10

AGRICULTURE

Before societies developed technology that spurred exploration, they developed agricultural practices providing them with ample food stuffs. Chapter Ten details the origin of farming as well as world regional differences. The size and output of a region's farms can indicate the general level of development found in that area. Additionally, with populations on Earth continuing to grow, even more food will be needed in coming years.

Agriculture: Geographers study *where* agriculture is distributed. In LDCs agricultural products are consumed near where they are produced while in MDCs agricultural products are sold and consumed away from where thy are produced. Geographers also study *why* farming practiced vary around the world. The are elements of the physical environment which limit agricultural production. *Local diversity* is shown in the environmental and cultural mix influencing agricultural practices. *Globalization* influences farmers to grow profitable rather than practical crops.

Key Issue 1: Where Did Agriculture Originate (337): Agriculture originated before written history so all information is speculation reconstructed from the archaeological record.

Origins of Agriculture (337): *Agriculture* is the modification of the Earth's surface through cultivation of plants and rearing of animals to obtain sustenance or economic gain. A *crop* is any plant cultivated by people.

Hunters and Gatherers (337): Before organized agriculture, people collected plants, hunted animals, and fished—a practice called *hunting and gathering*. Small groups would collect food often and, depending on resources, it might take a few hours or all day. Usually men hunted animals and women gathered plants and relocated often.

Contemporary Hunting and Gathering (337-338): Today, about 250,000 people (0.005 percent of world population) employ hunting and gathering as their primary means of survival. They live in Africa, Australia, South America, and the Arctic.

Invention of Agriculture (338): Through generations, people observed that seeds they threw away reappeared, especially near watered areas and places with manure. Accident and experimentation contributed to formal agriculture.

Two Types of Cultivation (338): *Carl Sauer*, prominent cultural geographer, proposed *vegetative planting* (the planting of cut stems and divided roots) occurred first, and was followed by *seed agriculture* (the planting of fertile seeds) which is more prominent today.

Location of Agricultural Hearths (338): Different agricultural techniques emanated from their respective hearths.

Location of First Vegetative Planting (338): *Carl Sauer* believed vegetative planting originated in Southeast Asia because the climatic and topographical elements encouraged the vegetative planting technique to be used with the taro, yam, banana, and palm. Vegetative planting may have diffused into China, Japan, India, Southwest Asia, Africa, and the Mediterranean. There may have been independent hearths in West Africa and northwestern South America.

Location of First Seed Agriculture (339): Western India, northern China, and Ethiopia were apparently the hearths for seed planting. People in Southwest Asia were the first to integrate seed agriculture and domestication of animals.

Diffusion of Seed Agriculture (339-340): Seed agriculture diffused from Southwest Asia into Europe, north and central Asia, North Africa, and northwestern India. Plants and animals were often brought from Southwest Asia. Millet diffused south and east from China. Rice has an unknown hearth, though it is speculated to be Southeast Asia. Millet and sorghum was domesticated in Ethiopia. There are two independent seed agriculture hearths in the Western Hemisphere--south Mexico, the hearth for squash and maize, and northern Peru, the hearth for squash, beans and cotton. The only domesticated animals were the llama, alpaca, and turkey. Vegetation, animals, climate, and cultural preferences influenced domestication. However, improved communication and transportation have encouraged the diffusion of plants to areas away from their hearths. For example, Old World and New World plants now are seen in opposite sides of the world from their original hearths.

Classifying Agricultural Regions (340):

Differences Between Subsistence and Commercial Agriculture (340): Farming which provides food primarily for consumption by a farmer's family is called *subsistence farming*. *Commercial farming*, predominating in MDCs, is the production of food primarily for sale off the farm. There are five main distinguishing factors between subsistence and commercial farming.

Purpose of Farming (340): In LDCs, subsistence farmers produce food for their own consumption. Incidental surplus is sold. Commercial farmers raise crops and animals for sail off the farm. Products are rarely sold to consumers, but to food-processing companies.

Percentage of Farmers in the Labor Force (340): In MDCs less than 5 percent of the labor force are farmers while in LDCs, 60 percent are farmers. In the U.S. and Canada, only 2 percent of people are farmers yet they are the most productive in the world. The number of farmers is declining in 20th century MDCs.

Use of Machinery (340): In LDC countries much of the work done on farms is done by hand. Farmers in MDCs rely on machinery to perform much of the work. In the late 1700s, the iron plow was created and it, and other metal tools, replaced wooden ones. Mechanized machines (tractors, combines, corn pickers, planters) and transportation networks (to transport crops and animals) also allowed farmers to be more productive. Commercial farmers also promote and rely on scientific advances in fertilizers, herbicides, and hybrids of plants and animals.

Farm Size (340-342): Commercial farms in MDCs, especially in the U.S. and Canada are large. Farm sizes have steadily become larger in the U.S., with the average farm occupying 469 acres. Since 1900, the amount of farm land has remained almost constant, although some *prime agricultural land*—some of the most productive farm land in the U.S.—has been lost to suburbs expanding away from city cores.

Relationship of Farming to Other Businesses (343): LDC farmers sell most of their goods directly to people who will consume them. U.S. commercial farmers sell their produce to specialized food processing firms. For example, a farmer may sell harvested wheat to General Mills who, in turn, makes cereal to be sold in the retail market. The group of businesses that process, package, store, distribute, and retail food products are collectively known as *agribusiness*.

Mapping Agricultural Regions (343-344): *Derwent Whittlesey*, in 1936, prepared one of the most widely used maps of world agricultural regions. He identified 11 regions plus a region where agriculture was nonexistent—5 were for LDCs and 6 for MDCs (Figure 10-5). He sorted regions by climate, and then by crops and animals.

Key Issue 2: Where Are Agricultural Regions in Less Developed Countries

Shifting Cultivation (344-345): Shifting agriculture predominates in tropical climates.

Characteristics of Shifting Cultivation (345): *Shifting cultivation* relies on slash and burn techniques for clearing fields that will be cultivated for a few years and then left *fallow* so the soil and vegetation can recover. *Slash and burn agriculture* entails burning the vegetative cover of land and then using the resulting nutrients to grow crops.

The Process of Shifting Cultivation (345): In some areas villagers find a desirable piece of land to farm, they clear the trees and other vegetation from the area by cutting them down, and burning the fallen plant cover. The cleared land is called *swidden*. Fields are prepared by hand, minimally fertilized (often from potash), and minimally weeded. In many areas such swidden can only support plants for three years or less; the nutrients in the soil are quickly depleted. Once an area is depleted, a new area is chosen for clearing.

Crops of Shifting Cultivation (345-346): Local cultural preferences determines the crops though they can include rice, corn, millet, sorghum, sugar cane, plantain, and vegetables. Crops are planted to take advantage of height, nutrient, and shade or sun requirements.

Ownership and Use of Land in Shifting Cultivation (346): Land is owned by an entire village and allocated to individual families. Private ownership of land is becoming more common. One-fourth of the world's land area is in shifting agriculture, and relied on by about 5 percent of the world's population. Shifting cultivation is declining in land area because of development.

<u>**Pastoral Nomadism (346):**</u>
Characteristics of Pastoral Nomadism (346-347): Subsistence agriculture based upon herding animals is called *pastoral nomadism*. It predominates in dry climates where planted crops are impossible. Approximately 15 million people are pastoral nomads and occupy 20 percent of the Earth's land area. Sometimes part of the group may plant crops at a fixed location. Most agriculture occurs from following and relying on sparse rainfall.
Choice of Animals (347-348): From their animals pastoral nomads gain hides, meat, milk, and trading power which, in turn, provides them with tents, clothing, food, and prestige. Goats, sheep, and camels are typically found in the herds of nomads, as well as horses (important to the wanderers of Central Asia). Each of the animals has particular needs for water and care.
Movements of Pastoral Nomads (348): Pastoral nomads do not wander aimlessly across the landscape; they have territorial boundaries which they respect. *Transhumance*, seasonal migration between mountain and lowland pastures, is still practiced by some nomads. *Pasture* is grass or other plants grown for feeding grazing animals, as well as the land itself.
The Future of Pastoral Nomadism (348): Due to competition for land, the pastoral nomads way of life is decreasing. Mining and petroleum companies, governments, and farmers increasingly pressure the nomads to give up their way of life and the land on which they depend. They are encouraged to settle down or their territory is restricted to fixed boundaries.

<u>**Intensive Subsistence Agriculture (348):**</u> *Intensive subsistence agriculture* occurs where farmers must intensively work their land to harvest enough food to meet their family's needs. This category of farming is found in the densely populated East, South, and Southeast Asia. Because the population density is so high, farmers have no choice but to produce much food on small plots of land. Consequently, virtually no land is wasted by these farmers, planting crops on every piece of land available. Paths and roads are kept very narrow, so as not to take up land that could be producing food.
Intensive Subsistence with Wet Rice Dominant (348-350): *Wet rice* is a labor intensive process. It begins with nursing rice plants in a nursery, and then planting to seedlings in a flooded field in which they grow and mature. A farmer plows the land with the help of oxen or water buffalo and plants rice plants. The field, called a *sawah*, is then flooded with water and regulated by the farmer using irrigation. After they mature, rice plants are harvested by hand with knives; the husks, known as *chaff*, are separated from the seeds. Lighter chaff is blown away by the wind, or *winnowed*. In regions where warm winters are common, some farmers get two harvests per year, *double cropping* the ground by planting rice and wheat or barley in alternating cycles.
Intensive Subsistence with Wet Rice Not Dominant (350-351): In climates where water is less common wheat and other grains may be intensively grown. This

land is worked primarily by human power. In order to keep from exhausting the soil, *crop rotation* takes place in which different crops are used in consecutive years so that certain nutrients in the soil are not depleted. In China, the communist government tried to make farmers work in communes. The program was dismantled because the harvests decreased substantially since people preferred to work for themselves as they had for centuries.

Key Issue 3: Where Are Agricultural Regions in More Developed Countries

Mixed Crop and Livestock Farming (351): The most common form of agriculture in the U.S. in the Great Plains and in Europe from France to Russia.

Characteristics of Mixed Crop and Livestock Farming (351): In *mixed crop and livestock farming* most of the crops are fed directly to livestock to fatten them for slaughter. Manure is used as fertilizer for the crops. Nearly all land is used for crops and three-quarters of the income comes from the sale of animal products—beef, milk, and eggs. By having cattle and crops, farmers may more fully use time throughout the year with fewer hours of inefficient time spent waiting for crops to mature. Diversity spreads the risk in business and provides a steadier income.

Crop Rotation Systems (351-352): Farmers often divide their land into fields and then plant different crops in two, three, and four year cycles. *Cereal grains* (oats, wheat, rye, barley), root crops, and rest crops (such as clover) are alternately planted so that the nutrients in the soil are replenished every few years. Sometimes the ground is left fallow for a year or two, which allows it to rest. This method of nutrient preservation is crop rotation.

Choice of Crops (352): *Corn* is most common because of the high yield per area and it can be consumed by people or by animals. A belt from Ohio to the Dakotas, with Iowa as its core, is the corn belt, where half of the U.S. corn is grown. *Soybeans* are the second most important crop in the U.S.. Soybeans are used in many food products such as tofu, and are increasingly used as an ingredient in other food products.

Dairy Farming (352): In the Northeast U.S., Southeast Canada, and Northwestern Europe, dairy farming is very important. These areas are also home to large urban populations that consume the milk, cheese, and other products derived from milk. Transportation technology allows people more access to milk and milk products which has increased consumption.

Why Dairy Farms Locate Near Urban Areas (352-353): The ring surrounding urban areas from which they receive their stocks of milk is called a *milkshed*. Historically, milksheds radiated no more than thirty miles from a city though refrigerated transportation means milk can be transported more than 300 miles.

Regional Differences in Dairy Products (353-354): Milk produced further away from cities is usually used for the production of cheese, butter, and other products, since milk products stays fresh longer than drinking milk. Some countries such as New Zealand devote most of their milk production to cheeses and butter, because their location makes the shipping of drinking milk very difficult, due to the relative isolation of New Zealand from the markets of Europe and North America. However, other places like Great Britain, with a large market base, can devote more dairy resources to milk production.

Problems for Dairy Farmers (354): Distribution of milk makes it difficult for dairy farmers to make a profit. In the winter, dairy cows must be fed when they can't graze. Low profitability and excessive workloads are dissolving many dairy farms in the U.S..

Grain Farming (354): *Grain* is the seed from various grasses such as wheat, corn, oats, and barley. Most grains are grown for human consumption. *Wheat* is the primary crop and is used for the manufacture of bread. Wheat has a high price, may be stored for long periods of time, and may be grown profitably in remote regions.

Grain Farming Regions (354): Large grain farm operations are found in the U.S., Canada, Australia, Argentina, France, and the United Kingdom. In the U.S., wheat is found in three areas. The *winter wheat* belt is found in Texas, Oklahoma, Kansas, and Colorado. This wheat is dormant in the ground during winter. Farther north is the *spring wheat* belt in the Dakotas, Montana, and Saskatchewan. Because of severe winters wheat must be planted in the spring and harvested in late Autumn. Another important wheat territory is the Palouse region of eastern Washington state. The *McCormick reaper* first allowed large scale growing and harvesting of wheat. Today, the *combine* reaps, threshes, and cleans wheat immediately after it is harvested in the field.

Importance of Wheat (354-355): Wheat is extremely important because it is exported by many people and is universally consumed.

Livestock Ranching (355): *Ranching* is the commercial grazing of livestock over an extensive area.

Cattle Ranching in U.S. Popular Culture (355): Cattle ranching in the U.S. transcends the economic benefit of livestock, for the popularity of the cowboy and ranching in popular culture is extensive.

Beginning of U.S. Cattle Ranching (355): Columbus brought cattle to the New World on his second voyage. Immigrants from Spain and Portugal began ranching in the Americas, for they were the only Europeans with a tradition of cattle ranching.

Transporting Cattle to Market (355-356): Due to population growth in the Eastern U.S., cattle became a profitable commodity. Thus, cattle were shipped to Chicago from the plains upon which they were fattened and eventually, shipped East as slaughtered meat products. Towns in the Old West such as Abilene, Kansas became famous for their reputations as centers of wildness (prostitution, gambling, and gunfights were rampant). The most famous route from the grazing plains of Texas to the railroads of Kansas was the Chisholm Trail, which today corresponds roughly with U.S. Route 81.

Fixed Location Ranching (356): Early cattle ranchers owned cattle and very little land.

Range Wars (356-357): Range wars became common between farmers and ranchers (who wanted to drive their cattle across all land). With the invention of *barbed wire* in 1873, farmers began winning this war, and cattle ranchers eventually settled on their own large plots of land, which were often ill-suited for agriculture. Today, 60 percent of all ranch land is leased from the U.S. government.

Changes in Cattle Breeding (357): Herefords breeds imported from England have replaced the Longhorn cattle stocks of the Old West. Cattle are still raised on ranches but regularly sent to farms to be fattened by eating corn. Ranching is less profitable per acre of land, so many acres have been converted to irrigated crop growing. Today, many ranching operations are owned by companies in the meat-packing industry.

Cattle Ranching Outside the United States (357-358): Europe has few cattle ranches outside of Spain and Portugal. Latin America does have significant cattle operations in southern Brazil, Uruguay, and on the Pampas of Argentina. Ranching has declined in Argentina because farming is more profitable. Ranches in the Middle East, Australia, New Zealand, and South Africa tend to have more sheep than cattle.

Mediterranean Agriculture (358): Mediterranean farming takes place in areas bordering the Mediterranean Sea as well as in California, Central Chile, and Southwestern Australia. They all have similar climates and hilly or mountainous terrain. A small amount of income is derived from animal products. *Transhumance*, moving animals from along the coastal plains in winter to the hills in summer, is less and less common.

Mediterranean Crops (358-359): These regions often practice *horticulture*, growing fruits, vegetables, flowers, and tree crops for human consumption. Most of the world's olives, grapes, fruits, and vegetables are grown in these regions. Cereal crops are grown along the Mediterranean Sea; after harvest, cash crops can be planted. Wine is also produced in these climates from France to California to Chile. *Irrigation* is very important to farming in this climate because precipitation is not plentiful, and tends to come in the winter.

Commercial Gardening and Fruit Farming (359): Commercial gardening and fruit farming predominate in the U.S. Southeast. *Truck farmers* are highly efficient and take advantage of machines because they tend to make farming more profitable. Crops that are increasing in demand are strawberries, asparagus, peppers, and mushrooms. Costs are kept down buy hiring undocumented immigrants to perform much of the labor-intensive duties such as harvesting and planting crops by hand. *Specialty farming* is growing popular in New England where specialty crops are grown for wealthier consumers.

Plantation Agriculture (359): *Plantations* are large farms which specialize in one or two crops, and are found primarily in Latin America, Africa, and Asia. They are usually found in sparsely populated areas; they usually import, house, and entertain their workers because plantations usually are in remote locations. Today, crops are often processed at the plantation, reducing their bulk and weight and making them cheaper to transport to distant markets. After the abolition of slavery in the U.S. in 1863, plantations became less important components of the economy of the South. *Eli Whitney's* cotton gin, created in 1793, further reduced the need for laborers.

Key Issue 4: Why Does Agriculture Vary Among Regions (359): There are environmental, cultural, and economic reasons for agricultural regions.

Environmental and Cultural Factors (360): Climate is the biggest influence on agricultural practices. There is a relationship between subsistence and commercial agricultural regions and climatic zones. Cultural preferences help explain agricultural differences between similar climatic areas.

Economic Issues for Subsistence Farmers (360): Subsistence farmers either grow crops for consumption or for sale and trade.

    Subsistence Farming and Population Growth (360-361): *Ester Boserup*, offered an explanation of the distribution of subsistence farming. Subsistence farming provided food for people until the population started growing. Boserup speculated people had to intensify production either through shorter times of fallow, or through adopting new farming methods. There are five stages of intensified farming—forest fallow (clear forest, grow for 2 years, and fallow for 20 years), bush fallow (clear land, grow for 8 years, and fallow for 10 years), short fallow (clear land, use for up to 2 years, and fallow for 2), annual cropping (plant fields every year, few months of fallow with legume and root plantings), and multicropping (continuous plantings, no fallow time). New farming methods include ploughs, weeding, applying manure, terraces, and irrigation.

    Subsistence Farming and International Trade (361): Expanding production may include higher-yield seeds, fertilizer, pesticides, and machinery. Crops are traded to urban dwellers for goods and supplies. LDCs may manufacture things for export to LDCs to raise funds to invest in agricultural supplies. In LDCs, women may grow food for the family while men grow crops for export or work at jobs in the cities. The more land is devoted to cash crops, the less can be used for growing food.

    Drug Crops (361-361): Large population increases are found in many countries where people practice subsistence farming. Due to the expanding populations, there is often not enough food to provide for the entire country's populace. If these countries are going to meet the demand for food, they may be forced in the future to switch to more automated modes of agricultural production. Coca leaves which are processed into cocaine originate from South American countries like Peru, Bolivia, Colombia, and Ecuador. Most of the processing and distribution takes place in Colombia. Most of the marijuana imported into the U.S. originates in Mexico, Colombia, and Jamaica. Opium used to manufacture heroin is grown mostly in Asia, though Mexico produces some of this crop also. The sales of such crops brings hard currency into developing countries, though the U.S. pressures countries to destroy drug crops.

Economic Issues for Commercial Farmers (362): The most

Access to Markets (362): When deciding which crops to plant farmers use site factors (the abilities of the soil to produce crops) and situational factors of the land (their relative distances to markets and distributors).

Von Thünen's Model (362): Johann Heinrich von Thünen, a farmer, designed a model in northern Germany to help farmers decide upon which crops to plant, depending upon the location of the farm land itself. The Von Thünen model heavily weighs two factors in its decision-making process: the cost of the land and the cost of transporting the harvest to market. In order to have a profitable crop, a farmer must be sure the cost of transportation does not outweigh the prices paid to the farmer for the crop. Consequently, perishable crops with high transportation costs are located in concentric rings close to cities (markets), while other goods that are less perishable or are cheaply transported may be grown further from the city, for they are still profitable at such longer distances. So, milk and gardens are located near the city while animal grazing is far-removed. The Von Thünen model can be applied to places and nations outside of Germany; it is a conceptual observation which holds true in most areas which possess agriculture.

Example of Von Thünen's Model (362-363): Wheat production is profitable only when it doesn't have to be shipped a long distance. Profit is determined by the value of the yield per hectare and the cost of transporting the yield per hectare.

Application of Von Thünen's Model (363): Von Thünen developed rings of production out from the central city—horticulture and dairying, forestry, and crop rotation. He didn't consider site or human factors and assumed uniformity across the landscape.

Overproduction in Commercial Farming (363-364): Commercial farming suffers from lower prices, thus lower profitability because they produce more crops than the U.S. market can absorb. Because of more productive plant breeds, management practices, chemicals, and equipment, production of crops in the U.S. is very high. The result of this efficient production is very low crop prices. Food supply has increased in MDCs though consumption does not change significantly with commodity prices.

U.S. Government Policies (364): In order to soften the impact of low crop prices, the U.S. government subsidizes farmers. For example, if a farmer doesn't receive a market price of a certain level, the government pays the difference to the farmer. The government also pays farmers not to grow certain foods that are saturated in the market place. Ironically, the U.S. government attempts to suppress food production while may other governments struggle to increase their food production.

Summary: The world has a wide variety of types of farming and levels of production. Some places annually produce more food than its population needs, while other countries, mostly less developed countries, struggle to feed their rapidly expanding populations. Without diffusion of modern technology and a lowering of population growth rates, many LDCs will continue to struggle to feed their respective populations.

CHAPTER 10
KEY TERMS AND CONCEPTS

Agriculture: The deliberate effort to modify a portion of Earth's surface through the cultivation of crops and the raising of livestock for sustenance or economic gain. In MDCs fewer people participate in this activity than in the past.

Crop: Grain or fruit gathered from a field as a harvest during a particular season. The harvest is culturally very important to many societies.

Hunting and Gathering: Practice of finding food as it occurs in the landscape—hunting animals, gathering plants, and fishing.

Carl Sauer: Very prominent cultural geographer who proposed vegetative planting occurred as the first form of domesticated plants and was followed by seed agriculture.

Vegetative Planting: Reproduction of plants by direct cloning from existing plants. This is often performed when growing rice plants.

Seed Agriculture: Growing food from planting or scattering fertilized seeds. Grain production is initiated using seeds.

Subsistence Agriculture: Agriculture which provides food for direct consumption by the farmer and the farmer's family. LDCs rely mainly on subsistence agriculture.

Commercial Agriculture: Agriculture undertaken primarily to generate products for sale off the farm. U.S. farmers mostly belong to this category.

Prime Agricultural Land: The most productive farmland. In the U.S., it is being rapidly consumed for residential housing construction and suburban development.

Agribusiness: Commercial agriculture characterized by integration of different steps in the food processing industry, usually through ownership by large corporations.

Derwent Whittlesey: Created a map of world agricultural regions based on climate, crops, and animals. He created 5 categories for LDCs and 6 for MDCs.

Shifting Cultivation: A form of subsistence agriculture in which people clear a field, burn the vegetation, and plant crops in the newly cleared area. Each field is used for crops for a relatively few years, and left fallow for many years.

Fallow: Land ordinarily used for cultivation when it is left tilled and planted with a crop that restores soil nutrients, or left unplanted for a growing season or part of a growing season.

Slash-and-Burn Agriculture: Another name for shifting agriculture, so named because fields are cleared by slashing the vegetation and burning the debris. Its practice has been opposed by many environmentalists, though when practiced appropriately with enough available land for a long fallow period, it can be a long-term, viable agricultural practice.

Swidden: A patch of land cleared for planting through slashing and burning. Rarely are swiddens used for more than three years.

Pastoral Nomadism: A form of subsistence agriculture based on herding domesticated animals. Pastoral nomadism usually takes place in very arid regions.

Transhumance: The seasonal migration of livestock between mountains and lowland pastures. Transhumance allows for seasonally balance feeding on the land.

Pasture: Grass or other plants grown for feeding grazing animals, as well as land used for grazing. It is important not to overgraze pastures, or else erosion will occur.

Intensive Subsistence Agriculture: A form of subsistence agriculture in which farmers must expend a relatively large amount of effort to produce the maximum feasible yield from a small parcel of land. Southeast Asia has much land allocated to this type of agricultural practice.

Wet Rice: Rice grown for much of the time in deliberately flooded fields. This crop is very important to East Asians and Western Indians.

Sawah: A flooded field for growing rice. Irrigation helps flood the sawah and regulate the water level.

Paddy: Malay word for wet rice. It is often incorrectly used by Westerners to describe a sawah.

Chaff: Husks of grain separated from the seed by threshing. Usually chaff is discarded by U.S. farmers.

Winnow: To remove chaff by allowing it to be blown away by the wind.

Double Cropping: Harvesting twice a year from the same field. It is difficult to do if the region has a long dry season.

Crop Rotation: The practice of rotating fields from crop to crop each year to avoid exhausting the soil. Nitrogen-injecting crops such as sweet clover are occasionally used to strengthen the soil.

Mixed Crop and Livestock Farming: The agricultural practice in which crops are fed directly to livestock to fatten them for slaughter. Crops and animals are both raised in order to diversify the risk of the farm, provide the family with necessary products, and maintain a steadier income through the year.

Cereal Grain: A grass yielding grain for food. Wheat, barley, and corn are cereal grains.

Corn: Most common crop for mixed crop and livestock farming. It has a high yield per area.

Soybeans: Second most important crop in the U.S. after corn. Soybeans are grown all over the world because of their versatility and high nutritional content. They can be processed into a variety of food products.

Milkshed: The area surrounding a city from which milk is supplied. Thirty miles was the general limit for a city's milkshed though milk can now be shipped across long distances.

Grain: Seed of a cereal grass. The most valuable part of the harvest, with the chaff and straw being by-products. Grains are grown primarily for human consumption.

Wheat: The most important of the grain crops and is used for the manufacture of bread.

Winter Wheat: Wheat planted in the Fall and harvested in the early Summer. This dominates the Kansas, Colorado, and Oklahoma region.

Spring Wheat: Wheat planted in the spring and harvested in the late summer. Places where harsh winters are common usually plant Spring wheat.

Reaper: A machine that cuts grain standing in the field. Its invention by Cyrus McCormick made wheat production more lucrative.

Ranching: A form of commercial agriculture in which livestock graze over an extensive area.

Barbed Wire: Invented in 1873, it allowed people to fence off large open areas where there was a shortage of trees and lumber.

Horticulture: The growing of fruits, vegetables, flowers and tree crops for human consumption.

Irrigation: Watering crops in areas where crops might not otherwise grow.

Truck Farming: Commercial gardening and fruit farming, so-named because truck was a Middle English word meaning bartering or the exchange of commodities. Crops are grown as efficiently as possible using machines, hired labor, and specialization.

Plantation: A large farm, sometimes in tropical and subtropical climates, that specializes in the production of one or two crops for sale, usually to a developed country. U.S. plantations declined sharply after the Civil War and were located in the Southeast.

Eli Whitney: Inventor of the cotton gin, in 1793, which greatly decreased the amount of labor needed to grow cotton.

Ester Boserup: Explained subsistence farming in five steps which depended on the original ground covering and the intensity and duration of farming each plot.

Johann Heinrich von Thünen: A German who published "The Isolated State" in 1826, which informed farmers of the best location in which to plant their crops in relation to the nearest city.

CHAPTER 10
PROGRESSIVE REVIEW

1. The world "_____" means "to care for."   cultivate

2. Any plant cultivated by people is called a _____.   crop

3. Two-thirds of the people in the world are _____, but less   farmers
   than _____ percent of the U.S. population are farmers.   two

4. 469 acres is the average size of a farm in the _____   United States
   _____.

5. Agriculture is deliberate modification of the Earth's surface
   for the rearing of _____ and the growing of _____ .   animals, plants

6. Today, 250,000 people in the world survive by _____ and   hunting
   _____.   gathering

7. Two types of cultivation are _____ planting and _____   vegetative, seed
   agriculture.

8. The hearth of vegetative planting is probably in _____   Southeast Asia
   _____ according to Sauer.

9. In the Western Hemisphere, southern _____ and northern   Mexico, Peru
   _____ were the two hearths of agricultural development.

10. When people use different plots of land each year to
    plant their crops, they use _____ _____.   shifting cultivation

11. _____ and _____ agriculture is the process of clearing a   Slash, burn
    piece of land, burning the vegetation and planting crops.

12. Swidden describes _____ land.   cleared

13. People who live in arid regions sometimes travel over
    large tracts of land searching for food and water for their
    livestock, a practice called _____ _____.   pastoral
                                                                             nomadism

14. Cassava and Maize were domesticated in the continent   South America
    of _____ _____.

15. The size of a nomad's herd is a sign of _____, _____, and _____ in many cultures.   power, prestige, wealth

16. In Central Asia, the _____ is important to nomadic herders.   horse

17. Today, the number of nomads in the world is _____ because of intense competition for land and programs to settle them in permanent locations.   decreasing

18. To maximize food production, _____ _____ farmers waste virtually no land.   intensive subsistence

19. A flooded field is called a _____, and not a paddy as is commonly believed.   sawah

20. _____ _____ is grown most easily on flat land for water management is more easily performed on level ground.   Wet rice

21. When two harvests are taken in a year it is called _____ _____.   double cropping

22. After 1949, _____ redesigned its farms around communes which proved ineffective for motivating workers.   China

23. _____ agricultural _____ is being expropriated by U.S. cities to expand their suburbs and built on.   Prime, land

24. _____ is the system of commercial farming and related industries found in the U.S. and other more developed countries.   Agribusiness

25. _____ factors affect farmers' decision on which crops to plant due to their proximity to a city.   Situational

26. The ring around cities where milk production is found is called a _____.   milkshed

27. Oats, wheat, and barley are called _____ grains.   cereal

28. The second most important agriculture crop in the U.S., due to its wide array of uses, is the _____.   soybean

29. Dairies which produce cheeses and butters are found _____ distances from the cities they supply compared to milk-producing dairies.   long

30. _____ _____ is the world's largest producer of dairy products.   New Zealand

31. Dairies are _____ in number in the U.S. in recent years.   decreasing

32. Today, _____ perform most of the harvesting of wheat in the U.S. and Canada.   combines

33. Kansas and Oklahoma are in the _____ wheat belt.   winter

34. The invention of _____ _____ in 1873 helped farmers combat the territorial aggressions of ranchers.   barbed wire

35. The _____ Trail was the main cattle drive between Brownsville, Texas and the railways in Kansas.   Chisholm

36. Most of the world's wine is produced in the lands adjacent to the _____ _____ or in similarly named climatic zones.   Mediterranean Sea

37. _____ farming is practiced widely in the U.S. Southeast and produces many varieties of fruits and vegetables.   Truck

38. _____ leaves are the fundamental ingredient in the manufacture of cocaine.   Coca

39. Most of the marijuana that reaches the U.S. is grown in _____.   Mexico

40. Today, plantations are found mainly in Latin America, _____, and _____.   Africa Asia

CHAPTER 11

INDUSTRY

When one observes the origin of products–automobiles, computers, and clothing, as well as the components that form the products–it becomes obvious that countries all over Earth's surface play a major part in our everyday life. Mexico, Taiwan, Malaysia, and Italy can be found labeled onto goods used everywhere in the U.S.. Chapter Eleven discusses origins of the industrial revolution, how industry is distributed worldwide, locational influences, and problems that face industry in today's global society. As comparative advantages of different locations become more influential with the dissolution of tariffs that impede international trade, geographical analysis of countries and their territories will help explain current conditions and determine locations of future industrial growth.

Industry: In January, 1985 GM announced that it was designing the Saturn model automobile, and was searching for an ideal location for new assembly plants. Intense competition between states and cities followed, because of the great economic benefits that would be derived from the plant. Spring Hill, Tennessee was chosen after a seven month search. Spring Hill was close to the market, accessible by -parts suppliers, and was a good community. In other words, Spring Hill beat out the competition because it was the best *geographic site* for the automobile plant, according to GM decision maters. The community had *locally diverse* characteristics which made it appealing for the plant to compete in the *global economy.*

Key Issue 1; Where Did Industry Originate?

The Industrial Revolution (371-372): In *Britain,* during the late 1700's, the industrial revolution was born. Innovations in manufacturing and efficiency brought higher quantities of high-quality goods to consumers for lower prices than ever before. Goods such as guns, food, tobacco, and textiles were processed and manufactured very efficiently. *Cottage industries* predominated; manufacturing was done by hand in people's homes. Merchants would contract to home-based workers who would be supplied with materials by *putters-out,* the "middle men" employed by merchants to conduct transactions. The *steam engine,* invented in 1769 by *James Watt,* is the most important example of the technology wrought by the industrial revolution. It is only one example of the mechanical devices created in the industrial revolution.

Diffusion of the Industrial Revolution (372): The iron industry relied on new technologies and the textile followed.

Diffusion from the Iron Industry (372): The iron industry was the first to benefit from Watt's new invention. Iron ore mined from the ground was smelted in *blast furnaces*, poured into casts, then transported for further refinement from the *pig iron* form. The steam engine to kept the furnaces hot during the heating and cooling of the iron and steel during production. *Henry Cort* developed a new way of purifying iron—*puddling*, which effectively purified pig iron. Cort and Watt's inventions increased iron-manufacturing capabilities, which directly affected many other key industries.

Coal (372-373): Prior to the industrial revolution, the primary source of energy was wood. However in addition to heat, wood was being used for many other purposes—ship building, construction, and furniture. Wood was becoming scarce. The solution was to switch from wood to *coal* for fuel. The furnaces, forges, and mills scattered throughout Britain became clustered into four large, integrated centers, all situated near coal fields (Staffordshire, South Yorkshire, Clydeside, and South Wales).

Engineering (373): In 1795, *Watt* and *Matthew Bolson* began their own business, producing hundreds of new machines that greatly increased the efficiency of the industrial process, giving birth to modern engineering and manufacture of machine parts.

Transportation (373): There were transportation inventions—canals and railways. In 1759, the Duke of Bridgewater began construction on a canal between Manchester and Worsley which was completed in two years. The canal allowed goods to be transported inexpensively and quickly. Soon, however, canals were eclipsed by the invention of the railway or "iron horse" invented by *William Symington* and *William Murdoch* in 1784. The railway symbolized the impact of engineering on the industrial revolution. The first public railway ran between Stockton and Darlington in the north of England in 1825.

Diffusion from the Textile Industry (373-374): The textile industry benefited from the industrial revolution. Inventions created between 1760 and 1800 transformed the textile industry into a complex factory system from a cottage industry. *Textiles* are woven fabrics. *Richard Arkwright* improved the process of spinning yarn by inventing a *spinning frame* and by patenting the process of *carding* to separate fibers. His factory designs were powered by Watt's steam engine. Other inventions mechanized weaving.

Chemicals (374): Cotton clothing had to be bleached and dyed for final production, bringing about the chemical component of the industrial revolution. At first chemicals were used primarily to bleach and dye clothing. As research developed the ability of chemistry to accomplish this task, new uses were found. It was discovered that, by combining natural-fibers, such as wool and cotton, with various chemicals, new *synthetic* materials could be formed. Today, the largest textile factories in the world are owned by chemical companies.

Food Processing (374): The workers of the industrial revolution could not grow their own food and work factory jobs. *Nicholas Appert* developed the canning method in 1810. Although fermenting, drying, and pickling had been used since ancient times, *canning* preserved food by killing the bacteria that spoil food. The *tinned can*, invented in 1839 by *Peter Durand*, made canning cheaper than earlier glass bottling techniques. When it was discovered that calcium chloride, when added to water, reduced sterilization time, canning increased tenfold in 1861.

Diffusion from the United Kingdom (374): The Crystal Palace of the 1851 World Fair in London symbolized Britain's dominance in the industrial revolution. At that time Britain produced half of the world's cotton fabric and iron, and mined two-thirds of the coal being used in the world. The small island nation had far outpaced the rest of the world. The industrial revolution spread eastward to Europe and westward to the U.S..

Diffusion to Europe (375): Europeans contributed to the early efforts of the industrial revolution. For example, the Belgians were coal-mining experts, the Germans made the first industrial cotton gin, and the French had the first coal-fired blast iron furnace. Unfortunately, the political disruptions of the French Revolution and the Napoleonic Wars delayed the spread of the industrial revolution to other European countries until the end of the nineteenth century, when it reached the Netherlands, Russia, and Sweden. These latter countries did not reach the level of industrialization of France, Britain, Belgium, and Germany until the twentieth century. Other southern and eastern European countries joined the industrial revolution later in the twentieth century.

Diffusion to the United States (375): The first U.S. textile mill was built in Pawtucket, Rhode Island in 1791 by *Samuel Slater*, a former worker at Arkwright's factory in England. To avoid entanglement in the Napoleonic Wars, the U.S. imposed a trade embargo with Europe in 1808. The embargo sparked the U.S. domestic industrial development. In the twentieth century industrial technology spread to Canada, Japan, and many former British colonies. However industry remains concentrated in four regions: eastern North America, western Europe, eastern Europe with Russia, and East Asia (See Figure 11-3).

Key Issue 2: Where Is Industry Distributed? (375-376): Three-fourths of the world's industrial production is concentrated in four regions. Industrial distribution covers one percent of all land area and differs from agriculture which occupies one-fourth of all land area.

North America (376): Manufacturing in North America is concentrated in the northeastern quadrant; it comprises only five percent of the land area, and accounts for one-third of the population and two-thirds of the industrial output. This area was industrialized partly because it was highly populated; it was the principal region of European settlement in the U.S. and Canada. Additionally, the raw materials--coal and iron—essential for development were found in the area. Transportation along the rivers and Great Lakes connected the East with the expanding frontier.

Industrialized Areas Within North America (376):

New England (376): The oldest area in the U.S. specialized in textile manufacturing, due to an abundance of cheap labor, and access to European markets. Today there is a highly skilled labor force.

Middle Atlantic (376-377): Located between New York and Washington, industries in the Middle Atlantic take advantage of the large consumer market and the importation of materials through several excellent ports.

Mohawk Valley (377): Industries that are located along the Hudson River and Erie Canal in upstate New York use cheap electricity from Niagara Falls. Large amounts of steel and food processing dominate the area.

Pittsburgh--Lake Erie (377): Between Pittsburgh and Cleveland steel production dominates. Ore from Minnesota and Appalachian coal constitute the industrial base.

Western Great Lakes (377): Toledo, Detroit, Chicago, and Milwaukee comprise this district. Formed because of its location as a distribution and manufacturing center, these places have great locational advantages for business, especially Chicago. Chicago is the third-largest urban area and the dominant market in the middle of the U.S.. Chicago is a break of bulk point with many different forms of transportation. Automobile manufacturing, machine tools, transportation equipment, clothing, furniture, and agricultural machinery and food products located along the Great Lakes to take advantage of the transportation network.

St Lawrence Valley—Ontario Peninsula (377): Canada's most important industrial area. Centrality to the Canadian market and proximity to Niagara Falls (cheap electricity) and the Great Lakes (cheap transportation) enticed business to locate here.

Changing Distribution of U.S. Manufacturing (377): In recent times, southeastern states of the U.S. have attracted investment because of *right-to-work* laws; such laws hamper unions and increase company profits. Los Angeles Seattle, San Diego, and San Francisco on the West coast developed many industries in the twentieth century, many of which are supported by government contracts.

Western Europe (377-378): Like the North American manufacturing belt, Western Europe appears as one industrial area but, due to different countries in competition with each other, four distinct regions developed there (See Figure 11-6).

The Rhine-Ruhr Valley (378): The most important region which stretches from northwestern Germany into parts of Belgium, France, and the Netherlands. Industry is rather dispersed across the landscape. The Rhine River provides transportation through most of the region and coal is found in high quantities which stimulated industrial growth through heavy-metal industries.

The Mid-Rhine (378-379): This area includes southwestern Germany, northeastern France, and Luxembourg. This area does not have abundant raw materials, but does have a large consumer population which sustains industry. Frankfurt, Stuttgart, and Mannheim are located here. Frankfurt became Germany's financial and commercial center and the hub of its transportation networks. The French portion of this area contains Europe's largest iron ore field which provides two-thirds of France's steel. Luxembourg is a leading steal producer because the French Lorraine iron-ore field extends into the country.

United Kingdom (379): The original region of the industrial revolution, most of its industry today is in the south of England at the core of the country's population and wealth. During the twentieth century Britain lost its global industrial lead due to global competition from other areas in the world. The factories tend to be old and out dated. Interestingly, the losers of World War II, Japan and Germany, received financial assistance from the U.S. with which they built new factories to replace those destroyed by the war; they now lead the world in industrial output, along with the U.S..

Northern Italy (379): The Po River Basin of northern Italy has much industry developed with access to cheap hydro-electricity and cheap labor. Textiles, raw-material processors, and mechanical-parts assemblers dominate the industrial base.

Eastern Europe and Russia (379-380): Four regions are in Russia, one in the Ukraine, and one is divided between southern Poland and northern Czech Republic. The first three and Silesia became manufacturing centers in the 1800s and the Volga and Urals, by the Communists, in the twentieth century.

Central Industrial District (380): Russia's oldest district, which doesn't have many natural resources but serves a large population center in and around Moscow. High-value bulky textiles are made by 30 percent of Moscow's labor force.

St. Petersburg Industrial District (380): An early node of innovation in Eastern Europe. Due to the proximate Baltic Sea, shipping is an industrial base as are food processing, textiles, light industrial goods, and chemicals.

Eastern Ukraine Industrial District (380): Endowed with generous deposits of coal, iron ore, manganese, and natural gas, this area has many plants which utilize these assets. The area is Eastern Europe's largest producer of pig iron and steel.

The Volga Industrial District (380): The largest oil and natural gas fields in Russia are located here. German occupation during World War II enhanced the industrialization of this area. Motor vehicles, oil refining, chemicals, metallurgy, leather, and fur are produced in this area.

The Urals Industrial District (380): Although this area is home to more than 1,000 types of minerals, it is difficult to process them because energy sources must be imported at great expense.

Kuznetsk Industrial District (380): Russia's important manufacturing center east of the Urals which possesses much coal and iron ore.

Silesia (380): The leading manufacturing center outside of Russia in Eastern Europe situated in southern Poland and northern Czech Republic. The area has rich coal fields and must import iron ore.

East Asia (380-382): East Asia has many different levels of industrial development, size of economies, and per capita GDPs. China has abundant reserves of coal, iron ore, and minerals while other countries in East Asia have few resources. East Asia has taken advantage of an abundant labor force. After World War II, Japan produced large quantities of cheap goods by relying on its labor force. Japan's economic planners foresaw more competition in the low-end consumer goods market, so it changed its industrial base to higher-end electronic goods and precision instruments made by a more educated work-force. Today, Japan leads the world in the export of consumer goods. China has been increasing production of steel, farm machinery, construction materials, and clothing. In Japan, industry is concentrated in the central region between Tokyo and Nagasaki.

Key Issue 3: Why Do Industries Have Different Distributions?

Situation Factors (382): *Situational factors* are related to the transportation of materials into and from a factory. An optimal location will provide the low costs of transportation to a firm. A company will tend to either locate its factory near the greatest source of its inputs or near its consumer base, whichever is more profitable.

Location Near Inputs (382): Inputs are either raw materials, or parts and materials made by other companies.

Copper Industry (382): Copper ore in North America is low-grade, with most of it being less than one percent copper. The result is a very heavy ore which is expensive to transport. Copper concentration is a *bulk-reducing industry* which refines the ore, removing 98 percent of the impurities. Proximity to copper mines determines the locations of copper smelters, refineries, and mills because high transportation costs would make other alternatives not profitable. The only major exception is Baltimore; it imports its copper from foreign countries into its port.

Steel Industry (382-384): Steel-making is another bulk-reducing industry. In the mid-1800's steel making was concentrated in southwestern Pennsylvania around Pittsburgh because both of its inputs, coal and iron ore, were mined there. However, the discovery of high-grade ore in the Mesabi Range of northern Minnesota near Lake Superior, as well as technology that decreased the proportion of coal in the manufacturing process, shifted steel-making to many cities on the shores of the other Great Lakes, such as Toledo, Cleveland, Chicago, and Gary. The Great Lakes provide very cheap transportation for the bulky iron ore and coal. Minimills are an emerging player in the steel-making industry; proximity to market determines successful mills today, as well as the fact that scrap metal derived from that same market is available.

Location Near Markets (384):

Bulk-Graining Industries (384-386): *Bulk-gaining industries* produce a commodity that gains weight and/or volume during the production process and thereby affects transportation costs. For example, the soft drink industry uses cans and bottles, syrup, and water. Syrup is concentrated and easy to transport, empty bottles and cans are relatively light, and water is found in any population center. Soft drink companies and beer bottlers tend to locate their industries in local markets to reduce transportation costs of the final product. More commonly, bulk-gaining products gain more volume than weight. When the sum of all the parts of a product, such as a car, surpass the individual components in weight, it becomes critical to locate assembly plants near the consumer market.

Perishable Products (386-387): Food products such as bread and milk are perishable so they must reach consumers as quickly as possible. *Perishable products* are processed near the consumer market. Perishable goods that are frozen, canned, or preserved can be transported long distances. Newspapers are a perishable product because they are only valuable when the information is current.

Accordingly, many newspaper publishers in the U.S. publish papers in the same areas that dually act as distribution centers to reduce transportation costs. Still, with the innovations in satellite technology, the New York Times, Wall Street Journal, and U.S.A.. Today can electronically transmit their papers' contents to regional publishers.

Single-Market Manufacturers (387-388): *Single market manufacturers* make products that are sold in one market. For example, several times a year, buyers from individual clothing stores come to New York from all over the world to order clothing that they will retail in department stores in the coming fashion season. Therefore, high-style clothing makers tend to cluster around New York.

Ship, Rail, Truck, or Air Transportation (388): There are four primary modes of freight transportation. In general, the farther the distance traveled, the cheaper per kilometer cost. The costs per kilometer differ because of loading and unloading costs. For short distances, trucks are most frequently used; trains have an advantage for medium and longer distances across land. Extremely long distances are cheaper by ship transport. Air transport is expensive, but it is quick and is used when time efficiency is a must, as with perishable and time-sensitive goods.

Break-of-Bulk Points (388-389): *Break-of-bulk points* are places where transfer among transportation modes is possible. Each unloading and reloading of goods increases transportation costs. For example, a steel mill near Baltimore may receive coal via rail from Appalachia and South American iron ore by a ship in its port. Though situational factors remain important, their relative importance has declined over time due to increasing importance of site factors.

Site Factors (389):
The actual location of industries is becoming more dependent on *site factors*, factors related to the costs production inside the plant such as land, labor, and capital.

Land (389-390): *Land* is an important factor because it varies much in cost, potential for expansion, proximity to energy, and amenities. Generally, modern factories tend to be located in rural or suburban areas, where large tracts of land may be obtained substantially cheaper than land in the central part of a city. The ability to add more buildings in the future is also a consideration for obtaining real estate in these areas. In the past, factories were located near rivers and forests because energy was ordinarily gained from those sources. Today, electricity has replaced wood and running water as an energy source, so it is a important variable in factory location. It should be noted that hydro-electricity from running water is a cheap source of electricity today. Some businesses locate in places like the American Southwest because of climate, sports franchises, topography and other amenities that are to their liking.

Labor (390): *Labor-intensive* industries must be located near large, cheap labor pools.

Textile and Clothing Industries (390-392): Textiles are labor-intensive industries. There are three steps involved in textile production—spinning, weaving or knitting yarn into fabric, and cutting and sewing fabric into other products. Natural fiber textile industries are located where natural fibers are produced. Approximately half of all synthetic fiber products are produced in LDCs. LDCs produce three-fourths of the world's woven fabric and two-thirds of the spun yarn. Most cotton goods are produced in Asian markets and most cotton clothing are produced in Europe and North America.

U.S. Textile and Clothing Industries (392-393): Textile producers have relocated to gain access to low-cost labor. Most cotton textile and clothing manufacturing has moved from the Northeast U.S. to the Appalachian Mountains and Piedmont of the Southeast. The wool industry requires more skilled laborers and has remained in the Northeast.

Skilled Labor Industries (393-394): Skilled labor industries require skilled laborers to perform highly skilled tasks using complex equipment or performing precision tasks. The automobile industry was built by having each worker perform one task repeatedly, called the *Fordist approach* after the Ford Motor Company model. Wider ranged activities performed by workers is called the *post-Fordist approach*.

Capital (394): In order to initially set up a factory or plant in a given place, *capital* needs to be secured for financing of the venture. In LDCs where monies cannot be secured, industrialization is stalled which impairs development. Unstable political systems, high debt levels, and ill-perceived economic policies retard the flow of investment into LDCs.

Obstacles to Optimum Location (394-395): Many industries have become *footloose*, meaning that many places can accommodate them without any major negative impacts upon their costs in transportation, land, labor, and capital. Proficiency in identifying the best of all potential sites varies widely, thus one executive in charge of such a task may actually find the best possible site, another less-competent executive unaware of modern technologies such as Geographic Information Systems (GIS), may find an acceptable site. Since locational searches are somewhat expensive, demand and time constraints force some companies to make less-than-perfect locational decisions.

Key Issue 4: Why Do Industries Face Problems? (395):

Industrial Problems from a Global Perspective (395):
Stagnant Demand (395-396): During most of the last two centuries an increasing amount people are being added to the world's consumer market. As more factories were opened throughout the world, more employees gained disposable income. By the 1970's demand slowed considerably in MDCs, mainly because of market saturation and stabilized population growth rates. Also, consumers matured, requiring quality goods that are replaced less frequently than in the past. Technology decreased the relative importance of steel which is substituted by plastics and other substances.

Increased Capacity Worldwide (396-397): While demand for products such as steel stagnated in the mid-1970's, the efficiency of the global economic production has increased, thus reducing the number of production facilities and, consequently, bringing unemployment to some economic sectors. For example, during most of the 1800's, the United Kingdom out-produced the rest of the world in industrial goods. As more countries entered competition with Britain for market share of industry, Britain's world domination was reduced. Today, the world has many industrial bases. LDCs have had a similar effect upon MDCs; LDCs have enlarged their industrial bases and MDC industrial market share has declined. LDCs such as India, Brazil, South Korea, and China have increased their steel production while MDCs have decreased steel production.

Industrial Problems in More Developed Countries (397):

Impact of Trading Blocs (397): As different countries in the world face increasing competition brought about by technology and cheaper transportation throughout the world, three regional blocs of countries have formed alliances, *trading blocs,* to ensure exports and to insulate themselves from competition.

Cooperation Within Trading Blocs (397): In the Western Hemisphere, most trade barriers have been eliminated between the U.S. and Canada. The *North American Free Trade Agreement (NAFTA)* was implemented in 1994 and will eventually negate all tariffs on goods traded between member countries which currently include the U.S., Canada, and Mexico. The European Union has eliminated most barriers between member countries. Japan dominated the informal East Asian bloc.

Competition Among Trading Blocs (397-399): The three blocs encourage trade within the bloc and restrict trade with other regions.

Transnational Corporations (399): Transnational corporations, also known as *multinational corporations,* have parts of their operations located in a number of different countries which, ideally, reflect the comparative advantage yielded by each country. Historically, the U.S. dominated this type of company, but Japan, Germany, France, and the United Kingdom have recently entered this realm of capitalism. For example, some firms have located labor-intensive industries in Mexico because, due to existing low wages and proximity to the U.S. market, Mexico is more profitable as a factory site than most places. Japanese auto companies, using the same philosophy, have located some factories in the U.S. because labor is cheaper than in Japan.

Disparities Within Trading Blocs (399): Countries or areas within a bloc may be at a disadvantage because of lower levels of industrial development

Disparities Within Western Europe (399-400): In France, areas near Paris have large concentrations of wealth and industry while the south and west suffer poorer economic realities. The northern part of Italy has three times the per capita income of the southern reaches of the peninsula and Sicily. In order to develop under-developed parts of the European Community grants, tax reductions, and other forms of government aid are often furnished as incentives to invest in less-prosperous areas.

Disparities Within the United States (400): In the U.S. the historically poor South has witnessed much economic growth due to government policy and evolving site preferences. The formerly solid core of industry in the U.S. has experienced little or no economic growth in recent decades.

Industrial Problems in Less Developed Countries (400):
Old Problems for LDCs (400):

Distance from Markets (400-401): If LDCs are to mature economically into MDCs then they must develop their economies in similar ways. Even so, obstacles hinder this evolution. Most LDCs in Latin America, Africa, and Asia are far from the wealthy markets of the trading blocs. Due to their geographic remoteness, LDCs must invest scarce resources in transportation that could otherwise be invested in education, infrastructure, or national strategic (long term) planning.

Inadequate Infrastructure (401): *Infrastructures* include universities, communications, roads, and utilities. LDCs still face the high cost of initially installing the expensive amenities that facilitate industrial growth.

New Problems for LDCs (401):
Economic geographers have named two phenomena indispensable for industrial growth; raw material access and favorable site factors: A country will more likely be developed if it has good access to coal, oil, iron, and other raw materials that can be used as an industrial input. During the twentieth century, multinational companies have selected locations, using labor as a weighted variable called the *new international division of labor*. Consequently, places with inexpensive labor have attracted the firms wanting to locate factories.

Summary: The industrial revolution began in Britain around 1750 due to a series of innovations in technology, and has since diffused throughout many parts of the rest of the world. Yet, many countries yearn to become more fully integrated into it. Still, most of Earth's industrial output remains in the most intensely industrialized parts of Europe, Asia, and North America. In today's world, firms are better served if they locate close to cheap labor sources. Nevertheless, in today's world of declining demand due to market saturation and other factors, industrial development is difficult.

CHAPTER 11
KEY TERMS AND CONCEPTS

Maquiladoras: Factories built by U.S. companies in Mexico near the U.S. border, to take advantage of much lower labor costs in Mexico. New maquiladoras are often located outside of the border area due to incentives given by local governments.

Cottage Industry: Manufacturing based in homes rather than in a factory, commonly found before the Industrial Revolution. **Putters-out** conducted transactions between workers and merchants. An important cottage industry was textile manufacturing.

Steam Engine: An efficient engine patented by **James Watt**, a Scot from Glasgow, in 1769. It was the most important single development in increasing capacity and profitability of factories during the Industrial Revolution.

Blast Furnace: A furnace that is blasted with air, thus made extremely hot for the smelting of iron. In blast furnaces semi-refined **pig iron** is cast castings to be later refined and made into products. **Henry Cort** purified iron by **puddling** it.

Coal: Replaced wood as the primary fuel source during the Industrial Revolution. It burns hotter and is more efficient for smelting iron and making steel.

Walt and Matthew Bolson: Created many machines during the Industrial Revolution. Their work was the beginning of modern engineering and manufacture of machine parts.

Railway System: The locomotives and iron rails upon which they are operated. The invention of the locomotive symbolized the impact of engineering on the industrial revolution. **William Symington** and **William Murdoch** invented the modern railway in 1784 using a steam engine.

Textiles: A fabric made by weaving, used in making clothes. In the U.S. the textile base has shifted from the Northeast to the Southeast due to cheaper, more cooperative (less unionized) work forces. **Richard Arkwright** made textile manufacturing more efficient with his inventions and powered the operation of carding, spinning, and weaving machines with **Watt's** steam engine.

Synthetic Fibers: Natural fibers that are combined with chemicals produce synthetic fibers. Today, the largest textile companies are owned by chemical companies.

Canning: A method of preserving food in glass bottles that had been sterilized in boiling water invented by **Nicholas Appert** in 1810. The invention of the more versatile, cheaper tin can in 1839 by **Peter Durand** made this process expand.

Samuel Slater: Former employee at **Richard Arkwright's** textile factory in England who built the first U.S. textile mill in 1791.

Right-to-Work State: A U.S. state that has a law preventing the negotiation of a contract that requires workers to join a union as a condition of employment. They are prevalent in the Southeast.

Situational Factors: Location factors related to the transportation of materials into and away from a factory. For example, a copper smelter would likely be located close to a copper mine where the ore could be bought inexpensively to the smelter, and the refined material transported inexpensively to plants for further processing.

Site Factors: Location factors related to the costs of factors of production inside the plant, such as land, labor, and capital. For example, the site characteristics of a maquiladora tend to be dominated by cheap labor.

Bulk-Reducing Industry: An industry in which the final product weighs less or comprises a lower volume than the inputs. The refinement of petroleum or steel is such an industry.

Bulk-Gaining Industries: An industry in which the final product weighs more or comprises a greater volume than the inputs. The manufacture of automobiles is an example of this industry.

Perishable Products: An industry for which rapid delivery of the product to consumers is a critical factor. Food and newspapers (which become value-less as time goes by) are examples.

Single Market Manufacturers: Manufacturers that make products sold in one market. The fashion industry is centered around New York.

Break-of-Bulk Point: A location where transfer is necessary from one mode of transportation to another. Airports and seaports are examples; they make excellent locations for distribution centers.

Labor-Intensive Industry: An industry for which labor costs comprise a high percentage of total expenses. Low-skilled, labor-intensive industries are often exported from MDCs to LDCs.

Skilled Labor Industry: An industry relying on highly skilled laborers to perform high-tech or precision oriented tasks.

Fordist: Form of mass production in which each worker is assigned one specific task to perform repeatedly. It is named after automobile mogul Henry Ford.

Post-Fordist: Form of mass production where each worker performs a wider range of activities and acts as part of team.

Footloose: An industry that has many locations that can accommodate their needs.

Trading Blocs: Regional economic affiliations which increase trade between member countries by reducing tariffs amongst themselves and blocking trade with countries outside the bloc. The three major blocs are the Western Hemisphere, Western Europe, and East Asia.

North American Free Trade Agreement (NAFTA): The regional trading bloc which includes the U.S., Canada, and Mexico. Other countries of the Western Hemisphere are likely to join.

Transnational Corporations: Also known as **multinational corporations**. Firms which operate different parts of their companies in different locations around the globe.

Infrastructure: The school and medical systems and the transportation and communication networks of a country.

New International Division of Labor: Transfer of some types of jobs, especially those requiring low-paid less skilled workers, from relatively developed to developing countries. Many people believe that freer trade will lead to an exodus of low-skilled jobs to LDCs where labor is cheaper.

CHAPTER 11
PROGRESSIVE REVIEW

1. _____ are plants located in Mexico due to the cheap labor found there.   Maquiladoras

2. The Industrial Revolution began in the _____ _____ around 1750.   United Kingdom

3. The root of the Industrial Revolution describes rapid advances in _____ brought about by innovative ideas.   technology

4. In 1769 James Watt invented the _____ _____, which greatly increased the capacity of factories.   steam engine

5. Before the Industrial Revolution manufacturing was often performed in people's homes and called the _____ _____.   cottage industry

6. In order to process iron into steel, _____ replaced charcoal (made from wood) for heating the iron.   coal

7. Due to the interdependence of coal and iron, steel mills tended to be located near _____ fields.   coal

8. _____ _____ and Matthew Boulton established the Soho Foundry in Birmingham, England in 1795.   James Watt

9. The invention of the _____, or "iron horse," replaced the canal as the dominant mode of transportation.   railway

10. _____, or woven fabric, were tremendously affected by the Industrial Revolution.   Textiles

11. Advances in _____ technology grew from finding industrial methods for bleaching cotton fabric.   chemical

12. Nicholas Appert of France developed _____ in 1810 to preserve various food products.   canning

13. The _____ _____ of the 1851 World's Fair symbolized the Industrial Revolution to that point.   Crystal Palace

14. The continents of _____ and _____ _____ were the first and second to benefit from the industrial revolution.   Europe, North America

15. Ironically, the infrastructures of _____ and _____ were rebuilt with aid from the U.S. after World War II, which aided their industrial development.

Germany, Japan

16. The first textile mill in the U.S. was built in 1791 in Pawtucket, Rhode Island by _____ _____.

Samuel Slater

17. When natural fibers and chemicals are combined, _____ _____ result.

synthetic fibers

18. Today, the largest textile companies in the world are owned by _____ companies.

chemical

19. Industry in North America is concentrated in _____ Canada and _____ U.S., though the _____ region in the U.S. is rapidly gaining in importance.

southeastern, northeastern Southeastern

20. Industrial development is occurring in the Southeastern states because of _____-_____-_____ laws making it illegal to require employees to join a union.

right-to-work

21. _____ is the dominant city of the U.S. between the two coasts. It is a break of bulk point, the third largest city in the U.S., and a major industrial city.

Chicago

22. The Rhine-Ruhr Valley is the most important industrial area in Western _____.

Europe

23. Throughout the twentieth century, _____ _____ has lost market share due to increases in global competition.

Great Britain

24. Most of _____ industries and population are concentrated in the Po River valley, in the northern part of the country.

Italy's

25. Over 1,000 minerals are found in the _____ _____ of Russia.

Ural Mountains

26. _____ has few natural resources and is far-removed from the markets of North America and Europe, but is a powerful industrialized country.

Japan

27. The actual location of industries are dependent on _____ factors—land, labor, and capital.

site

28. _____ factors are related to the transportation of materials into and from a factory.

Situational

29. The steel industry is a _____-_____ industry.

bulk-reducing

30. The _____ Range of Minnesota supplies high grade iron ore to the steel mills situated along the shores of the Great Lakes.

Mesabi

31. Fresh food and newspapers are known as _____ products because they quickly lose value.

perishable

32. _____ is the most expensive mode of transportation for any distance.

Air

33. Ships are the cheapest mode of transportation for _____ distances.

long

34. Many modern factories have relocated to _____ or _____ areas.

suburban, rural

35. A _____-_____ industry is one in which the cost of labor makes up a high percentage of the total operating costs.

labor-intensive

36. Local and national governments attempt to lure industry within their boundaries by offering financial _____.

incentives

37. The management philosophy whereby one worker performs a single task is called _____.

Fordist

38. Regional economic differences within are known as _____.

disparities

CHAPTER 12

SERVICES

People are not uniformly dispersed across the landscape. Some people prefer to live in comparatively isolated areas while others prefer to live near other humans in settlements. Settlements are further divided into a number of sub-groupings because of diverse locations, sizes, and shapes. Chapter Twelve describes the variety of settlements and their available services that have developed in the world. Chapter Thirteen takes a closer looks at settlements and urban patterns.

Services: In MDCs, people work in shops, restaurants, hospitals, and businesses which are all tertiary sector, or the service sector of the economy. A *service* is any activity that fulfills a human want or need and returns money to those who provide it. Geographers are interested in *where* services are located. A *settlement* is a permanent collection of buildings *where* people reside, work and obtain services. They range in size and populations and occupy less than one percent of the world's land area and contain nearly all people on Earth. Geographers are also interested in *why* services are clustered in settlements. Services are dependent on a market and must consider their site and situational factors. *Globalization* of services means they are increasingly evenly distributed in settlements. *Local diversity* of services when fast food restaurants and chain stores are so visible is seen in the clustering of services in a particular location. Every location is distinct in some way.

Key Issue 1: Where Did Services Originate?:

Types of Services (409): There are three types of services—consumer services, business services, and public services.

    Consumer Services (409): *Consumer services* provide services to individuals who desire them and can afford to pay for them.

    Retail Services (409): *Retail services* provide goods for sale to consumers. In the U.S. 25 percent of jobs are retail service jobs and off that group, 25 percent are wholesale; 25 percent in restaurants; 25 percent selling food, motor vehicles, or clothing; and 25 percent selling other goods.

    Personal Services (410): *Personal services* provide services for the well-being and personal improvement of individual consumers. In the U.S. 20 of jobs are personal and social services and of that group 40 percent are in health care, and about 10 percent each in education, social services, recreation, hotels, membership organizations, and other personal services.

Business Services (410): *Business services* facilitate other businesses.

Producer Services (410): *Producer services* provide services primarily to help people conduct other businesses—agriculture, manufacturing, or other services. In the U.S. about 15 percent of jobs are in producer services and of that group, 45 percent are in financial services, 20 percent are in professional services, 10 percent in employment agencies and temporary help agencies, 5 percent in computer and data processing services, and 20 percent in supporting services (advertising).

Transportation and Similar Services (410-411): *Transportation, communications, and utilities services* diffuse and distribute services. In the U.S. this group accounts for 5 percent of jobs. Of this group, transportation includes trucking (30 percent), aviation (10 percent), and 20 percent in railway and other transportation. About 25 percent of jobs are in communications and 15 percent in utilities (gas, electric, water, sanitary services).

Public Services (411): *Public services* provide security for citizens and businesses. In the U.S. 15 percent of jobs are in the public sector, and of that group 15 percent are employed by the federal government, 25 percent by a state government, and 60 percent in local government jobs.

Changes in Number of Employees (411-412): From 1960 to 1995 employment in services (tertiary sector) has increased by 143 percent, increased in manufacturing (secondary sector) by 13 percent, and declined in agriculture (primary sector) by 46 percent. Producer services have increased the most because of computers, data processing, advertising, and employment agencies. Personal services have also increased rapidly because of increased health care services. Retail services have modestly increased and mostly in restaurants and specialty shops have increased more than have department stores. Transportation has increased moderately because new technology has replaced old technology. Communication has increased because of technological advances. Public services has grown the least, contrary to the misconception that the number of government jobs has increased.

Origin of Services (412-413): Services are clustered in settlements. The origin and impetus for people to settle in permanent settlements is unknown though it is speculated that settlements provided services and had cultural significance.

Early Personal Services (413): Permanent settlements may have provided personal services like burial places and religious services. Buildings may have been constructed for ceremonies. Dwellings may have housed a more permanent population so that males could travel longer distances in search of food. People may have also started manufacturing goods. The variety of services expanded as people specialized.

Early Public Services (413): As the permanent population of a settlement increases, they need specialized their activities. Early cities organized and developed defenders for the vulnerable cities. They built walls to help defend themselves. Cities no longer have walls though they do have military and political services.

Origin of Other Services (413-414): People in settlements needed food and transportation services may have originated to provide food. Retail functions as people brought their diverse resources and goods for storage and for sale. Groups could safely come to settlements for trade goods and services. Officials may have provided producer services to regulate transactions, set prices, keep records, and create a currency system.

Services in Rural Settlements (414): Today, more people live in rural areas than in urban areas. *Clustered rural settlements* exist where a number of families live in close proximity to each other with fields surrounding the collection of houses and farm buildings. *Dispersed rural settlements*, characteristic of the North American rural landscape, are characterized by farmers living on individual farms isolated from neighbors rather than alongside other farmers in settlements.

Clustered Rural Settlements (414): When people reside in a clustered village or hamlet, they work in surrounding fields. Often the inhabitants of these settlements will be responsible for farming a few pieces of land, which may be held by an individual or a landowner who dictates farm activity. If the population grew too large to be supported by the fields, new settlements were started nearby. Satellite settlements in England were named similarly to the original settlement.

Circular Rural Settlements (414-415): *Circular rural settlements* have an open central space surrounded by structures. They are used in Africa by the Masai and southern Africans to protect their cattle in the kraal (corral) in the center of the settlement. Germans used circular settlement patterns as a way of organizing homes and agriculture.

Linear Rural Settlements (415): *Linear settlements* feature buildings clustered along a road, river, or dike to facilitate communications with fields extending beyond the buildings in long, narrow strips. Linear settlements describe places settled by the French; property would extend back from the linear settlement for long distances creating *long lots*.

Dispersed Rural Settlements (415-417): Dispersed rural settlements are common in Anglo-America and the United Kingdom. They are more efficient than clustered settlements in more developed societies. Farmers, after centuries of land inheritance, owned very fragmented pieces of land. Between 1750 and 1850 the British government began the *enclosure movement* which consolidated many of the fragmented farms in Britain. Consequently, many people moved to cities in England to be employed by the engines of the industrial revolution.

Key Issue 2: Why Are Consumer Services Distributed in a Regular Pattern?

Central Place Theory (417): The market center to which people come for the exchange of goods and services is called the *central place*. The central place is located so that it maximizes accessibility by the people living in its dominion. Conceived by *Walter Christaller* and further refined by August Losch and Brian Berry, *central place theory* is the geographical concept which explains the significance of central places.

Market Area of a Service (417-418): The *market area* or *hinterland* is the area surrounding a service from which customers are attracted. A market area is a nodal region. Although circles can be drawn to represent the markets of various firms, six-sided hexagons fit easily together and tend to be less confusing. Four hierarchies of hexagons represent, in ascending order: hamlets, villages, towns, and cities, shown in Figure 12-5. The size of the hexagon is determined by its market.

Size of a Market Area (418): The market area of services vary; the range and threshold of a service determine the market area.

Range of a Service (418-419): The *range* is the maximum distance people are willing to travel to obtain a service. More common services (groceries, video rentals) have a small range and more unique services (concerts, specialized health care) have a larger range. Range is dependent on distance as measured in the time it takes to get to the service.

Threshold of a Service (419): The *threshold* is the minimum number of people or the minimum income needed to support the service. The threshold may be dependent a certain number of consumers or a minimum amount of income it must take in. Services also appeal to different portions of the population; age, income, gender, proximity, and interest are all indicators about the group of people a service is targeting or that it appeals to. Consumers produce revenue, which makes the firm profitable. By using Census data, computer software, and performing marketing research a firm may ascertain these figures.

Market Area Analysis (419): *Market area analysis* is the study of a market area to assess optimal locations for services as well as the comparison of data generated by the business to the market area population.

Profitability of a Location (419): The range and threshold of a service determine the profitability of a potential location. Convenience stores have a 15 minute range and a $10,000 threshold. They need approximately 5,000 people within the range of the location in order to make a profit.

Optimal Location Within a Market (419): Once an acceptable threshold and range has been found, the precise location for a business or service can be established.

Best Location in a Linear Settlement (419-420): Geographers use the gravity model to locate businesses in areas of maximum potential. A *gravity model* predicts that the optimal location of a service is directly related to the number of people in the area, and inversely related to the distance people must travel to access it. In a linear settlement, the best location for a business is the geographic midpoint between the extreme corners of population along the dominant transportation corridor.

Best Location in a Nonlinear Settlement (420): The gravity model can be applied to nonlinear settlements by comparing several locations and choosing the one that maximizes the number of potential customers as measured by the total customers and the average travel distance for all customers in the range.

Hierarchy of Services and Settlements (421): Small settlements have services with small thresholds, ranges, and market areas. Large settlements can support larger services.

Nesting of Services and Settlements (421-422): MDCs have diversely sized services and are less reliant on a few large settlements as are LDCs. Figure 12-8 shows a grid of varying sizes of hexagons representing four levels of market areas—hamlets, villages, towns, and cities. *Nesting market areas and services* models the ranges of settlement sizes and their interaction across the landscape.

Rank-Size Distribution of Settlements (422-423): The *rank-size rule* is applicable when a country's Nth largest city contains 1/N of the population of the largest settlement; it is a way of evaluating the hierarchy of settlements in a country or region. The *primate city rule* exists when the largest city in the country, the *primate city*, possesses over twice the population of the next largest city. LDCs tend to have primate cities more often than MDCs. A regular hierarchy means goods and services are available to people throughout the country. Countries that have a few large settlements do not have the wealth to make services available to all people.

Key Issue 3: Why Do Business Services Locate in Large Settlements?

World Cities (423): Cities are a modern phenomena because people were depended on the agricultural products from surrounding fields. Services were limited.

Ancient World Cities (423):
Earliest Urban Settlements (423): One of the oldest cities on Earth is Ur, located in modern day Iraq. The city contained a temple known as a ziggurat, 250 acres, and was encircled by a wall. Titris Hoyuk, in present-day Turkey dates from 2500 BC and suggests a well-planned community. Public buildings were in the center of the city, it occupied a 125 acre site, had a population of 10,000, and was occupied for 300 years and then abandoned.

Ancient Athens (423-424): The Mediterranean began having settlements in about 2500 BC, and included Knossos on Crete, Troy in modern Turkey, and Mycenae in Greece. They were *city-states*—self-governing units that provided a variety of services. Settlements grew in number of size in the eighth and seventh centuries BC in Italy, Sicily, and Spain. Athens was probably the first city to attain a population of 100,000; the city contributed to many elements of Western civilization.

Ancient Rome (424-425): The rise of the Roman empire encouraged urban settlement which helped the Romans manage their territory. Roads were constructed to facilitate transportation to Rome. Rome, its administrative, cultural, and commercial center was integral to the empire's success.

Medieval World Cities (425-426): In the eleventh century new settlements began to appear in Europe. Feudal lords allowed their serfs to move to cities in exchange for periodic military service. By the fourteenth century Europe had many settlements and a network of connecting roads. The typical European city was compact, densely settled, and surrounded by a wall. Palaces, churches, and public buildings were arranged in the center of town. Until the Industrial Revolution the five most important cities in the world were in Asia: Baghdad, Constantinople, Kyoto, Changan, and Hangchow (both in China).

Modern World Cities (426-427): Although most of the planet's people reside in rural areas, the percentage of people living in urban areas is rapidly increasing because of the perception that urban areas offer a higher standard of living. Concentrated populations encourage the concentration and development of services through developments in communication and transportation.

Business Services in World Cities (427-428): Business services cluster in cities because of the industrial revolution. Factories had a board of directors to make decisions and reduce the liability of each owner. Financial businesses are located in major cities and include stock exchanges, banks, and insurance companies. Professional services—lawyers, accountants, advertisers marketers, and others—help corporations make decisions and anticipate changes. Transportation services have hubs in large cities.

Consumer Services in World Cities (428): Retail services can have large market areas in world cities. Wealthy people cluster in world cities so there is a clustering of highly specialized products and services. World cities have personal services like theater events, restaurants, bars, sports events, libraries, and museums.

Public Services in World Cities (428): World cities are centers of national and international power; they are often capitals. There are offices for foreign representatives, trade associations, labor unions, and professional organizations.

Hierarchy of Business Services (428): Geographers enumerate four different levels of cities based on their roles in global services: world cities, regional command and control centers, specialized producer-service centers, and dependent centers.

World Cities (428): London, New York, and Tokyo are in the first class of world cities. A second tier of world cities includes Chicago, Washington, Los Angeles, Brussels, Frankfurt, and Paris. Secondary world cities are spread across the world.

Command and Control Centers (428): These cities include regional and command centers and also act as the headquarters for many large corporations. There are regional and subregional centers.

Specialized Producer-Service Centers (429): Third tier cities specialize in producer-service centers with highly specialized services. A city or group of cities may specialized in management and research and development, and another group specializes as centers of government and education.

Dependent Centers (429-430): Fourth tier cities are dependent city centers and provide relatively unskilled labor. There are four types of dependent centers in the U.S.—resort, retirement, and residential centers; manufacturing; industrial and military centers; and mining and industrial centers.

Economic Base of Settlements (430-431): Cities often specialize their industrial base in specific ways. *Basic industries* sell their goods and services outside of the community and *non-basic industries* sell their goods and services mainly to people within the community. Basic industries are very important because they inject money into the local economy, allowing non-basic industries to develop which directly serve the populace. A community's unique collection of economic industries define its *economic base*. Different regions in the U.S. have different economic bases. For example, the Southeast is more likely to have textile industries as their base than are other areas in the U.S..

     Specialization of Cities in Different Services (431-432): Basic industries used to mainly be manufacturing but have increasingly been replaced by service industries. Cities have often structured themselves around unique economic bases. The San Jose and Boston areas specialize in computing and data processing industries while cities like Austin and Orlando distinguish themselves with high-technology industries and many cities are changing to high-tech industries.

Key Issue 4: Why Do Services Cluster Downtown? (432): Services have historically dominated the center of town called the *downtown* and known more precisely as the *central business district (CBD)*.

Central Business District (432): CBDs are generally the oldest and most distinct areas of cities. The CBD is compact and takes up less than 1 percent of urban land area. It is the center f transportation in most cities.

     Retail Services in the CBD (432):

     Retail Services with a High Threshold (432): Retail services with a high threshold can be established in CBDs and traditionally included department stores. As the CBD has declined in importance, many department stores and businesses with a large threshold have relocated to suburban malls.

     Retail Services with a High Range (432, 434): Retail services with high ranges tend to be stores that are very specialized and not found in many places so draw infrequent customers and consumers travel long distances. Specialty and larger malls can thrive in CBDs if they combine retail with recreational activities.

     Retail Services Serving Downtown Workers (434): Shops serving CBD businesses and workers include copy stores, shoe repair, and computer stores. They often have limited hours in the evenings and on weekends. The diversity of shops is increasing in many CBDs. Revitalization plans for CBDs may include creating pedestrian streets to encourage shoppers.

     Producer Services (434): Business persons such as lawyers, financiers, journalists and advertisers are often clustered in the downtown for they are interdependent and must have face-to-face meetings.. Locating these types of businesses within proximity of each other facilitates meetings between the various professionals. Central locations also allow employees to choose between a variety of housing and neighborhoods, all reasonably accessible to the city center.

     High Land Costs in the CBD (434-435): Because land is very desirable in the CBDs and its area is relatively small, property prices in downtown areas are exorbitant. Tokyo's land prices are the highest in the world, as high as $250,000 per square meter. Prices are inflated by a shortage of available, open land.

Intensive Land Use (435): The intense demand for land in CBDs has caused people to utilize spaces both below and above the ground's surface. Under the ground exist subways, parking garages, and utility lines. Toronto and Minneapolis have created subsurface corridors for shopping areas. Utility and communication lines are typically below the surface.

Skyscrapers (435): Skyscrapers have been built in the world's largest cities creating distinctive urban skylines. The first skyscrapers were built in Chicago in the 1880's. Skyscrapers have caused traffic problems because they house large numbers of people, bringing many cars into small areas. Washington, DC doesn't have a high skyline like other cities of its size because zoning laws restrict the height of all buildings to no higher than the capitol building.

Activities Excluded from the CBD (435):

Declining Manufacturing in the CBD (435-436): Manufacturing facilities today desire very large, one-story plots of land for industrial plans. Since CBDs tend to have expensive rents, many manufacturers have left for the cheaper real estate of the suburbs or outlying small towns. In response to the exodus of industries from city cores, city planners have often redesigned cities for recreation and retail shops. For example, formerly deteriorating waterfronts have been torn down and rebuilt with the tourist and suburbanite shopper in mind.

Lack of Residents in CBDs (436): CBDs have experienced an overall reduction in population because of associated poor social statistics of crime and poverty. Yet, in Europe people are more likely to live in CBDs. Many people in the U.S. must commute daily from the suburbs to the CBD, creating the *rush hour*–a time period when transportation areas are acutely crowded.

European CBDs (436): The structure of streets and buildings in European cities tends to be more irregular and smaller than in American cities. This is a legacy from medieval times. European cities have also tried to preserve the historical character of their cities; consequently, renovations are more common in European cities. Demand for space in European CBDs is even higher than in American urban areas and, logically, so are the rents.

Suburbanization of Services (436):

Suburbanization of Retailing (436): Since World War II suburbs have grown in the U.S. and people have moved from the CBDs. Suburban sales have increased by an annual rate of 5 percent.

Shopping Malls (437-438): Because richer and larger consumer bases are more frequently found in the suburbs, firms have located shopping malls in them. *Shopping malls* are elaborate, multilevel structures which house many retail establishments. They are frequently at road intersections and occupy more than 100 acres of land. A developer buys the land and constructs the mall, centering it around an anchor. An anchor is a large discount store or supermarket which attracts consumers who then frequent other shops in the mall.

Suburbanization of Factories and Offices (436): As with retailing, many factories and offices have moved to the suburbs because of low-rents, availability of parking, and more space. Offices that do not require face-to-face contact find the suburbs to be more desirable with less congested roads and more readily available parking.

Summary: Settlements were originally established for cultural reasons. The importance of a solid economic base for settlements has become very important, especially after the Industrial Revolution. Due to changing technology, economic success is more often found in urban settlements. Consequently, the world's population has steadily been migrating to cities during the last two-hundred years. Cities are not only attractive because of lucrative jobs, but also because of the many services and goods provided.

CHAPTER 12
KEY TERMS AND CONCEPTS

Service: Any activity that fulfills a human want or need and returns money to those who provide it. In recent years this economic sector has grown faster than any other.

Settlement: A permanent collection of buildings and inhabitants. Cities are born from settlements.

Consumer Services: Provide services to individuals who desire them and can afford to pay for them.

Retail Services: Provide goods for sale to consumers.

Personal Services: Provide services for the well-being and personal improvement of individual consumers.

Business Services: Provide services facilitate other businesses.

Producer Services: Provide services primarily to help people conduct businesses which produce things.

Transportation, Communications, and Utilities Services: Diffuse and distribute services.

Rural Settlement: A settlement in which the principal occupation of the residents is agriculture. Rural settlements are very common in less developed countries.

Urban Settlements: A settlement in which the principle economic activities are manufacturing, warehousing, trading, and provision of services.

Clustered Rural Settlement: A rural settlement in which the houses and farm buildings of each family are situated close to each other and fields surround the settlement. Farming villages are classified as this type of settlement.

Dispersed Rural Settlements: A rural settlement pattern characterized by isolated farms rather than clustered villages.

Circular Rural Settlements: Settlements with an open central space surrounded by structures.

Linear Settlements: Have buildings clustered along a road, river, or dike which facilitates communications with fields extending beyond the buildings in long, narrow strips.

Long Lots: French linear settlements were often located along rivers and the long strips of land extended back from the river.

Enclosure Movement: The process of consolidating small land holdings into a smaller number of larger farms in England during the eighteenth century. The English farms were made more efficient by the changes.

Central Place: A market center for the exchange of goods and services by people attracted from the surrounding area.

Central Place Theory: A theory developed by **Walter Christaller** that explains the distribution of settlements based on the fact that settlements serve as market centers for people living in the surrounding area. Larger settlements are fewer and farther apart than smaller settlements and serve a large population base.

Market Area (Hinterland): The area surrounding a central place, from which people are attracted to use the place's goods and services. Its size determines the number of businesses which may exist in the area's core.

Range: The maximum distance people are willing to travel to use a service. The less common the service, generally, the longer people will travel to use it.

Threshold: The minimum number of people needed to support the service. Due to high population densities, thresholds are more easily found in urban areas than in rural areas.

Market Area Analysis: The study of a market area to assess optimal locations for services as well as the comparison of data generated by the business to the market area population.

Gravity Model: A model that holds that the potential use of a good or service at a particular location is directly related to the number of people in a location and inversely related to the distance people must travel to reach the good or service.

Nesting Market Areas: A model explaining how the diversely sized settlements and service areas interact with each other.

Rank-size Rule: A pattern of settlements in a country, where the nth largest settlement is 1/n the population of the largest settlement. Countries where this rule holds true tend to be more developed.

Primate City: The largest settlement in a country if it has more than twice as many inhabitants as the second-ranking settlement. Paris, France is an example.

City-State: An independent state comprised of a city and immediate environs. San Marino and the Vatican are contemporary examples.

World Cities: Large cities in the world that play an important role in the global economy.

Basic Industries: Industries that sell their products primarily to consumers outside the settlement. These businesses inject fresh currency into the local economy.

Nonbasic Industries: Industries that sell their products primarily to consumers in the community. A large number and variety indicate a high standard of living for the populace.

Economic Base: A community's collection of basic industries. Often cities have created a special niche as an economic base.

Central Business District (CBD): The area of the city where retail and office activities are clustered. In large cities, the suburbs are often drawing CBD businesses away from the city center.

Rush Hour: The times through the week when transportation areas are crowded because of commuting.

CHAPTER 12
PROGRESSIVE REVIEW

1. A _____ is any activity that fulfills a human want or need. service

2. A permanent collection of buildings and inhabitants is a _____. settlement

3. Settlements are theorized to have began around _____ grounds and religious buildings. burial

4. _____ services facilitate other businesses. Business

5. Places where groups met to barter goods that were not widely available were called _____ _____. trading centers

6. _____ is the main economic activity in rural settlements. Agriculture

7. A clustered rural settlement is commonly known as a _____ or _____. village, hamlet

8. _____ villages in southern Africa have enclosures (kraal) for livestock. Masai

9. The _____-_____ is a pattern of settlement common to the French settled areas in North America. long-lot

10. The _____ _____ brought greater agricultural efficiency to Britain by consolidating farms, but destroyed the self-contained village way of life. enclosure movement

11. _____ rural settlements are common in the U.S. where farmers live on individual farms. Dispersed

12. The part of the city people come to for exchange of goods and services is the _____ _____. central place

13. _____ _____ created the original theory about the location of places that maximizes accessibility for the consumers in the market or service area. Walter Christaller

14. The _____ of a service is the maximum distance people travel for that service. range

15. The _____ is the minimum amount of people or income a business must have to support it.   threshold

16. Stores needing a large customer base are said to be _____ threshold businesses.   high

17. A _____ _____ is used to asses the optimal location for a service by looking at the number of proximate customers who will travel to obtain the service.   gravity model

18. A _____ area is the surrounding domain from which customers are attracted.   market

19. A _____ _____ is a city with more than twice the population of any other city in that country.   primate city

20. One of the oldest settled cities is _____ and was in Mesopotamia.   Ur

21. Knossos and Troy were early _____-_____ in the Mediterranean.   city-states

22. _____ was probably the first city in the ancient world to reach 100,000 people.   Athens

23. The fall of the _____ Empire saw a decline in urban settlements in their realm of influence.   Roman

24. Prior to the Industrial Revolution, the world's five largest cities were found on the continent of _____.   Asia

25. Cities which dominate the global economy are _____ cities.   world

26. Cities which provide relatively unskilled labor are _____ centers.   dependent

27. _____ _____ are industries which sell products primarily outside of their community while _____-_____ industries sell products internally.   Basic industries non-basic

28. A community's unique collection of basic industries comprise its _____ _____.   economic base

29. CBD stands for a city's _____ _____ _____.   central business district

30. The city of _____ is acknowledged to have the highest land prices of any urban area on Earth.   Tokyo

31. High-rise structures which symbolize the American metropolitan area's downtown are called _____.   skyscrapers

32. The first skyscrapers in the U.S. were built in the city of _____.   Chicago

33. The city of _____, _____ has no buildings higher than thirteen stories, the level of the U.S. Capitol's dome.   Washington, DC

34. The renovation of older buildings is more prevalent in _____ cities, than in the U.S..   European

35. Many Europeans prefer to live in CBDs but Americans prefer the _____ of their urban places.   suburbs

36. There are problems traveling in cities during the _____ _____, or time when most people are commuting to and from work.   rush hour

CHAPTER 13

URBAN PATTERNS

The core of a city has traditionally been its downtown. Religious centers, government, businesses and public spaces are often found in the center of cities. Geographers are interested in the distribution of settlements and the distribution of people with urban areas. Chapter Thirteen describes different characteristics of urban areas and their peripheries and how urban areas differ around the world. People tend to live near other people who share similar geodemographic traits. This chapter also describes the different living arrangements between poor and rich people in urban areas.

Key Issue 1: Where Have Urban Areas Grown?: In 1800 only 3 percent of the world's population lived in cities and most were relatively small. Today nearly half the world's population lives in cities and over 100 have more than 2 million inhabitants.

Urbanization (445): During the last 200 years people have increasingly migrated to urban areas; cities have experienced more natural increase causing urbanization. *Urbanization* is the increase in the number and percentage of people living in cities.

    Increasing Percentage of People in Cities (445): A large percentage of people living in urban areas is a measure of the country's development. MDCs tend to have higher proportions (three-fourths) of their populations in cities than LDCs (just under half). In MDCs the industrial revolution and the increase in services has increased urbanization. People have migrated to the cities to work in factories and services located in the cities. Increased efficiencies in agricultural production freed people to work in other economic sectors. MDCs are now *fully urbanized*, meaning urban areas have approached their maximum capacity and everyone interested in moving to cities has already done so. In LDCs people are moving to cities though they are pushed off the farms with no assurance of urban jobs.

    Increasing Number of People in Cities (446-447): Urban areas in less developed countries are attracting large numbers of rural people because, although their economic opportunities are not great, they are still better than the economically desolate countryside. The U.S. Census Bureau estimates seven of the ten most populous cities are in LDCs. New York, Tokyo-Yokohama, and Osaka-Kobe-Kyoto are the only ones in MDCs. Estimates of LDC city populations differ, though Mexico City, São Paulo, Shanghai, Beijing, Rio de Janeiro, and Buenos Aires are the largest cities in LDCs. In 1900 London was the world's largest city and five of the top ten largest cities were in Europe, three in the U.S., and Tokyo, Japan was the only pre-industrial city. Most increases in population in LDCs are not fueled by increases in job availability, but by natural population increase.

Defining Urban Settlements (447):

Social Differences Between Urban and Rural Settlements (447): *Louis Wirth*, in the 1930s defined a city as having a large size, high population density, and socially heterogeneous people and that the way of life for urban and rural dwellers is different. His ideas may still be applicable in LDCs, though the urban/rural distinctions have blurred in MDCs.

Large Size (447): Urban areas are very large, allowing one to personally know few people relative to the overall population, whereas in rural areas people often know very high percentages of the populations.

High Density (448): Higher population densities in cities make people more competitive for virtually everything from living space to jobs. The stronger groups dominate. Higher densities also promote specialization.

Social Heterogeneity (448-449): In large, urban centers there is a greater variety of people; there are more lifestyle choices. Differences in religion, sexuality, or personal appearance are more tolerated in large cities.

Physical Definitions of Urban Settlements (449):

Legal Definition of a City (450): A *city* is a urban settlement which has been formally incorporated into an independent, self-governing unit. A city can collect taxes, elect officials, and must provide essential services. Cities are not given rights in the U.S. Constitution, as are counties and states. Boundaries delimit the area of the city.

Urbanized Area (450): An *urbanized area* is the area in a city, its *central city*, as well as the built-up, surrounding suburbs where population density exceeds 1,000 people per square mile. Approximately 60 percent of the U.S. population lives in an urban area.

Metropolitan Statistical Area (450-451): The U.S. Census Bureau has created the *metropolitan statistical area (MSA)* to denote a central, urban county and its dependent areas. An MSA has a central city county with a population of at least 50,000, and adjacent counties where 15 percent of the residents work in the central city county, a population density of 60 persons per square mile, 65 percent of its residents working in nonfarm jobs, a population growth rate in the 1970s of at least 20 percent and at least 10 percent (or at least 5,000 people) living in an urbanized area. MSAs are popular for analysis because data is available for counties, the building blocks for MSAs. MSAs often overlap and include much non-urban land.

Consolidated Metropolitan Statistical Areas (451-452): A long, continuous urban complex which combines several MSAs is often called a *megalopolis*, coined by geographer *Jean Gottman*. The long stretch of urbanization between Boston and Washington, DC is a megalopolis. Boundaries between metropolitan areas of the megalopolis overlap and do not have significantly large, continuous rural areas separating them. The downtown areas of the cities may be distinct. If MSAs are adjacent and overlap commuting patterns, they may be combined into *consolidated metropolitan statistical areas (CMSAs)*. Within a CMSA, the MSA that exceeds 1 million population may be classified as a *primary metropolitan statistical area (PMSA)*. A PMSA has at least one county with a population of more than 100,000, at least 60 percent of the population working in nonfarm jobs, and less than 50 percent of the workers commuting to jobs outside the county.

Importance of MSAs (452): It is important to many counties to be designated as MSAs and CMSAs because the federal government uses the county to award funds. Exposure due to statistical data at that level is also an important factor in attracting economic investment by business.

Key Issue 2: Where are People Distributed Within Urban Areas?

Three Models of Urban Structure (452): Sociologists, economists, and geographers have developed three models to depict the locations of where people live in urban areas.

    Concentric Zone Model (452): The _concentric zone model_ was the first to describe social structures of areas surrounding CBDs. It was developed by _E. W. Burgess_ in 1923, and postulated that a city grows outward from a CBD. The second ring is in transition between industry and poor housing. Stable, working class families occupy the third ring. Newer, more spacious homes occupy the fourth ring. Finally, the fifth ring includes small villages and bedroom communities populated by commuters.

    Sector Model (452-453): _Homer Hoyt_ designed the _sector model_, which says cities develop in a series of sectors, not rings. He believed that activities evolved in a wedge shape with the most narrow tip being the CBD. The model is, to some extent, a refinement of the concentric zone model. Interestingly, the layout of Chicago was used to support the concentric zone and sector models.

    Multiple Nuclei Model (453-454): _Chauncy Harris_ and _Ed Ullman_ developed the _multiple nuclei model_ stating a city is a complex place in which different nodes develop. Nodes may be represented by parks, universities, ports, or business centers. Different types of nodes tend to attract certain types of people to them depending on offered services.

    Geographic Applications of the Models (454): In order to understand and digest the data concerning people's locations, the U.S. Census gathers information by _census tracts_, neighborhood areas each containing about 5,000 people. Demographic information is collected which can be analyzed.

    Social Area Analysis (454-455): The study of population characteristics and distributions to create an overall picture of where various types of people tend to live is called _social area analysis_. Models help describe spatial attributes of race, income, and transportation needs which contribute to better strategic decisions made by public and private sector institutions.

Use of the Models Outside North America (455):

    European Cities (455-456): Europe's wealthy tend to live in the inner cities while poor people, often immigrants, are relegated to dense public housing structures in the suburbs. European officials endorse building high density suburban housing so the countryside will be preserved from development. By living in the central part of the large metropolitan areas, Europe's upper classes have access to the best shops, historical places, and restaurants. However, due to the congestion which prevails, they must share green spaces (public parks). Some urban people purchase country homes to gain more private space which they may visit on weekends or holidays.

Less Developed Countries (456): The rich people in LDCs also reside in the city cores of their respective countries. The poor are located in the more remote suburbs.

Pre-Colonial Cities (456): During pre-colonial times, cities were formed around a religious core, such as a church or mosque. Businesses were arranged in concentric or hierarchical patterns--distance from the center depended on the business's perceived value. Cities might be organized by grouping ethnic or religious groups.

Colonial Cities (457-459): Europeans expanded the existing cities in their colonies to provide colonial services. Wider streets, grid street plans, and open spaces are the trademarks of European influence while old quarters have narrow, winding streets, little open space, and cramped residences. .

Cities Since Independence (459, 461): Modern cities were planned. *Ernest Griffin* and *Larry Ford's* analysis of Latin American cities show the elite often settled along spines of development that contain restaurants, theaters, and other amenities attractive to richer people. The physical environment influences settlement and development patterns with the wealthy building in more desirable places.

Squatter Settlements (462): LDCs are not able to provide housing for all residents. Many desire to live in the cities and are forced to dwell in shanty towns which occupy the fringes of many cities in Latin America, Africa, and Asia. Squatter settlements are known as barrios, favelas, bustees, and bidonvilles in different parts of the world. *Squatter settlements* initially begin as camp grounds where new immigrants live. Often, over long periods of time, their infrastructure improves. Sadly, many cities in the world have significant portions of their populations living in squatter settlements. Early immigrants to the U.S. and to London lived in terrible conditions though they improved because of an expanding economy and an adequate supply of jobs; the opportunities and prospects are not available in many large LDC settlements.

Key Issue 3: Why Do Inner Cities Have Distinct Problems?

Inner-City Physical Problems (463):

Process of Deterioration (423): City neighborhoods can shift from middle-class to low-income occupants in a few years.

Filtering (463): Large houses built by wealthy people are often divided among poorer families. As time goes by the houses are neglected and eventually become abandoned because taxes exceed the income collected by the landlord. The process of home division and rental is known as *filtering*. Through the filtering process many poor families move farther from the city center to find less-deteriorated houses.

Redlining (463): *Redlining* occurs when banks delineate areas within the urban area to which they will not loan money because of high financial risk. The *Community Reinvestment Act* requires banks to keep track of the geographic locations of loans to ensure inner-city neighborhoods in each bank's service area receive a fair share of loans.

Urban Renewal (463): *Urban renewal* was a policy whereby the government removed many city dwellers from blighted inner-city neighborhoods, and sold the property to public agencies or private developers. It has become very unpopular and no longer receives funding from the U.S. government.

Public Housing (463-464): Much old, low-quality housing in the U.S. and Europe has been demolished and replaced by *public housing*-- units reserved for low-income people who must pay a percentage of their income, such as thirty percent, for rent. In the U.S. only two percent of all housing is public, but in the United Kingdom public housing accounts for over thirty percent of all housing. Since the 1970's, funding from the U.S. government for public housing units has nearly stopped. The government does subsidize some rents.

Renovated Housing (464-465): Islands of wealthy people have maintained exquisite neighborhoods in the midst of the inner-city. *Gentrification* occurs when people move back to the inner-city to renovate homes. Nice architecture, inexpensive prices, and access to the downtown draw many suburbanites back into the city. Cities encourage gentrification through low-cost loans and tax breaks. Cities in the U.S. and Western Europe try and reduce the financial impact for poor families forced to relocated by reimbursing moving expenses and rent increases for a 4-year period. Cities also renovate houses for poor families which helps keep the poor dispersed throughout the city.

Inner-City Social Problems (465): Many people in the inner-city are a permanent underclass living in a culture of poverty.

Underclass (465): Inner-city residents are referred to as the *underclass* because they are trapped in an unending cycle of economic and social problems— high unemployment rates, alcoholism, drug addiction, illiteracy, crime, deteriorating schools, expensive housing, and a lack of basic infrastructure of fire, police, and health facilities.

Lack of Job Skills (465): Inner-city residents lack job skills which would let them compete for better jobs. Employers needing more skilled labor are locating in the suburbs, increasing the distance between inner-city residents and even low skilled jobs.

Homeless (465-466): The *homeless*, people with no permanent housing, are now a fixture of the inner-city environment. Sadly, many of these people cannot afford housing and have no regular income or have been released from hospitals and institutions, and fail to cope with the modern world.

Culture of Poverty (466): Many people in the inner-city have low incomes and many children. A lack of child care facilities makes mothers choose between working or taking care of their children. Many fathers don't make their child support payments and if they are living in the home, may cause mothers to lose their welfare benefits.

Crime (466): Drug use is a problem in cities and rates of drug addiction are increasing more rapidly in the inner cities. Money is obtained through criminal activities with gangs forming to control drug distribution and territories within the city. In high density inner cities people are likely to sell drugs on street corners while in suburban drug sales take place behind closed doors.

Ethnic and Racial Segregation (466): Many neighborhoods are segregated by ethnicities. Whites, African-Americans, and Hispanics are generally segregated; African-Americans and Hispanics tend to dwell in the inner cities while whites are found more often in the suburbs. People choose neighborhoods which match their own socio-economic conditions. Voting patterns are affected by the division of cities into ethnic neighborhoods.

Inner-City Economic Problems (466-467): City services cost money. When wealthier, employed people move out of the inner cities fewer taxes are collected. Cities have two choices—reduce services or raise tax revenues. Reduction in services includes closing libraries, eliminating transit routs, and delaying school improvements all of which further encourage middle-class residents and industries to relocate. Raising tax revenues also drives out the desirable middle-class and industries. Improvements which would attract industries and wealthier residents are costly and can take money from other inner-city needs. State and federal funds have alleviated some inner-city fiscal problems.

Annexation (467-468): Until recently, cities could expand their sphere of influence through *annexation*, the addition of new land to within city boundaries. In the 1800's many people desired annexation because that meant better services than were previously provided. Today, high taxes and less authority over large bureaucratic government encourage many areas to remain independent of large urban areas.

Key Issue 4: Why Do Suburbs Have Distinct Problems? (468): Population in upper Midwest central cities has declined by 40 percent; the middle-class and industries have declined by an even higher percentages. In the U.S., suburbs have grown much faster than the overall population from 1950 to the present. Suburban population is growing reflecting people's desire for suburban living—detached dwellings, land, parking, and home ownership opportunities for space and privacy. Families with children are especially attracted to suburbs with lower crime rates and less traffic than the inner-cities.

The Peripheral Model (468-469): Developed by *Chauncy Harris*, the *peripheral model* suggests an urban area consists of an inner-city surrounded by large suburban residential and business areas tied together by a *beltway* or ring road. Suburban areas have fewer severe physical, social, and economic problems. The peripheral model points out the problems found in suburban areas. In the beltway there are *edge cities* or nodes of consumer and business services. They began as housing areas and have diversified to include office parks, manufacturing centers, shopping malls, and specialized nodes of hotels, warehouses, theme parks and distribution centers near the beltway and major interstate intersections.

Density Gradient (469): The housing density, and thereby housing lots, become larger further from the city core. This density change is called the *density gradient*.

Changes in Density Gradient (469): The number of people living in city cores is decreasing. Density has decreased in heavily urbanized areas because of population decline and abandonment of housing. Density has increased along the periphery where low-cost housing and apartment buildings are being built. Europeans have used zoning laws to make density gradients flatter, which encourages a more uniform population density across the urban area.

Cost of Suburban Sprawl (469): *Sprawl* is the progressive spread of development across the landscape. Suburbs often exist on former farmlands.

Suburban Development Process (469): Land at the urban fringe is being developed by individual builders to accommodate suburban housing preferences. Detached, isolated sites are cheaper which further encourages sprawl. Road and utility networks must be expanded and funded through new taxes or installed by the developer and passed along to the home owner. Agricultural land is lost to sprawl which affects the ability of the city dweller to go to the country for recreation. Excessive energy is spent because automobiles are required for all transportation. Mandatory open spaces often encircle cities in Great Britain and are called *greenbelts*.

Suburban Segregation (469-472): Laws that prevent mixed land use such as commercial and residential overlapping property are called *zoning ordinances*. U.S. suburbs are criticized because poor people, often minorities, can not afford to live in them because housing prices are kept uniformly high.

School Busing (472): In 1954, the U.S. Supreme Court ruled that segregation is unconstitutional. Afterwards, many white and black students were bussed to schools in areas outside their neighborhoods to promote integration. Many white parents reacted to this by enrolling their students in private schools often requiring them to be bussed to the private school.

Contribution of Transportation to Suburbanization (472): Urban sprawl makes people more dependent on transportation.

Motor Vehicles (472-473): Because of urban sprawl, people have become more dependent on automobiles. Before the automobile, people lived in dense cities with no option for living in suburbs because the means for transportation simply did not exist. The automobile is responsible for 95 percent of all trips within U.S. cities. Public transit is not available outside the big cities. Highways paid for by the U.S. government have helped encourage the purchase of automobiles by the U.S. population. Gasoline has price limits keeping the price at one-fourth those in Western European countries. The implementation of new highways has caused disruptions in many older world cities where there isn't room for road construction or expansion.

Public Transportation (473):

Rush Hour Commuting (473): *Rush hour* is the four consecutive 15 minute periods during the day that have the heaviest traffic. As much as 40 percent of all trips in or out of the CBD occur during a four hour period. Automobiles are very expensive to own and operate. Popularity must stem from convenience and privacy because public transportation is cheaper, less-polluting and more energy-efficient. The average city allocates one-fourth of its land area to roads and parking lots, and one-third of its high priced land. Commitment to the automobile decreased the number of people using public transportation in the last fifty years. Public transportation use declined from 23 billion per year in the late 1940s to 7 billion per year in the early 1990s.

New Rapid Transit Lines (473): New interest has developed in rapid transit lines. Funds earmarked for highways have recently been invested in the expansion and modernization of rapid transit systems. The trolley, fixed light transit, is making a comeback in North American cities. California leads in the construction of new light rail systems.

Service Versus Cost (474): Reduced subsidies to rapid transit lines threaten their existence. Low-income people in inner-city neighborhoods rely on public transit though transit still doesn't take them to where the jobs are found—in the suburbs. The U.S. doesn't fully recognize the importance of public transportation.

Public Transit in Other Countries (474): Unlike the U.S., Western European countries and Japan maintain and expand rapid transit because it is perceived as an important and desirable amenity as well as a necessity.

Local Government Fragmentation (474): Due to the enormous number of governments in the U.S., it is very difficult to coordinate them in a team effort to solve regional problems such as traffic, solid-waste disposal, and affordable housing.

Metropolitan Government (474-475): Metropolitan areas in the U.S. are commonly managed by a council of government that is authorized to perform overall planning of the entire area which local governments cannot do. A *council of government* is a cooperative agency consisting of representatives of the various local governments in the region. There are two kinds of metropolitan-wide governments.

Federations (475): *Federation governments*, such as the one ruling Toronto's area, divide duties of government between two tiers: one regional and several local component governments.

Consolidations (475): *Consolidated governments* are formed when cities and their respective counties combine governments as is the case for Indianapolis and Miami.

Metropolitan Governments in the United Kingdom (475-476): In the United Kingdom the federal government has the power to redefine the boundaries of local governments. In the 1980s' the UK redefined many of its cities' borders. It was decided London would be better governed by 32 local boroughs than by one regional government.

Summary: The U.S. economy has shifted from an agricultural economic base to a manufacturing base, and is now shifting to the service sector—an indicator of contemporary economies in MDCs. Along with changes in the economic base as well as the infusion of different technologies, the cities have adjusted to the shift. In the U.S., most upper class people prefer to live in the suburbs and the suburbs are increasingly attractive for industries. Europe's elite often live in the central cities of their urban complexes with poorer classes living on the fringes in densely populated suburbs. Although planners may wish to create a more egalitarian living structure through planning, prices dictated by taxes and supply and demand prohibit such an urban structure from existing.

CHAPTER 13
KEY TERMS AND CONCEPTS

Urbanization: The increase in the number of urban dwellers as well as the increase in the overall percentage of urban dwellers. It has drastically increased in the last two hundred years.

Fully Urbanized: Describes countries whose urban areas are approaching their maximum capacity and all the people interested in moving to cities have already done so.

Louis Wirth: In the 1930s he investigated the differences between urban and rural residents and their lifestyle. He defined a city as having a large size, high population density, and socially heterogeneous people.

City: An urban settlement which has been formally incorporated into an independent, self-governing unit.

Urbanized Area: Includes the central city and the built-up surrounding areas where population density exceeds 1,000 people per square mile.

Central City: The core of a large, urbanized area. Los Angeles is the core of a large urbanized area which contains many other cities.

Metropolitan Statistical Area (MSA): In the United States, a central city with at least 50,000 people, the country within which the city is located, and adjacent counties meeting one of several criteria indicating a functional connection to the central city.

Megalopolis: Continuous, adjacent MSAs which form a massive urban complex, such as the urban corridor between Boston and Washington. Term was coined by geographer **Jean Gottman**.

Consolidated Metropolitan Statistical Area (CMSA): Two or more adjacent MSAs with overlapping commuting patterns.

Primary Metropolitan Statistical Area (PMSA): The MSA within a CMSA that exceeds 1 million population with at least one county with a population of more than 100,000, at least 60 percent of the population working nonfarm jobs, and at least 50 percent of the workers commuting to jobs outside the county.

Concentric Zone Model: A model of the internal structure of cities in which social groups are spatially arranged in a series of rings. **E. W. Burgess** developed it in 1923.

Sector Model: A model of the internal structure of cities in which social groups are arranged around a series of sectors or wedges radiating out from the CBD. **Homer Hoyt** developed this model in 1939.

Multiple Nuclei Model: A model of the internal structure of cities in which social groups are arranged around a collection of nodes of activities. **Ed Ullman** and **Chauncy Harris** developed this model in 1945.

Census Tracts: An area delineated by the U.S. Bureau of the Census for which statistics are published. In urbanized areas, census tracts correspond roughly to neighborhoods and contain about 5,000 people.

Social Area Analysis: The study of population characteristics and distributions to create an overall picture of where various types of people tend to live. Also called geodemographics.

Ernest Griffin and Larry Ford: They analyzed Latin American cities and showed the elite often settled along spines of development with amenities that attract the wealthier people.

Squatter Settlements: An area within a city in a less developed country in which people illegally establish residences on land they do not own or rent and erect home-made structures. Rio de Janeiro, Brazil has extensive squatter settlements which are known as favelas.

Filtering: A process of change in the use of a house, from single-family owner and occupancy to abandonment. The house costs eventually exceeds its income.

Redlining: A process by which banks draw lines on a map and refuse to lend money to purchase or improve property within the boundaries. Such properties are deemed as high financial risks by the banks.

Community Reinvestment Act: An act requiring banks to evenly distribute loans across their service area which ensures inner-city neighborhoods receive a fair share of loans.

Urban Renewal: A process where cities identified undesirable inner-city neighborhoods, relocated the occupants, cleared the site, and developed the land privately or publicly.

Public Housing: Housing owned by the government. In the United States, it is rented to low-income residents, and the rents are generally set at 30 percent of the families' incomes. Public housing in the U.S. has declined in recent years.

Gentrification: A process of converting an urban neighborhood from a predominantly low-income renter to a predominantly middle-class owner-occupied area. Classic architecture and low-prices are two things that encourage gentrification by the middle-class.

Underclass: A group in society prevented from participating in the material benefits of a more developed society because of a variety of social and economic characteristics. Poor education and high crime rates are often prevalent in such groups.

Annexation: Adding land area legally to a city. Many people in the U.S. resist annexation because it usually brings higher taxes.

Peripheral Model: Developed by **Chauncy Harris** which suggests an urban area has an inner-city surrounded by large suburban residential and business areas tied together by a beltway.

Beltway: A ring road that travels around the city.

Edge City: A large node of office and retail activities on the edge of an urban area. Their lucrative traits are cheaper rents and room for expansion.

Density Gradient: The change in density in an urban area from the center to the periphery. As one moves outward from the city core, densities in the U.S. tend to decline.

Sprawl: Development of new housing sites at relatively low density and at locations that are not contiguous to the existing built-up area.

Greenbelts: A ring of land maintained as parks, agriculture, or other types of open space to limit the sprawl of an urban area. They have driven up housing prices in Europe.

Zoning Ordinances: A law limiting the permitted uses of land and maximum density of development in a community. These statutes attempt to prevent the mixing of land uses in neighborhoods.

Rush Hour (peak hour): The four consecutive fifteen-minute periods in the morning and evening with the heaviest volumes of traffic. The suburbs have less congestion than the CBDs of most cities.

Council of Government: A cooperative agency consisting of representatives of local governments in a metropolitan area in the United States. Planning powers are often held by councils.

Federation Government: Divides duties of government in a city between a regional tier and several local governments.

Consolidated Government: Combined government for both the county and city.

CHAPTER 13
PROGRESSIVE REVIEW

1. Today nearly _____ the world's population lives in cities and over _____ have more than 2 million inhabitants.

½
100

2. _____ is the increase in the number and percentage of people living in cities.

Urbanization

3. A country is _____ _____ when its urban areas are approaching their maximum capacity and all the people who want to move to cities have already done so.

fully urbanized

4. _____ cities are attracting large numbers of people and their population is growing largely due to natural increase rather than expanding economic conditions and increased numbers of jobs.

LDC

5. Cities can be described, according to Louis Wirth, by their _____ _____, _____ _____, and _____ _____ and the description is now more applicable to LDC cities than to MDC areas.

large size, high density, social heterogeneity

6. MSAs are popular for city analysis because their building blocks, _____, have abundant data.

counties

7. An area is considered urban if it has a population density of _____ people per square mile.

1,000

8. The _____ city is experiencing declines in population and, as a whole, is considered the middle of a city.

central

9. The daily traverse from the suburbs to the CBD by workers in their automobiles is known as _____.

commuting

10. _____ _____ coined the term _____ to describe a large urban area with no real rural areas between the built up areas.

Jean Gottman, megalopolis

11. The percentage of _____ settlements has been steadily increasing for 200 years.

urban

12. The observation developed by Homer Hoyt which explained the spatial array of economic activities in urban areas is called the _____ _____.

sector model

13. E. L. Ullman and C. D. Harris develop the _____ _____   multiple
model that said different urban activities are clustered near   nuclei
nodes.

14. If a city grows outward from a CBD in rings, it can be
described by the _____ _____ model.   concentric zone

15. _____ _____ _____ uses data from census tracts to   Social area
analyze the distribution, patterns, and characteristics of urban   analysis
dwellers.

16. In Europe, suburbs often have _____ crime rates than do   higher
cities because the wealthy elite tend to live in the central city.

17. According to the U.S. Census Bureau, the largest urban
area in the world was found in the country of _____.   Japan

18. A larger variety of cultures and lifestyles are found in   urban
_____ areas than in rural areas.

19. _____ _____ are located in areas not considered   Squatter
desirable by wealthy people and have different names   settlements
depending on where they exist in the world.

20. The time of heaviest traffic in the day is called the _____ rush
hour.

21. The subdivision of large houses and occupancy by lower
income people is known as _____.   filtering

22. _____ is the process by which banks refuse to lend   Redlining
money for houses situated in specific geographical areas.

23. Most North American and European cities have turned
away from urban _____ since the 1970s.   renewal

24. When older housing in the inner-city is purchased and
renovated by younger, higher income people, _____ occurs.   gentrification

25. Inner-city residents who seem trapped in their low-income
social group are called the permanent _____.   underclass

26. People who have no permanent housing and no regular
income are called _____.   homeless

27. _____ occurs when people of different races and ethnicities live apart from one another.

Segregation

28. Over _____ percent of Americans polled prefer to live in the suburbs.

90

29. As one leaves the central city, the population density in U.S. cities usually _____.

declines

30. Progressive urban spread over the landscape is _____.

sprawl

31. Rings of parks around British cities are called _____.

greenbelts

32. Laws, called _____ _____, encourage spatial separation of different urban activities.

zoning ordinances

33. Cities legally add territory to their area through the process of _____.

annexation

34. Many _____-_____ and _____ people can not afford to move into suburban housing in the U.S..

low-income, minority

35. The invention of the _____ significantly reduced the percentage of people who used public transportation in the U.S. during the twentieth century.

automobile

36. The average U.S. city allocates one-fourth of its area to parking lots and _____.

roads

37. Elaborate, multiple-level _____ _____ are located in the suburbs where their consumers tend to live.

shopping malls

38. Urban areas have many different forms of _____ to try and control the urban area and provide services.

governments

39. Most U.S. metropolitan areas have a _____ form of government, which includes representatives from many different local governments.

council

CHAPTER 14

RESOURCE ISSUES

Humans make many choices about the world around them. They must decide everything—what to make the house out of and how to get to work. As economies have grown more complex, industry and manufacturing have risen to the challenge of providing everything wanted: televisions, automobiles, fertilizers, paints, and wrist watches. There is a negative side to development. Cars produce air pollution. Fertilizers contribute to water pollution. Disposal of paints contributes to soil pollution. By-products (heat, light, chemicals, acids, toxins, and sludge) are produced for everything manufactured and consumed. With more people come more wants. More wants mean more consumption. More consumption means more pollution. Taking care of the Earth now is perhaps one of the greatest challenges of all times.

Resource Issues: Mexico City is an example of a city with extreme urban pollution. Among its worst forms of pollution is its poor air quality. The elevation of Mexico City at 7,400 feet makes the air thin but, added to this, are pollutants from automobiles, factories, refineries, and other sources, which are constantly compacted against the valley walls which form the perimeter of the city on all but one side. Winds from the open north side of the valley compact the pollutants against the other three sides of the valley, causing very unhealthy smog. Most of the emissions in the air come from automobiles. Factories add to emitted pollutants. The Mexican government has restricted car use and has closed some industrial facilities to lower the toxicity of the air in their capital. Sewage flows openly into nearby rivers, and 30 percent of the city's homes have no connections to the public sewer system.

Humans frequently do not live harmoniously with nature. Invariably resources are not properly used by humans; waste and pollution are the consequences. Geographers say that humans misuse resources through depletion of scarce resources, destruction of resources through pollution, and inefficient use of resources. The study of planetary resource is a feature of globalization; resources extend around the Earth and are used by everyone.

Key Issue 1: Why Are Fossil Fuel Resources Being Depleted? (483): The use of power by humans or animals is named *animate energy*. Power from machines is called *inanimate energy*.

Dependence on Fossil Fuels (483-484): Historically, *biomass* (wood, plant material, and animal waste) has been and continues to be a very important source of energy. It is burned directly or converted into methane gas, charcoal, or alcohol.

Energy is important to businesses, homes, and transportation. A *fossil fuel* is the residue of plants and animals buried for millions of years. Fossil fuels are finite; they are limited in supply. They are also unevenly distributed throughout the world. Oil, natural gas, and coal provide over ninety percent of the energy in the U.S..

Finiteness of Fossil Fuels (484): *Renewable* energy is limitless in amounts such as wind, solar, fusion, and hydroelectric. *Nonrenewable* energy can only be used once and will not be replaced within the life of a human being. Fossil fuels and fission nuclear energy are nonrenewable sources of energy.

Remaining Supply of Fossil Fuels (484-485): A *proven reserve* is the remaining amount of a nonrenewable resource. Reserves that are thought to exist, but not proven, are called *potential reserve*. At current consumption rates the Earth's oil reserves will last another forty years and natural gas will last for about 80 years. Coal is plentiful compared to oil and natural gas.

Extraction of Remaining Reserves (485): As time passes, the extraction of fossil fuels will become more difficult and costly. Coal mined today comes from seams which are relatively poor in quality compared to those mined in the past. The future will see the refinement of *oil shales* (rocks saturated with oil) and *tar sands* (oil-saturated sand). It is currently not profitable to process these energy sources as cost-effective extraction technology has yet to be developed.

Uneven Distribution of Fossil Fuels (485): Global distribution of fossil fuels is uneven and consumption is higher in some regions than in others.

Location of Reserves (485-486): Fossil fuels were formed from tropical swamps which, because of tectonic movement, migrated poleward producing oil, coal, and natural gas. The U.S. and Russia each have a quarter of the world's reserves of coal. Europe has about twenty percent and China ten percent. Most of the world's oil supply is found in Saudi Arabia (25 percent) and other countries located near the Persian Gulf (40 percent). Countries such as Russia, Turkmenistan, and Uzbekistan possess one-third of the world's reserves of natural gas. Most places in Africa, Latin America, and Asia are relatively fossil fuel poor.

Consumption of Fossil Fuels (487): Today a handful of countries consume seventy-five percent of the world's energy. As LDCs develop (increasing per capita consumption of resources) and their populations increase, they will place an even greater demand upon the reserves of fossil fuels in the world. The U.S. and Western Europe import more than half of their petroleum. Japan imports more than 90 percent. Competition for fuel is likely to increase as LDCs increase their usage and dependence on them.

Control of World Petroleum (487-488): MDCs import most of their petroleum from the Middle East. Many of the reserves were controlled by Western European and U.S. oil companies until the 1970s when operations were either nationalized or more tightly controlled.

OPEC Policies During the 1970s (488-489): To reduce competition that drove down oil prices, a cartel was formed to set high prices for the MDC customers. This cartel is known as OPEC, Organization of Petroleum Exporting Countries; OPEC has used its influence to increase the price of oil. In 1973, these countries caused an energy crisis in the West when they boycotted oil exports as a form of protest for Western countries aiding Israel in the 1973 Arab-Israeli War. MDCs suffered in the 1970s because of the rapid increases in oil prices. LDCs were hurt even more because they relied on low-priced oil to fuel industrial development.

Reduced Dependency on OPEC (489-490): OPEC's effectiveness has been reduced in the last two decades because of disputes between member countries. After the Persian Gulf war between the U.S., Kuwait and Iraq the price of oil fell after briefly rising at the onset of the war to over forty dollars per barrel. More efficient motor vehicles and development of oil in other regions in the world have reduced world dependency on OPEC.

Problems with Coal (490): Coal is a resource for which large reserves exist, enough to serve U.S. needs for hundreds of years.

Air Pollution (490): *Air pollution* is caused when coal is burned, releasing sulfur oxides, hydrocarbons, carbon dioxides, and particulates into the atmosphere. Scrubbers are placed on smoke stacks to minimize the amount of pollution emitted into the air.

Mine Safety (490-491): In the past, thousands of miners perished annually in mining accidents. They were prone to black lung disease. Improved ventilation and mine safety rules have reduced the reported annual number of deaths to below 100.

Subsidence and Erosion (491): Coal mines cause land to subside and to erode more easily. Water is often acidified after exposure to coal mines and can pollute grown water sources. Clearing the land of vegetation contributes to erosion.

Economics (491): Coal is costly to transport because it is bulky and heavy; a great deal of resources are spent moving coal to locations where it will be used.

Powering Motor Vehicles (491): Electric cars are ultimately powered by the coal burned to produce the electricity. Electric cars are expensive to purchase and operate; few people are willing to pay to save energy and reduce pollution. They also have a limited range, further reducing their appeal.

Alternative Energy Sources (492):

Nuclear Energy (493): Large amounts of energy are produced by small amounts of material when nuclear energy is produced through fission. Western Europe is largely powered by nuclear facilities. In North America and Europe, about 25 percent of electricity is from nuclear facilities.

Potential Accidents (492-494): *Fission* is the splitting of atoms, producing nuclear reactions that heat water, turn turbines, and result in electricity. Another result is *radioactive waste,* which can be deadly if humans are exposed to it. Reactions may runaway, causing a meltdown as happened at Chernobyl in the Soviet Union, killing 31 people and extending its impacting most of Europe.

Radioactive Waste (494): Nuclear waste does not lose its radioactivity for thousands of years, hence permanent storage facilities are difficult to find. People don't want storage facilities near their communities.

Bomb Material (494): Nuclear bombs are being developed by countries around the world. Pakistan and India are a matter for serious for global concern. No nuclear conflict has occurred because people recognize such a war could terminate human civilization.

Limited Uranium Reserves (494): Uranium has a limited supply, only about sixty more years at current levels of use. A *breeder reactor* turns uranium into plutonium as a renewable resource. But plutonium is far more lethal and may be more easily placed into nuclear bombs.

Cost (494): Nuclear plants are also extremely expensive to build and maintain. *Costs and risks* are the main impediments to more nuclear facilities.

Solar Energy (494-495): Solar energy is free and will be present for about 5 billion years. *Passive solar energy systems* collect energy without special devices such as human skin or dark clothing. *Active solar energy systems* collect solar energy and convert it either to heat energy or electricity. Heat conversion uses mirrors to reflect sunlight into lenses that heat water or rocks. Indirect electric conversion heats oil, running turbines on steam. Direct electric conversion uses *photovoltaic cells* to convert light energy directly into electricity. Solar energy is popular in the U.S., Israel, and Japan.

Other Energy Sources (495):

Hydroelectric Power (495-496): Water may be used to turn turbines as it falls, causing electricity. This is called *hydroelectric power.* This is the world's second most common form of electricity after coal. Dams are sometimes built which flood land and upset ecosystems, making hydroelectric plants less desirable.

Geothermal Energy (496): *Geothermal energy* is the steam and hot water from naturally occurring hot water heated by underground forces. It is found in active volcanic regions of the world.

Biomass (496): *Biomass* in the form of sugar cane, corn, and soybeans may be processed into motor vehicle fuels. Biomass is not likely to be increased as a source of fuel because it is inefficient to convert biomass into refined fuel sources, and most biomass is already fulfilling many other purposes.

Nuclear Fusion (496): *Fusion* is a potentially limitless source of energy, but temperatures created by such reactions can not yet be controlled, and other risks are increased.

Key Issue 2: Why Are Resources Being Polluted? (496): Air, water, and land disperse human waste. When more waste is added than a resource can accommodate there is *pollution.* Pollution is greater where people are concentrated. Waste can either be collected and reused, or discarded into the environment. Natural sources of pollution include volcanoes and erosion from floods.

Pollution Sources (497): Discarded waste can go into the air, water, or land.

Air Pollution (497):

Global Warming (497-498): *Air pollution* is the concentration of trace substances at a level greater than that which occurs in average air. Carbon monoxide, sulfur dioxides, and nitrogen oxides are common pollutants of air. Cars, industry, and power plants cause most of the air pollution in the world. On a global scale human pollution of the Earth's air may be causing the temperature of the Earth to rise. Earth's surface temperatures have increased by one degree Celsius during the last 100 years. Many people attribute the rise in temperature to the *greenhouse effect.* If temperatures rise significantly more, the ice caps could melt and climate patterns around the planet would be disrupted.

Global-Scale Ozone Damage (498): The _ozone_ is a layer of air within the stratosphere which absorbs much of the ultra-violet rays from the sun. _CFCs (chlorofluorocarbons)_ produced by people have damaged this zone, causing higher surface levels of UV exposure than in the past.

Regional-Scale Acid Deposition (498): _Acid precipitation_ is produced when industry emits sulfur and nitrogen oxides into the atmosphere. Acid deposition damages water bodies and biomass. In the U.S., acid deposition originates in the highly industrialized areas around the Great Lakes. Eastern Europe has also suffered environmental damage because of acid rain and deposition.

Local-Scale Urban Air Pollution (498-500): At a local level, carbon monoxide causes much biological damage to humans as it reduces oxygen in the blood when inhaled. Hydrocarbons and nitrogen oxides can form _photochemical smog_ when released into the atmosphere, causing respiratory problems in exposed people. Particulates include dust and smoke as from factories and diesel truck exhaust. Denver has the worst air in the U.S. according to the EPA. Denver is situated along the Rocky Mountains and gases get trapped and produce a permanent temperature inversion. Many LDC cities such as Santiago, Chile experience very intense air pollution. Air is becoming cleaner in MDCs where legislation is enforced. In countries where the population is beginning to drive, more air pollution grows accordingly.

Water Pollution (500): Water is imperative to human survival, yet it is frequently polluted by humans. Pollution of waterways is widespread. Rivers, lakes, and the ocean are very accessible to humans both for use and for waste disposal.

Pollution Sources (500-501): Industries pollute waterways used as part of the industrial process in manufacturing or in chemical production. Municipal sewage pollutes water because it is difficult to extract all of the pollutants in the treatment stage. Fertilizers and pesticides used for agriculture runoff from watersheds to concentrate in streams and lakes, causing damage to the aquatic ecosystems. Nonpoint polluters are hard to stop, for their area of pollution is large and unfocused.

Impact on Aquatic Life (501): _Biochemical oxygen demand_ occurs when oxygen is consumed by organic waste, depleting the amount of oxygen that may be utilized by animal life in the water system.

Wastewater and Disease (501): In MDCs today, diseases caused or carried by polluted water are relatively rare. In LDCs diseases are common because of the lack of good water treatment facilities in urban areas. Waterborne diseases such as cholera, typhoid, and dysentery are major causes of death.

Land Pollution (501-502): Products consumption has solid waste byproducts that are incinerated, put into a dump, or recycled. In the U.S. 4 pounds of solid waste per person is generated daily. About five-sixths of solid waste is put into landfills or incinerated. Only one-sixth of solid waste is recycled.

Sanitary Landfills (502-503): _Sanitary landfills_ are the most common disposal for solid waste in the U.S.. Solid wastes are concentrated into small areas of land, possibly affecting ground water supplies. They also drive down land prices. Consequently, many urban areas export waste to poorer parts of the country where disposal is overlooked because of financial gains.

Incineration (503): Incineration burns solid waste and reduces bulk by about three-fourths so the ash demands less space in landfills. This can be helpful when energy is derived from incineration. Sometimes toxins are released into the atmosphere during this process.

Recycling Solid Waste (503-504): Recycling solid waste prevents it from being placed in a landfill or incinerated. Many U.S. communities have forced people to recycle certain products. Recycling has increased to 22 percent of all solid waste in 1994. About 97 percent of auto batteries are recycled and only 2 percent of plastics.

Toxic Pollutants (504): Toxic wastes found in heavy metals are harder to dispose of than other materials. People fear being near toxic waste sites because they can be very harmful. Many toxic substances are known to cause health problems in the human body even in small concentrations. This was the case at Love Canal, New York. Some U.S. and European firms have exported toxic wastes to West Africa to avoid domestic government and public scrutiny.

Alternatives for Reducing Pollution (505): There are two way to reduce pollution—reduce discharge or increase environmental capacity.

Reducing Pollution by Reducing Discharges (505-506): If the amount of waste is reduced or recycled, pollution can be decreased.

Reduce Waste Created (506): Changing the number and amount of inputs into a product will decrease the amount of pollution the product creates. If demand for a product is reduced, so will the pollution caused by creating the product.

Recycling (506): Recycling will also lower the number of inputs placed into a product. Waste can be reused in the same production system or used in a different production purpose.

Increasing Environmental Capacity (506-507): Increasing the ability of the environment to absorb pollution reduces the stress caused by pollution.

Use Resource More Efficiently (507): This can be done by increasing the efficiency of the resources currently receiving discharges. For example, smokestacks can be built in areas with high winds to disperse and weaken pollutants.

Discharge into Different Part of Environment (507): Residues can also be transformed and then expelled into other parts of the environment. For example, scrubbers are placed into the smokestacks of plants to make them more efficient and change air pollution into a solid waste than can be disposed of on land.

A Coking Plant: Using All Reduction Strategies (507-508): A coking plant can reduce the heat pollution it creates by transforming heat into liquid water and steam. It can reduce discharges by reusing water to cool hot coke and capturing gases, tars, and oils. Changing the mix of coal also reduces the amount of gases emitted.

Comparing Pollution Reduction Strategies (508): Humans can easily exceed the environmental capacity for a particular waste. Dispersed waste can remain harmful. Many forms of waste are mobile and move from soil to air to water.

Key Issue 3: Why Are Global Food Resources Expandable?

Alternative Strategies to Increase Food Supply (508-509):
Increase Food Supply by Expanding Agricultural Land (509): Only 11 percent of the world's land is cultivated. There is not a significant amount of land that can be put into agricultural production.

Land Removed From Agriculture (509-510): Agricultural production can be increased without negative effects. Restrictions can be placed on the amount of land consumed each year by urban sprawl. Housing is often built on premium farm land. Most scientists believe that shortages in world food supplies will not be compensated for by employing these measures. Desertification is constantly reducing the amount of farmable land.

Increase Food Supply Through Higher Productivity (510): The best way to increase food production is through research to develop more efficient genetic varieties of crops like wheat and rice.

The Green Revolution (510): The *green revolution* of the 1970s and 1980s greatly increased world food production through these techniques. Wheat varieties were developed which were better suited to harsh environments and matured quicker than other types. This created substantially increased harvests of wheat.

Need for Fertilizer and Machinery (510): Fertilizers that inject nitrogen into the ground are another way to increase yields. This re-energizes the ground after crops tire it. Current fertilizers are often derived from oil bases. If oil prices go up, it becomes harder to fertilize crops, and yields drop accordingly.

Increase Food Supply by Identifying New Food Sources (510):

Cultivating Oceans (510-511): The oceans can probably supply a much larger percentage of our food. The oceans are vast, covering three-fourths of the Earth's surface. If fishing is kept efficient, preventing over fishing, harvests from the sea can consistently be very large.

Higher-Protein Cereals (511): Since much of the world doesn't consume very much animal protein, it is important to develop cereal grains that have high protein contents. If varieties of corn and wheat had higher levels of protein, many people in LDCs would maintain better health.

Improve Palatability of Rarely Consumed Foods (511): Improving the variety of goods consumed improves diet and health. Americans would be healthier if soybeans were part of the daily diet.

Increase Food Supply by Increasing Exports from Other Countries (511-512): More balanced crop exports to needier places on the planet would alleviate pressure to grow large amounts of food in places which are naturally agriculturally disadvantaged. The U.S. could export crops and surpluses to African countries. Russia is the world leader in grain imports. Japan and Russia together account for one-half of the world's corn imports and Russia and China together account for one-fourth of the world's wheat imports.

Africa's Food Supply Crisis (512-513): Sub-Saharan Africa cannot produce
enough food for its population. It is estimated that 70 percent of Africans do not have enough food to eat. Agricultural production today is lower than it was in the

1950s. Farmers over planted, land was overgrazed, and the soil was exhausted. Governmental price fixing kept the sale of farm commodities from making a profit decreasing incentives to increase productivity.

Summary: In the ultimate analysis, the resources available to humans, and how they use resources, will determine the human geography of the future. The twentieth century will be remembered as the century in which most natural petroleum resources were consumed. Almost certainly the twenty-first century will see an increase in per capita use of resources, but without petroleum resources to provide the base as it did during the twentieth century. Coal will be available, but its threat to the environment may render it less useful. Alternate energy sources will be explored and exploited. Chapter Fourteen lays a foundation for understanding what might happen and where, as a capstone for the body of human geography provided by the previous thirteen chapters.

CHAPTER 14
KEY TERMS AND CONCEPTS

Resource: A substance in the environment useful to people that is economically and technologically feasible to access and socially acceptable to use.

Animate Power: Power supplied by people or animals. Today, it is used more in LDCs than in MDCs.

Inanimate Power: Power supplied by machines. This type of power dominates today's automated world.

Biomass: Fuel derived from plant material and animal waste. Animal wastes can be "fermented" to produce methane gas, used in some areas where wood fuel is difficult or impossible to obtain.

Fossil Fuel: Energy source formed from the residue of plants and animals buried millions of years ago. They will be gone within 100 years, except coal, if used at current rates of consumption.

Renewable Energy: A resource that has a theoretically unlimited supply and is not depleted when used by people. Sunlight is an example.

Nonrenewable Energy: A source of energy that has a finite supply. Oil and natural gas are examples.

Proven Reserve: The amount of a resource remaining in discovered deposits. China and Russia are not open about their reserves.

Potential Reserve: The amount of energy in deposits not yet identified but thought to exist.

Oil Shales: Rocks saturated with oil. They aren't yet cost effective for refining.

Tar Sands: Sand saturated with oil. They aren't yet cost effective for refining.

Air Pollution: Concentration of trace substances, such as carbon monoxide, sulfur dioxide, nitrogen oxides, hydrocarbons, and solid particles, at a greater level than occurs in average air.

Fission: The splitting of an atomic nucleus to release energy. It is the common technique used to create nuclear energy.

Radioactive Waste: Particles from a nuclear reaction that emit radiation. Contact with such particles may be harmful or lethal to people and must therefore be safely stored for thousands of years.

Breeder Reactor: A nuclear power plant that creates its own fuel from plutonium. They are more dangerous than other reactors and are not found in the U.S..

Passive Solar Energy Systems: Solar energy system that collects energy without the use of mechanical devices. Animal skin and dark clothing are examples.

Active Solar Energy Systems: Solar energy system that collects energy through the use of mechanical devices like **photovoltaic cells** or flat-plate collectors. Solar cells on roofs are examples.

Photovoltaic Cells: Solar energy cells, usually made from silicon, that collect solar rays to generate electricity. Enough cells can propel small cars.

Hydroelectric Power: Power generated from moving water. There is little expanded future opportunity for this power in the U.S. because most of the good sites are already being used.

Geothermal Energy: Energy from steam or hot water produced from hot or molten underground rocks. In the U.S., Yellowstone National Park has good geothermal energy potential.

Fusion: The creation of energy by joining the nuclei of two hydrogen atoms to form helium. It produces heat which can not be contained by modern laboratories.

Pollution: Addition of more waste than a resource can accommodate. It often decreases the value of other natural resources.

Greenhouse Effect: Anticipated increase in Earth's temperature, caused by carbon dioxide (emitted by burning fossil fuels) trapping some of the radiation emitted by the surface. The melting of the polar ice-caps could be a long-term result of this phenomena.

Ozone: A gas which absorbs ultraviolet solar radiation, found in the stratosphere, a zone between 15 and 50 kilometers above Earth's surface. It is widely thought that it is being depleted by chemical reactions.

Chlorofluorocarbon (CFC): A gas used as a solvent, a propellant in aerosols, a refrigerant, in plastic foams and fire extinguishers. Its presence is thought to be destroying the ozone.

Acid Precipitation: Conversion of sulfur oxides and nitrogen oxides to acids that return to Earth as rain, snow, or fog. It causes bodies of water to become acidified.

Acid Deposition: Sulfur oxides and nitrogen oxides, emitted by burning fossil fuels, enter the atmosphere where they combine with oxygen and water to form sulfuric acid and nitric acid and return to Earth's surface. Here they destroy many botanical surface features of the Earth.

Photochemical Smog: An atmospheric condition formed through a combination of weather conditions and pollution, especially from motor vehicle emissions. Denver has the worst in the U.S..

Biochemical Oxygen Demand (BOD): Amount of oxygen required by aquatic bacteria to decompose a given load of organic waste, a measure of water pollution.

Sanitary Landfill: A place to dispose solid waste, where a layer of Earth is bulldozed over garbage each day to reduce emissions of gases and odors from the decaying trash, minimize fires, and discourage vermin. It is difficult to open new ones because of public resistance.

Incineration: The burning of solid wastes to reduce their bulk.

Desertification: Degradation of land, especially in semiarid areas, primarily due to human actions like excessive crop planting, animal grazing, and tree cutting. Substantial desertification has occurred in Africa.

Green Revolution: Rapid diffusion of new agricultural technology, especially new high-yield seeds and fertilizers. Wheat and rice crops have increased substantially.

Sustainable Development: The level of development that can be maintained in a country without depleting resources to the extent that future generations will be unable to achieve a comparable level of development.

CHAPTER 14
PROGRESSIVE REVIEW

1. Mexico City suffers from extreme _____ pollution.   air

2. Animal and human power is also known as _____ power.   animate

3. Energy is used in businesses, homes, and _____.   transportation

4. Coal is an example of a _____ energy.   nonrenewable

5. Sunlight is an example of a _____ energy.   renewable

6. Mineral deposits that are known to exist are called _____   proven reserves
_____.

7. Mineral deposits which are thought to exist are known as
_____ _____.   potential reserves

8. _____ sands and oil _____ are oil-saturated.   Tar, shales

9. At current rates of consumption the world's oil supply will
dry up in _____ years.   40

10. _____ supplies will last much longer than oil and natural   Coal
gas.

11. Coal was formed millions of years ago in tropical _____.   swamps

12. MDCs tend to have a disproportionately _____   high, use
percentage of the world's fossil fuel.

13. Two-thirds of the world's oil reserves are found in the   Middle East
_____ _____.

14. OPEC largely controls the world's supply of _____.   oil

15. After the _____-_____ war, OPEC boycotted oil exports   Arab-Israeli
to the West.

16. The South American country of _____ is a member of   Venezuela
OPEC.

17. Annual direct mortality rates in _____ is now being   mining
reported as less than 100 annually for the entire U.S..

18. _____ is more difficult to transport than other fossil fuels.   Coal

19. _____ _____ produces a large amount of energy from a small amount of material.   Nuclear energy

20. The splitting of an atom in a nuclear reaction is called _____.   fission

21. The two primary radioactive materials used for nuclear reactions are _____ and _____.   uranium, plutonium

22. Power derived from moving water is called _____ _____.   hydro electricity

23. _____ energy heats water into steam which then runs turbines.   Geothermal

24. Atoms are combined in the process of _____, and is the most efficient way of producing energy, though the extreme temperatures have yet to be controlled.   fusion

25. Anticipated warming of the Earth is part of the _____ _____.   greenhouse effect

26. CFCs are thought to be destroying the _____ layer in the atmosphere.   ozone

27. Most solid waste in the U.S. goes into _____ _____.   sanitary landfills

28. _____ reduces solid waste to 25 percent of its original size.   Incineration

29. When arid land is overgrazed and deteriorates to a point where it cannot be used or maintain vegetative cover it experiences _____.   desertification

30. Genetic improvements made on plants which increase harvests are collectively referred to as the _____ _____.   green revolution

31. _____ could supply a large percentage of the world's food.   Oceans